D1369533

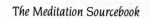

The Meditation Sourcebook

The
MEDITATION
S O U R C E B O O K
Meditation for Mortals

Holly Sumner, Ph.D

L O W E L L   H O U S E

LOS ANGELES

NTC/Contemporary Publishing Group

Published by Lowell House
A division of NTC/Contemporary Publishing Group, Inc.
4255 West Touhy Avenue, Lincolnwood (Chicago), Illinois 60646-1975
U.S.A.

Cover photograph copyright © 1992 Color Box/FPG International LLC

Lowell House books can be purchased at special discounts when ordered
in bulk for premiums and special sales. Contact Department CS at the
following address:
    NTC/Contemporary Publishing Group
    4255 West Touhy Avenue
    Lincolnwood, IL 60646-1975
    1-800-323-4900

Library of Congress Catalog Card Number: 98-75385
ISBN: 0-7373-0038-8

Roxbury Park is a division of NTC/Contemporary Publishing Group, Inc.

Managing Director and Publisher: Jack Artenstein
Editor in Chief, Roxbury Park Books: Michael Artenstein
Director of Publishing Services: Rena Copperman
Editorial Assistant: Nicole Monastirsky
Interior Design: Robert S. Tinnon
Typesetting: Ken Trickey

Printed and bound in the United States of America
10 9 8 7 6 5 4 3 2 1

To my son Scott Sumner, the love of my life:
I am proud of the man you have become.

To my parents Edward and June Senger:
Thank you for always being there for me from day one.

To my brother Michael Senger, and our friend Paul Johnson:
Thank you both for the patience and support you gave me.

To Barbara Sumner:
Still family after all these years.

To my agent, Nancy Crossman:
Thank you for believing in me and taking a chance.

To my editor, Michael Artenstein:
Just breathe! And may you keep doing
so for many more years to come.

To Nicole Monastirsky, Editorial Assistant:
Thanks for your enthusiasm—it helped.

Contents

Foreword

Scientific research has shown us that meditation can improve our lives in many ways. Meditation can reduce the number of stress response syndromes people suffer from. Experiencing the daily practice of meditation can slow the heart rate, reduce blood pressure, reduce risk for hypertension, and literally help you live longer.

Your daily meditation will do more than just give you physical benefits of course. Regular meditation will put you more at peace with yourself and the world. You will learn that meditation will help you be happier and more in control of your life. Experiencing meditation will allow you to gain new insights into yourself and it will change your life in ways you could only have hoped.

It is a great honor for me to introduce to you Holly Sumner and her brilliant book about meditation. Holly demystifies meditation and makes meditation accessible to anyone now. In my opinion, this is the ultimate resource book on meditation and one that I think you will find useful for many reasons and on many levels.

You will realize that Holly does not talk down to you as a disciple or student. She shares with you "secrets" that have been closely guarded for years and breaks through all the complexities of meditation and makes it simple. Holly has a wonderful sense of humor and a wide appreciation for her subject that shines through this entire tome.

What I like best about this book is that Holly leaves no stone unturned. She takes you through almost all of the forms of meditation from the simple to the complex and helps you discover which forms are most useful for you. Meditation is not really something you "learn to do." It is something you discover that you already do every day. There are many things you can more easily do with this skill you possess. Meditation will help you enhance your concentration, sharpen your thinking skills, and bring you more in touch with that part of you that makes you, "you."

It is my privilege and honor to present to you a brilliant teacher sharing with you her experience about this absolutely vital subject. Ladies and gentleman, allow Holly Sumner to begin to help you change your life and touch the universe.

KEVIN HOGAN
Author of
Life By Design: Your Handbook
for Transformational Living;
The Gift; and
The Psychology of Persuasion

Introduction

I imagine you've picked this book up because you are interested in learning how to meditate. Well, I have a secret to tell you . . . I can't teach you how to do it. Why? Because you already know how!

What I *can* teach you is how to produce the meditative state upon demand. Confused? Quite simply, meditation utilizes a state of mind that your brain produces naturally. This state of mind is actually brain wave patterns that you already produce many times throughout the day and night. It's not something you must learn or a magical state of being that only an elite group can accomplish. It's just a brain wave pattern. Therefore, meditation simply is the ability to bring oneself to that brain wave pattern on purpose.

LOVE AND KISSES

The practice of meditation does not have to be complicated. Do you know the acronym KISS? It stands for: *Keep It Simple Stupid.* No, I am not calling you stupid! The meaning behind that phrase is that with most anything, we can take something and make it far more complicated than it needs to be. We can add all kinds of things to meditation, such as certain rituals, sayings, body positions, and philosophies. But that is the key statement, we add those *to* meditation. We can make it complicated, or we can allow it to be simple, to exist in its simplest form. On its own, meditation is very simple.

There is a scientific and philosophic rule called *Occam's Razor*, which roughly states: "All things being equal, the simplest explanation tends to be the correct one." Taking this thought a bit further, "the simplest way simply works."

HAVE IT YOUR WAY!

While preparing to write this book, I asked many of my clients and friends what they most wanted to see in a book on meditation. The overwhelming response was, "I want to know how to do it right! My teacher told me I was doing it wrong." Or they would tell me, "The book I read said I *must* do it this way, or it wouldn't work."

The most important thing I feel I can teach is that there is no *one* right way. Whatever works for you is the right way. Your religion, beliefs, and occupation have nothing to do with the ability to meditate. You do not have to be a Buddhist monk, believe in New Age topics, or have any special talent or powers. Meditation does not "belong" to any particular sect or group; it is simply a brain wave pattern that all humans produce naturally. Period.

Therefore, I do not believe that any one group can decree that their way is the only way to meditate correctly. True, you will find many groups, religions, or belief systems that use meditation. However, it is used as a part of their practices and is styled to their particular system. To meditate incorrectly would only be in relation to their practices and beliefs. Meditation itself is something we all already are able to do in its purest and simplest form.

GOT A BUSY SIGNAL?

Now, here is where people might have difficulties. Some find that their minds are just too "busy" to practice passive meditation easily. Recently, I met a young woman at a local fair. We started discussing meditation and she told me that it had been recommended to her because of panic attacks and bouts of depression. Her counselor told her she must sit quietly and think of "nothing." When she tried to do just that, thoughts would immediately bombard her. She was told she had to have a quiet or an empty mind, therefore, she must be doing it wrong. She was made to feel like a failure.

Needing an "empty mind" to meditate is a misconception that the media have helped foster. The act of trying to empty your mind is surely the quickest way to fill your head with thoughts! Perhaps your doctor or health care practitioner has suggested it to relieve stress, but you think that meditation sounds boring or difficult to do. Sitting still for hours visualizing lotus leaves or fluffy clouds drifting by just isn't appealing for everyone. Meditation is that— but it's also not that—as well as so much more.

There are two styles of meditation. Most of us have heard of passive meditation, where one attempts to quiet or silence one's mind. However, this is not the only style. Countless people have told me that they "could not meditate" because their minds were too busy. I've got good news. There is also what is known as active meditation. You can be very active mentally and still be meditating. Both styles are valid and useful.

PRETZELS ANYONE?

You also may have read that you must follow certain rituals or use particular body positions. For instance, some of you may have heard that you must sit in a lotus position. Quite honestly, I can't even get into that position, much less meditate in it! But I can meditate successfully, and so can you.

Certain practices, such as Zen meditation, do require sitting in a half or full lotus position. Others require the hands to be positoned in a certain way or breathing to be done in a particular manner. These things are part of those practices and the way in which they use meditation. There are reasons for them, but they have to do with the concepts of the particular belief system and not meditation itself.

WHY SHOULD I MEDITATE?

Another question I am often asked is, "Why should I meditate?" There are as many answers to that question as there are people, but I feel the foremost reason is to allow time . . . just for you. In this day and age it seems we have less and less time for ourselves. Spending a few minutes a day relaxing is a gift you can give yourself. The benefits both mentally and physically are immeasurable. Indulge yourself—you deserve it!

HOW OFTEN SHOULD I MEDITATE?

Remember that we are all individuals. There is no set requirement or rule that says you must meditate for a certain amount of time each day or it won't work. Nor does the ability to meditate go away if you don't meditate each day. True, if you don't meditate for a while, it may take a little practice to stay focused, but there is no penalty for not doing it each day. It's not a case of "use it or lose it."

As for the amount of time you spend meditating, it is really up to you. Even five or ten minutes of meditation can be beneficial. Fifteen minutes to half an hour is better, but you may not be able to do that each day. Don't punish yourself. Meditation should be enjoyable, not just work or something you dread doing.

READY . . . SET . . . GO!

Don't know where or how to begin? There are always tapes, courses, and workshops, but you may not have the time or hundreds of dollars to spend. Learning meditation does not need to be an expensive proposition. After all, you already know how to do it! This book will cover a wide range of topics and offer dozens of easy techniques and tips to help you along the way. Follow them exactly, or blend bits and pieces of different techniques to find a style that suits you.

With such a wide-ranging book, there are bound to be topics that just do not interest everyone. Some readers may only be interested in stress reduction or health benefits. Others may want to know how to use meditation to discover more about their inner world and themselves. This book is not meant to be purely clinical, neither is it meant to be purely New Age. Yet, I felt that it would be beneficial to cover as wide a spectrum of uses as possible. Use what feels right for you.

JUST DO IT!

My experience with meditation has developed over many years of study, but I have learned much more by *doing*. It does not take years of study and tireless effort. This book will teach you to tap into what you already know how to do, and you will be meditating successfully in just a few short days, or even hours.

What *can* take time is exploring the myriad ways that meditation can be used! You can use it to relax, improve your memory, gain self-confidence, eliminate unwanted habits, and set goals. The list is limited only by the ways you can think of to use it. Feel free to experiment and make up your own techniques. Remember that the right way is *your* way.

The purpose of this book is to teach you how to use meditation your way. Consider it a private workshop just for you! The rest of these pages will cover the questions you are likely to have. If you are on the Internet, you can join a discussion group by e-mail. The instructions will be in the Resource section of this book. You will be able to ask further questions and share experiences with other members.

The rest of the Resource section will list many different places to learn more about meditation, such as magazines, and Internet Web sites and resources.

Acknowledgments

It's a rare book that has not been enriched by the input or assistance of others, and this book is no exception. I would like to thank and acknowledge those people.

Kevin L. Hogan, Ph.D., has been of immeasurable assistance, both as a colleague and a friend. My deepest gratitude goes to him for his willingness to share valuable time and expertise.

To all my wonderful friends in my E-mail listserve, The Psychic Discussion Group. Thank you for allowing me to pick your brains again and again.

Special thanks go to Kelli Whelan-Whitman, Susan Harkins, Phylameana Désy, and Nancy Barnett for their Web sleuthing.

What is the far greater journey?
To the stars and beyond . . .
Or the mind and within?

Part One

The Basics

Chapter One

The Mind and Meditation
Caution: Brain at Work

There's no doubt about it; the mind is a mysterious thing. Scientists have studied it for centuries, and it seems the more we think we know, the less we really do. How do the brain and the mind interact? Is the mind separate from the brain? Where *is* the mind? Who and what are we? These are some of the questions that humankind has meditated upon throughout the ages.

HOW OUR BRAIN WORKS

You do not need to know how the brain functions in order to meditate. It is after all, a natural process your brain already knows how to do. Those of you who do not care to know can safely skip over this part. You still will be able to meditate. (Watch out, though, there just may be a test at the end of the book!)

For those who are curious, the process is really not all that complicated. For meditation purposes, we are mostly interested in brain wave patterns and the functions of the two sides of the brain. Unless you are a medical doctor or a scientist, the basics will suffice. I'll keep it simple and easy. After all, it's nice to have some knowledge, and besides, you can use it to make scintillating conversation at parties.

Am I Right . . . ? or Am I Left . . . ?

The brain itself is a small organ weighing approximately three pounds. Not so very large for the big job it has! The parts of the brain itself are the cerebrum, the cerebellum, the hippocampus, the hypothalamus, the pituitary gland, and the brain stem. The cerebrum is divided into halves, each hemisphere controlling different human functions. You probably have heard the terms *left brain* and *right brain.*

The right half, or hemisphere, of the brain is associated with intuition, abstract ideas, colors, shapes, music, and symbolism. The left brain is associated with analytical thinking, logic, and mathematical thinking and controls our speech and language. We have a tendency to think in either a left- or right-brained manner. As A. M. Krasner points out in his book *The Wizard Within,* "Nobody is totally right-brained or left-brained. But just as most people tend to be right-handed or left-handed, they also tend to use one hemispheric mode of thinking over the other."

Understanding whether you tend to be predominately right- or left-brained can help you choose the kind of deepening technique for meditation that will work best for you. For instance, a left-brained person may find counting-down procedures such as stairs and elevators useful, whereas a right-brained person may prefer walking down paths or imagining floating down a river. Chances are, you can tell which ones will work best for you simply by your preference.

There are many question-and-answer tests available that will help you determine whether you are a lefty or a righty. If you are on the Internet, I'll include some Web sites that have some tests. However, a quick way to determine if you are left- or right-brained is to ask yourself a few questions:

Do you prefer to go over every detail before making a decision, or do you go with your gut instinct?

When traveling somewhere new, do you prefer written instructions or would you rather see a map?

If you picked the first choice in both, you most likely are left-brained. If you picked the second choice, you are most likely right-brained. This is by no means a comprehensive test to find your dominant hemisphere. But it does give clues as to how you think. For meditation purposes, you will quickly find out what works for you and what doesn't, no matter what your hemisphere dominance.

Brain Wave Patterns and Functions

The brain produces a pulsating electrical energy, known as brain wave patterns, which can be measured by an electroencephalograph, or as it's commonly abbreviated, an EEG. These patterns or rhythms have four frequency ranges: beta, alpha, theta, and delta. They are measured in cycles per second (CPS).

Actually, the brain produces all the patterns simultaneously; however, one is more predominant than the others. In the field, we tend to say that a person is "in" one of the patterns, such as being *in alpha,* or *in beta.*

Beta is more connected with our conscious minds, while alpha, theta, and delta are linked with our subconscious.

Beta Beta has a frequency of approximately 14 CPS and above. It's associated with being wide-awake, mentally and physically active. Your focus is on the world around you with all its distractions and excitements. It's your everyday real-world state of mind. You are out there doing as well as being done to. You are highly focused on what you are saying and what you are doing.

If you are highly stressed, upset, or excited, the CPS level can go quite high. The expression "I was so excited I could hardly think straight" is apt. The more stimulation your brain has, the higher the brain wave frequency is likely to be.

Alpha Alpha has a frequency of from 7 to 14 CPS. You may have heard of *the alpha state.* It's associated with light daydreaming, meditating, REM (rapid eye movement) sleep, most hypnosis, or "vegging out."

In the alpha state, you are more focused upon your inner world, what you think, feel, and imagine. You are still aware of your surroundings and have thinking ability. True, you are not as *concerned* with the outside world, but you are aware of it. Most hypnosis takes place while a person is in alpha. The hypnotist wants clients to be aware and have the ability to think.

My clients often ask if it is dangerous to be in a meditative state. Sometimes they are afraid that they would not be able to "come out of" meditation if something happened that needed their attention. Since meditation and daydreaming really have the same brain wave pattern, I often give this analogy:

> You are sitting at work daydreaming. It's a wonderful fantasy . . .
> George Clooney is smiling at you and walking toward you. Sigh . . .
> All of a sudden your boss walks into the office.

Trust me, you will quickly be aware of that fact! Very few people daydream so deeply that they will not be able to react.

Oh, all right, maybe George Clooney doesn't do it for you. Just insert Cindy Crawford or whoever else you would like. I'm sure you get my point, which is that we do have awareness while in alpha. If you are daydreaming or meditating and someone comes into the room and calls out your name, you *will* be able to hear them. You are not in some zombielike state. You are just more focused on your inner world, rather than the outside one. You can and will be able to shift gears and react should the need arise.

It is surprising how often and easily we drift into alpha. How many of you have been in your car and arrived at your destination with no real recollection of how you got there? Oh, you knew you were driving, you just don't recall the details.

Theta Theta has a frequency of 4 to 7 CPS and is associated with a deeper meditative state. A person under anesthesia is generally in a theta state. People in theta are usually not as aware of their surroundings as in an alpha state. They are more disassociated from the physical. Runners often produce a theta brain wave pattern. They have disengaged themselves from the physical task of running and are in a more mental world.

More experienced meditators can easily produce a theta meditative state. Some research indicates that people in a theta state become highly creative. Other research indicates that creativity occurs instead in alpha. I tend to think it varies from person to person and is likely to be right on the border between alpha and theta.

Interestingly, theta is also associated with shock or intense fear. For example, if a person is placed in a situation where he fears for his life, he will usually produce theta brain waves. True, theta is a slower brain wave pattern; one would think the frequency would be much higher. Actually the person enters into what is called the "flight or fight" syndrome. Instinctively, the brain slows down so he will act rather than think.

If you are walking across a street and a car suddenly heads straight toward you, it is best to act quickly. You certainly don't want to think: "Well, perhaps I should move? Or would it be better if I didn't?" Analyzing the situation for too long could be disastrous, if not downright deadly. A large number of our instinctual responses are for survival purposes.

As stated earlier, most hypnosis takes place in an alpha state. However, a hypnotist may train a client to enter into theta. For many purposes, it's too unresponsive a state for hypnotic suggestion. However, it can be useful for someone who needs to undergo surgery but cannot have chemical anesthesia.

Delta There isn't much data on what occurs when a person is in delta, which ranges in frequency from .5 to 4 CPS. You may have noticed that I said from point five rather than zero. A frequency of zero would be brain dead! Most studies suggest that it is a deep, dreamless state of sleep. Many believe that a yogi can lower their brain waves to almost a nil frequency.

RIDE A WAVE

Most who are new at meditating meditate mostly in alpha, although many people can attain a lower pattern as they go along. For example, in a fifteen-minute meditation, a person may be in alpha for the first ten minutes or so and in theta during the last few minutes. The more you practice meditation, the easier and quicker you will be able to produce a deeper meditative state. Yogis, for instance, are able to lower their brain waves to theta and possibly even delta.

There is much conflicting research on what exactly occurs in the various brain wave states, especially in alpha and theta. For instance, some researchers are positive that memory is triggered in an alpha state, while just as many feel it is in theta. And it's the same with creativity. Hypnotists also disagree as to the level and types of suggestibility in alpha and theta.

Authors Jodie Hadley and Carol Staudacher in their book *Hypnosis for Change*, liken the deepness of the trance state in hypnosis to the level of activity. For instance, in a light trance state a person may be idly thinking about playing tennis. In a somewhat deeper state the same person may actually visualize herself playing tennis. In an even deeper state, she can *feel* herself playing tennis. This analogy makes a lot of sense to me because the deeper the meditative state, the more involved and focused the subject is.

However, I believe that it's the end result that matters. Who cares if it's alpha or theta brain waves that you produce if you are accomplishing what you are setting out to do? If relaxation is your goal and you are able to achieve it, that is what matters. How do you feel when you stop meditating? Are you relaxed? If so, congratulations, you've done it! There are no brain wave police. If highly creative and useful ideas occur to you during meditation, again, that is what counts.

For a while, when I went to conferences, it seemed that people were getting to be "brain wave snobs." I'd hear people say, "Well *I* meditate in theta." They insinuated that if one meditated in alpha it wasn't good enough. Actually, when you begin to meditate, you do start out in a higher brain wave pattern. However, as you continue your meditation exercise, your brain waves slow down naturally. You will progress from beta to alpha, and many of you will indeed reach a theta state during meditations.

Your ability to focus will also improve as you practice meditation. At first, it may take a while before you can easily retain that focus. However, you will soon find that it takes less conscious effort.

THE SENSES

All of our senses, such as hearing, smell, sight, touch, and even taste, can play a part in meditation. Our senses operate on more than just a physical level. An often-cited example of this involves a lemon:

Close your eyes. Now, imagine that you are biting into a tart, ripe, juicy lemon.

Most people will salivate, and many will also have a tingling feeling in their tongue and jaw just as they would if they did bite into a lemon. It is as though the mind does not know the difference between reality and fantasy. In truth, it really doesn't. In the case of the lemon we, in effect, tricked our brain. It processed the information it received and then reacted accordingly. Information, whether from our inner or our outer senses, has equal validity.

We also use both inner and outer senses while meditating. All of the senses we have at our disposal in the physical world, such as sight, hearing, touch, taste, and smell, we also have in the world of the mind. Do you need a little proof of that? Let's try a few simple exercises. After reading each example, I want you to close your eyes and imagine each of the following:

Imagine walking by a rosebush. Stop to smell the fragrance of the roses. Inhale deeply, doesn't it smell heavenly?

Imagine being at a parade. Listen as the marching band plays a lively tune such as "The Saints Come Marching In." Listen to people applaud as each band goes by.

Imagine being at the beach. Curl your toes in the sand and feel how cool it is. Walk over to the water's edge and dip your toe into the water. Brrrrr, it's cold!

Imagine yourself at an ice cream parlor. Now, imagine placing a spoonful of a rich, cold ice cream sundae in your mouth. Savor the flavors of the nuts, the marshmallows, and the texture of the gooey chocolate sauce.

There are plenty more examples we could use. Think of your favorite song. Can you hear it playing in your head? What is your favorite food? Think of eating it and you may almost be able to taste it. Remember a time when you picked up an ice cube with your hands. I bet you can feel the coldness as well as the wetness of that ice cube.

Emotions can be recalled and used in meditation as well. Since the goal of meditation is to be relaxed and tranquil, let's do practice exercises that will achieve that type of emotional response. After reading each example, close your eyes and imagine each of the following situations:

> *You have just been told that you have won an all-expense-paid vacation to Hawaii. Imagine how you would feel. Picture it, feel it, sense it. See and feel yourself reacting.*

> *You are wearing a new outfit for the first time. Everyone you meet tells you how wonderful you look. Imagine how you feel when they tell you how great you look. Picture it, feel it, sense it.*

> *You've been working hard on your diet to lose weight. You finally achieve your goal. You now are able to fit into the clothing size you want to wear. Imagine how you feel when you put on that clothing. Picture it, feel it, sense it.*

Does this seem a bit like playacting? Well, remember that example of the lemon. As far as the mind was concerned, we really were biting into a lemon. The mind does not know the difference between reality and fantasy. The same principle applies in meditation. We want the mind to believe that we can do what we ask of it in our meditations, whether it's relaxation or achieving a goal. The more we can involve our senses and emotions in our meditations, the more real they will seem.

CHANNEL SURFING

There is a field of study called neurolinguistic programming (NLP) that delves into how we process information. We use our senses when we perceive the world around us. Scientists believe that we are more sensitive to, or aware of, one sense over the others—we predominately favor one. This is not to say that is the only way we do things, but it is the way we usually operate. Thus, we tend to learn and react to information primarily in one of the following ways:

1. Visual
2. Auditory
3. Kinesthetic

A visual person will represent things with pictures or symbols. Speech patterns can give a clue, as a visual person will use statements such as, "I can see that," "In my view," or "Looking at it that way." For meditation, visual people enjoy vivid imagery packed with color: "And as you see yourself looking at the field in front of you, you notice the profusion of colorful wildflowers."

Auditory people will use sounds as a basis for their perceptions. Their speech will likely contain statements such as these: "I hear you," "That sounds like a good idea," or "Listen, did you know that." Auditory people like melodic description, or imagery laced with sound clues. "As you relax, you hear the gentle chirping of the birds, the rustling of the leaves in the trees."

A kinesthetic person bases his perceptions on feelings and sensations. You'll hear him saying things like this: "I feel that is incorrect," "I don't grasp this concept," or "I'll hold you to that promise." Kinesthetics enjoy descriptions that include sensatory statements: "As you touch the water in the lake, you feel yourself becoming calm and relaxed, just as a light breeze feels gentle on your skin."

When we talk about visualization in relation to meditation, it is more than just a visual *seeing*. It's not just the imagery itself; it's how we approach that imagery. All three types of people can visualize, however, their perceptions tend to be based on their primary channel of learning.

ANALYTICAL VERSUS FEELING

Just as we tend to favor one of our senses when receiving input, we also have a tendency to be predominately analytical or feeling in our way of using that information. This correlates to whether we are left-brained or right-brained.

Does it really matter? Not really, although it can help you find the types of meditation that work well for you. Analytical types do well with step-by-step meditations that go from Point A to Point B to Point C. If an unrelated direction is thrown in, they are often uncomfortable. Take the following example:

> "Walk down the path until you come to a gate. Open the gate and step through it, and there you will meet a wise man."

Now alter the direction:

> "Walk down the path until you come to a gate. Look at the ocean gently rolling in and out. Now go through and you will meet a wise man."

This alteration might bother an analytical person, but might not be as big a deal for a feeling type of person. Analytical types are aware of the process, while feeling types are involved in the moment. The analytical person may have felt a step was missing, and that the direction didn't logically flow. The more feeling or kinesthetic person would go with how it makes them feel.

There, this wasn't so bad, was it? Now you have a bit of information about how your brain works while meditating.

Chapter Two

What We Say
Isn't What We Mean!

Communication and language are an integral part of our existence. In order to survive, we need to make our needs known to those around us as well as our thoughts, feelings, and wishes. Ask someone how we communicate, and the answer will usually be that we use language. However, language is actually only a small part of how we communicate. It is a tool for communication.

Language is a collection of sounds and/or gestures that form words or concepts to convey a message. Communication is interaction. Ironically, our definition of *language* has become fairly synonymous with *communication.* The purpose of language is communication, yet we do not communicate solely through language.

We can intuit someone's mood from her expression. We can tell a great deal by the way people sit or stand. Ironically, this is called body language. It is a way of communicating even though it's not a verbal language. There are universal gestures that people all over the world can comprehend. A smile is one such gesture. Crooking and wiggling a finger to say "come here" is another. I'm sure you can think of a few others.

Ballet is performed entirely without words. I once watched a performance and became so caught up in the feelings it conveyed that I cried. Opera can have a profound effect upon people even though they don't understand the words. How many times have you laughed at the antics of a mime or clown? Paintings can evoke a myriad of emotions. We can convey a wealth of meaning in just a look or a glance. Touch is often underrated as a method of communication; a comforting hug can do much to communicate love and security.

Years ago, I was at a conference where I didn't know anyone at all. I felt very much like a nameless face in the crowd. Worse, I felt inadequate because I thought everyone must know much more than I did. However, I did know that people tend to perceive us as we project ourselves. I decided to try an experiment. I smiled at each and every person I walked by. Not just a tiny little smile, but a great big one. At first I felt rather silly and a bit self-conscious. But as I smiled at people, I found the majority smiled back. Soon people were coming up to talk to me though I hadn't yet said a word. Of course, as I met and talked with people, I felt better about being at the conference. I found out that many others were in the same boat, feeling out of place and insecure.

Here are some interesting and fun communication exercises you can try:

> With another person or even a small group, set aside a time where you all agree to communicate without words—written or spoken. You can use any method you wish, such as gestures, posture, facial expressions, or movements, as long as you don't use words. Be creative.

> With another person or a small group, agree to communicate only by singing song titles. Not lyrics, just titles!

> Again, with one other person or with a group, agree to communicate only by drawings and pictures. Use no words in the drawings.

These exercises can be fun as well as entertaining, but they also serve to prove that we can successfully interact without the spoken word.

Yet language is a powerful way of communication. We must not and should not underestimate the impact of our words! We can easily see that the language we use has an effect upon others. After all, what we say often produces a direct and immediate result. Think about it for a moment. When we really want something from another person, we choose the words we will use carefully. We want to strengthen our chances for success. When we are angry, we often use words as weapons. When we want to be noticed, we use them to get attention.

For an exercise, write a short convincing paragraph for each of the following scenarios:

Convince someone to go out on a date with you. If you are married or involved, convince your partner to go ballroom dancing with you.

You are running for political office. Convince your neighbor to vote for you.

You haven't had a raise in quite a while. Convince your boss you deserve a raise, and a big one at that.

Now do the opposite for each example. Use language that would not be convincing. Sound a little strange? Well, think about how many times we do exactly that in real situations: "I know you probably won't want to, but ..." "I'm sure I don't really deserve it but ..."

When we don't think about our language, we also see results as well. How many times have you inadvertently hurt someone's feelings by careless words or been embarrassed by something you said without thinking? Conversely, what others say to us has as much of an impact upon us. The old saying "Sticks and stones may break my bones, but words can never hurt me" is just not true for many of us.

There are times when what we have to convey is less than positive or is something the other person might not want to hear. But if we think before speaking, we can get our point across without resorting to words that are hurtful.

For this exercise, write a sentence or a short paragraph telling the person in each example some not very pleasant news. Work to find the most positive way to do so:

A co-worker has gained a tremendous amount of weight. Today he is wearing an outfit that makes him look like a stuffed sausage. You've been elected to tell him not to wear it again, and tell him why.

A co-worker has body odor. You have to tell her about it and ask her to do something about it.

You have a friend whose every effort brings disaster. He wants to help you build a deck on your house.

For another exercise, take one day in which you stop and think for at least five to ten seconds before you speak.

Some of the communication exercises above may not seem to be very relevant; after all, this is a book about meditation. However, you will see their relevance if you consider that meditation requires effective communication with your subconscious mind. You will find it helpful to treat your subconscious as though it were a person. How can you best approach it for success?

If you were using meditation to lose weight, you certainly would not start out by saying, "I know it probably won't work, and I'm just a fat slob, but . . ." In each of the examples given above, we set out to convince someone to do something or worked to find the most positive way to say things. It's the same thing with meditation. We are setting out to convince our subconscious mind to do something.

We do so by our language, our imagery, and any method we can utilize to communicate. Even a smile can work well in meditation. In fact, in many of the meditations in this book, I will suggest that people smile at you. It feels good, and those feelings add to the completeness of the meditation experience. The more senses you can use in meditation, the more real it will seem. The more real meditation seems, the more effective it will be.

HIDING PLACES

We often hide behind language. What we say often isn't quite what we mean. Sometimes we are attempting to be polite and spare someone's feelings, or we don't want to be vulnerable by admitting our actual feelings. At other times we are outright deceitful and lie.

A more difficult concept to grasp is the impact our language has upon ourselves. Our brain processes information from many sources, and part of the information it receives is from our own words. When we talk and think, we are, in effect, also communicating with ourselves. We are interacting with our mind and specifically with our subconscious. The subconscious mind tends to translate words quite literally. It uses the meanings it has learned rather than what we sound like we are saying.

There are certain words we substitute for what we *really* mean. By using them in this fashion, our brain soon interprets the real meaning of these words. For example, when we say we will "try" to do something, it means that we don't *want* to do it, or that we don't think we *can*. How many times have you told someone you'd "try" to come to her party? At the time you knew darn well that you either didn't have any desire to go or that you already had other plans.

Perhaps someone has asked you to go mountain climbing. Maybe you would very much like to go, but you worry that you aren't athletic enough to do it. So you tell yourself that you will try. *Try* indicates a high probability of failure. If we say to ourselves "I'll try," our subconscious mind translates it literally as "I am likely to fail." Here is another instance in which you are reinforcing the word's negative meaning. You are giving yourself a strong suggestion that you will probably be unsuccessful.

Yes, I said suggestion—as in hypnotic suggestion. The mind listens to what we tell it and does its best to comply. The success of hypnotic suggestion has much to do with the rapport and trust between hypnotist and client. And who has the best rapport with your own mind? Who is the one you can trust the most? (One hundred points if you said yourself!) No, you will not fail every time you use the word *try*. But why purposely set yourself up for that possibility?

"*Can't* is another word we use in this fashion. In my opinion, it's an even stronger negative suggestion. Can't literally means cannot do, no way, nada. Period. No shades of gray here! How many times have you said something to this effect: "I can't remember names," or "I can't write well"? This is a strong, strong type of hypnotic suggestion. You are telling your brain, "Brain, I cannot do this," and it dutifully and cheerfully attempts to comply.

Slang expressions are minefields of hypnotic suggestion, and often not very nice ones at that. Have you heard the expression "So-and-so is a pain in the neck"? Or the ever popular, "So-and-so makes me sick to my stomach"? How about "I can't stand him"? Remember that our subconscious translates words quite literally. Now just the mere utterance of such a slang expression now and again isn't actually going to make you sick. But with enough repetition it can certainly do so. Associate "pain in the neck" with a person enough times, and you might just find yourself with a sore or stiff neck!

With a little bit of effort, you can clean up your language. As an experiment, make a list of words and expressions you often use, such as *try, can't,* or *I'm stupid.* Then, for the next couple of days pay close attention to what you say. Whenever you find yourself using one of those expressions, substitute a more positive phrase. The best way to do this is to use words that are closer in meaning to what you really mean.

Okay, maybe you still don't want to go to that party we mentioned above. Yet you don't want to hurt the host's feelings by telling them you have no desire to go. It would be far better to say, "I am not sure that I will be able to come," or "I'll have to check my schedule; I may already have made conflicting plans that I cannot cancel." In that way you are not reinforcing the association of sure failure with the word *try.*

AND THE SECRET PASSWORD IS . . .

Have you ever been at a gathering where everyone spoke a different language from yours? No matter how hard you try to be friendly and interested in what is being discussed, it's confusing! You don't quite understand what is going on and you feel left out. Or worse, you are afraid you will make some silly mistake that will upset everyone. So you either pretend you understand, or you smile and nod your head a lot.

The jargon and terminology often used in meditation can be much like that, an unknown language. Many of the terms if taken literally are confusing and misleading. Just when you think you know what a term might mean, you start thinking that you must be wrong. You feel like everyone but you knows the "secret code." You worry that you are missing an important piece of information.

It is all too easy for teachers, writers, or practitioners to become accustomed to using certain phraseology. We often don't even think about what we are saying; after all, we know what it means. Herein lies a very real chance of inadvertently putting stumbling blocks in the way of communication. To us, certain terms are crystal clear. To someone just starting out, those same terms can be minefields of confusion.

COME ON DOWN
TO THE DOUBLE D RANCH

Just about every meditation book or tape I've come across contains what I call the "Double D's." You're always being invited to "go down" or told to "go deep." But where exactly is "deep" and why must we "go down"?

When I first began studying meditation, the "deep" part especially bothered me. I have quite a vivid imagination and I would find myself thinking, "Is the mind like a cavern? Do I have to descend somewhere into a deep dark pit? Isn't there a better tourist spot? Can I bring a flashlight? What if I get lost? What if there are monsters there?"

In classes there always seem to be those who are not concerned about deep and how to get there. They just happily close their eyes and off they go. I know there are others like me. We want to know where deep is, what we will find there, and more importantly, how we will know when we get there.

In meditation, as well as hypnosis, the term *deep* isn't quite accurate. What is really meant is to be more focused and pay less attention to outside stimuli. Meditation is simply the ability to focus on one or just a few things. Since we tend to be introspective during meditation, it's been associated with going deep within ourselves. Therefore, using the term *deep* is apt. It makes perfect sense to me now that I know why.

Since meditation has a slower brain wave pattern, it's easy to associate it with *down*. We slow down the cycles per second; it's a lower frequency. You will find that many techniques use counting down, going down stairs, going down in an elevator, or some other method that suggests a direction of down. The reasoning is metaphorical. But I'll tell you a secret. You do not have to go down. You can go up if you like. You can go up those stairs, count up, or go up in that elevator. You can go sideways if you'd prefer. Actually, you don't have to go anywhere! It's simply a method of suggestion to help you produce a meditative brain wave pattern.

ONE, TWO, THREE . . . CONCENTRATE!

I do not like to use the word *concentrate* because it suggests that one must try hard to concentrate. That implies hard work! Meditation is supposed to be restful and peaceful. To add hard work to that equation seems to be an oxymoron. Concentration is really just being able to focus.

Look at a cartoon where concentration is being portrayed and you'll notice certain characteristics in the drawing. The character's face is all contorted, the eyes are shut tight, and the forehead is full of deep lines and grooves. Maybe the character grimaces or scowls. It doesn't look very relaxing to me. I prefer to think of concentration as thinking of one thing or just a few things.

WAKE UP AND COME OUT!

I've heard many meditation tapes that use a phrase similar to this at the end of the tape: "At the count of five you will wake up." You are not sleeping when you meditate. It may look like sleep; the eyes are usually closed, the breathing is slower, and the body is relaxed. It is true that some people become so relaxed they fall asleep while meditating. But meditation itself has nothing to do with sleep.

Another phrase you might hear in meditation tapes is this: "At the count of five (or three or ten) you will open your eyes and come out." This can be quite confusing since you didn't really go anywhere. Meditation is more like focusing inward—paying more attention to your inner rather than outer world. Yet, a phrase like that can scare some people because it implies that you have gone somewhere. What if you can't come back? The truth of the matter is that you can't get stuck in meditation.

The worst thing that will happen is that you will produce a lower brain wave pattern and fall asleep. No big disaster, your body and mind will get some rest. If you are using a tape, you will wake up naturally. If this worries you or you have to be somewhere shortly after meditating, set a clock for a wake-up call. If you are in a group meditation class or working one-on-one with an instructor, you will be awakened. When I've led meditation groups and someone has fallen asleep during the exercise, I've rarely had to wake them up at the end. When I've done the final "count up" most have awakened at that time.

PUTTING IT TOGETHER . . .
THE LANGUAGE OF MEDITATION

A friend recently commented to me, "You know, all this meditation stuff is weird. Have you ever listened to a tape? It's all fluffy, flowery, frou-frou stuff." I had to agree. There is a purpose however. We are creating a world for our subconscious mind. We are composing a symphony, painting a picture, and inspiring feelings of wonder, awe, and creativity. We are talking to the subconscious of the most important person in the world . . . you!

Chapter Three

The Styles of Meditation

If I had to pick the single most important statement I could make about meditation, it would be this: *Successful meditation does not require an empty mind.*

If you were to walk into a roomful of people right now and ask if anyone had tried meditation, you would undoubtedly hear statements such as this: "I tried meditation, but it didn't work for me. I couldn't do it because I could never empty my mind." This is the number one misconception about meditation. I teach meditation and I hear it repeatedly. So often, in fact, that if I had a penny for every time I've heard it, I could probably erase the entire national debt. So let me say it again, successful meditation does not require an empty mind!

Let me ask you a question. Why are you interested in learning how to meditate? Is it for stress reduction? Perhaps you've heard that you can use meditation to help achieve your goals? Or maybe you have heard you can improve your health and well-being with meditation? Memory improvement? Pain management? The list could go on and on. Well, meditation can help you do all that and more without ever needing an empty mind. Does that make you feel better? I hope so.

I don't doubt it could be possible to achieve a totally empty mind, although I have never met anyone who has. There are yogis who reportedly are able to do just that. However, they spend countless years doing little besides practicing deep meditation. I don't know about you, but I have a life to lead. I have no desire to spend all that time working to achieve an empty mind. Yet I successfully use meditation in my life, and so can you.

There are actually two styles of meditation: active and passive. Passive meditation is what most people think of when they hear the word *meditation*. But passive meditation does not mean an absence of thought. It simply means focusing on one thought or just a few thoughts.

It is also the most difficult form of meditation to do. Try this experiment: Close your eyes. Now just empty your mind of all thoughts.

I'm pretty sure that most of you will have had *some* thoughts while doing that exercise. Okay, maybe that wasn't quite fair—I just told you that passive meditation doesn't require an empty mind. Try this instead: Close your eyes and think of a cloud. Think only of that cloud.

You may have had better luck with that example. Yet some of you may have found other things creeping into your mind. Perhaps you saw birds flying by the cloud, and then you started thinking about flying. That made you think about your next vacation, which in turn made you think about the workload you have on your desk.

PASSIVE MEDITATION

Passive meditation is simply a matter of quieting the mind and shutting out the "chatter" we usually have going on in our heads. Focusing on one thought, one sound, or one picture is the best way to achieve it. Yes, it can be difficult, but it's not impossible by any means. It does get easier with practice.

What is the purpose of passive meditation? Passive meditation is a useful tool, especially for stress reduction. If we ever really took the time to listen to ourselves, we'd notice a lot of self-chatter going on. Our heads are a busy place! It's rarely quiet in there. Passive meditation is like a vacation from all that clutter.

There are some techniques that make passive meditation easier to achieve, such as focusing on a mantra. A mantra is a word or sound that is repeatedly verbalized or silently thought. Focus is directed totally on that sound, which helps to block out other thoughts. Breathing exercises are another good technique because the focus is placed solely on the breathing cycle.

Contemplative meditation is most often considered to be a form of passive meditation. It's usually associated with those who practice Zen meditative techniques. The contemplative style is probably the form of meditation closest to having a thought-free mind. Even so, a totally empty mind really wouldn't be desirable. The purpose of contemplative meditation is to detach oneself from the conscious/ego thought process. In this state, a person can be aware of himself, but have the ability to be objective. It is not emptiness, for there is thought within the process.

The *Microsoft Encarta 97 Encyclopedia* describes Zen meditation this way: "Zen is the peculiarly Chinese way of accomplishing the Buddhist goal of seeing the world just as it is, that is, with a mind that has no grasping thoughts or feelings (Sanskrit *trishna*). This attitude is called 'no mind' (Chinese *wu-hsin*), a state of consciousness wherein thoughts move without leaving any trace."

ACTIVE MEDITATION

It's important to remember that passive meditation is only one style. There is also active meditation. Active meditation more closely resembles our natural thinking process. When we think, our mind utilizes pictures, sounds, feelings, and emotions, as well as actions. The mind is rarely inert or immobile, yet countless people feel they cannot meditate successfully because they have an active mind. They feel like failures because they aren't doing it "right." Well, in my opinion, they are doing it exactly right!

Look at someone who is daydreaming. Daydreamers sit quietly and stare off into space. Their breathing is slow and regular. Their body is relaxed even though their mind may have quite an action scene going.

Daydreaming has the same brain wave pattern that is produced during meditation. Daydreaming is a natural process. Do you feel you can't daydream correctly? You probably have never given it much thought. Active meditation is also a natural process.

You might say, "But my doctor told me that I should meditate to relax. How can I relax if I'm still mentally active? Isn't that an oxymoron?" No, it isn't. The end result is what matters. If you are relaxed, does it matter if you didn't have completely passive thoughts? You've cleverly used to your advantage what you naturally do. Are you a failure? No, not by a long shot.

Interestingly, a by-product of an active meditation style is an increased ability to focus. Working with active meditation first increases your ability to sustain more passive meditations. It seems to me that a large number of books and classes teach meditation backward.

Actually, there is a very fine line between the two, for even passive meditation generally involves some action. Even imagining that you are floating on a cloud has some minor activity involved. Totally passive meditation would require focusing on the cloud and only the cloud. No action, thoughts, or feelings would be involved. With active meditation you might imagine being *on* that cloud, noticing how it feels, what it looks like, its texture, and more.

You may be thinking that active meditation sounds suspiciously close to self-hypnosis. The truth is, it is as close as you can get, even if it is not quite the same thing. At a conference, I overheard two colleagues discussing self-hypnosis and meditation. One stated that the two were close cousins. The other one disagreed and said they were siblings. I feel the two are fraternal twins.

In some cases it's simply a matter of semantics. Those who feel that meditation is a bit too "new-agey" may prefer the more clinical term self-hypnosis. Yet others may be mistrustful of hypnosis and therefore prefer the term meditation. They are almost one and the same thing. After all, they both have the same brain wave pattern.

Perhaps the only real difference between the two lies in the free-flowing contemplative benefits of meditation. Self-hypnosis techniques generally have a specific goal that is tangible, whether its relaxation, smoking cessation, or improving self-confidence. For example, with self-hypnosis you could give yourself suggestions that you are a creative person. With active meditation, you would give those same suggestions and then you would allow yourself to notice the flow of ideas while meditating.

Chapter Four

How to Get There

Well, hello there! I'll bet some of you skipped right to this chapter. Caught you! That's okay, I have to admit if I were looking at this book in a library or bookstore, this is the chapter I would turn to first.

If you have not read other parts of the book yet, I want to tell you that you already know how to meditate. It's simply a matter of producing certain brain wave patterns. You have produced them hundreds of thousands of times and continue to do so daily. This is nothing new for you. The difficulty lies in producing them on demand. And that is exactly what this chapter is all about. So feel free to charge ahead and be demanding!

THE FASTEST WAY TO MEDITATE

We like instant gratification. We are used to it. We turn on the television and instantly receive entertainment and information. We buy food that is instant or that we can quickly microwave. This is not meant to be judgmental, it is merely a fact of life. It's reality in this day and age. Our lives are hectic and busy and we want to know how to do things as quickly as possible. Is there a shortcut?

Okay, the quickest way to do meditation is just to do it! Close your eyes and meditate. That's correct, just plunge right in and meditate. Now, I can almost hear many of you thinking, "Well, if I could do that, why would I be reading this book?" Well, you can do it because you already do. Not convinced? Then let me ask you a question. Do you daydream?

Meditation is much like daydreaming. When you daydream you begin by thinking about something, perhaps what you did yesterday or the person you just met who is so gorgeous and exciting.

Maybe you think about the vacation you are planning or just enjoyed. The next thing you know, you are in full daydream mode. Which, by the way, happens to have the same brain wave pattern as meditation.

True, I know many of us don't purposely set out to daydream. It's not as though we are at work or home and think, "Hmm, I think I'll daydream." We don't quite realize how we went from being alert to daydreaming. One minute we are in the here and now, and the next we are off in some other place. We were just thinking . . . and then it happened. But that's exactly how we do it; we start thinking and imagining, and within moments, there we are in the middle of a full-blown daydream.

When I meditate, I don't always use a deepening method. I simply close my eyes and start thinking. After a minute or two I reach a meditative state. This is exactly what we do when we daydream: we focus on our thoughts. We shift from thinking about what is going on around us to what is going on in our mind. There has been a change from the outer world to our inner world. We may not do it on purpose, but that doesn't matter. As we are thinking, our brain wave patterns gradually shift downward. This brings about a meditative state of mind, and as we continue thinking, we reach an even deeper level. Meditation is simply focus.

Let's try an experiment. I want you to go ahead and attempt to daydream right now. Yes, right now. Mark your place and close this book for a moment. Then just close your eyes and start thinking about something you'd like to do this weekend, for example. Make it nice and juicy and interesting. Give yourself a few minutes to do this.

Some of you will easily be able to do this; others will find it a bit more difficult. If you try this experiment a few times, some of you will be able to do it at one time, but maybe not at another. There are times when it doesn't work for me either. I find that there are just too many distractions around me, or I have a lot on my mind. Don't be discouraged, for even experienced meditators have difficulty from time to time. It's a very common occurrence; therefore, I've included a whole chapter on the stumbling blocks you might face. Those are always around. For the moment, we'll concentrate on "how to get there."

WHAT DOES IT FEEL LIKE?

Do you remember what it feels like when you are daydreaming or are about to wake up? At those times you are producing alpha brain waves. You also are "in alpha" when you are deeply engrossed in a book or a television program. Alpha brain waves are produced when you daydream, meditate, or dream. As you can see, alpha is not some new and unknown territory. It's familiar, a place you have been many times before.

Most people report that it feels very good. So good, in fact, that I often hear, "I didn't want to come out, it felt so wonderful!" Think about that dreamlike state when you first wake up. Doesn't it make you want to go back to sleep and finish that dream?

But others say, "What's the big deal, I didn't feel all that different?" People often expect to feel something dramatic, as though being in a meditative state is a magic place and that something special and unusual is going to happen just by being there. Remember that it's a familiar state—you have been there many times before.

HOW DO I KNOW
WHEN I AM THERE?

A big concern for those new to meditation is, "How do I know when I am there?" There are no announcements or road signs that say "You are here." You won't feel dramatically different. Unless you are using biofeedback equipment or are hooked up to an EEG, you won't have actual data to show that you are there.

Let's go ahead and experiment. Take a few moments to do this exercise:

Sit comfortably in a chair. Close your eyes and mentally count backward from ten to one. Ten. As you say the number ten to yourself, take a deep, gentle, relaxing breath, hold it for a moment, and then exhale. Allow yourself to think of the number ten. Perhaps you can even see a number ten in your mind. Nine. As you say the number nine to yourself, take a gentle, relaxing breath, hold it for a moment, and then

exhale. Allow yourself to think of the number nine. Perhaps you can
even see the number nine in your mind. Eight. As you say the number
eight to yourself, take a gentle, relaxing breath, hold it for a moment,
and then exhale. Allow yourself to think of the number eight. You can
even see a number eight in your mind. Seven. As you say the number
seven to yourself, take a gentle, relaxing breath, hold it for a moment,
and then exhale. Allow yourself to think of the number seven. You can
even see a number seven in your mind. And as you continue to count
down, you feel yourself becoming more and more relaxed. Six. As you
say the number six to yourself, take a gentle, relaxing breath, hold it for
a moment, and then exhale. Allow yourself to think of the number six.
You can even see a number six in your mind. Five. As you say the
number five to yourself, take a gentle, relaxing breath, hold it for a moment, and then exhale. Allow yourself to think of the number five. You
can even see a number five in your mind. Four. As you say the number
four to yourself, take a gentle, relaxing breath, hold it for a moment,
and then exhale. Allow yourself to think of the number four. You can
even see a number four in your mind. And as you continue to slowly
count down, you feel yourself becoming even more relaxed. Three. As
you say the number three to yourself, take a gentle, relaxing breath,
hold it for a moment, and then exhale. Allow yourself to think of the
number three. You can even see a number three in your mind. Two. As
you say the number two to yourself, take a gentle, relaxing breath, hold
it for a moment, and then exhale. Allow yourself to think of the number
two. It's easy to see a number two in your mind. One. As you say the
number one to yourself, take a gentle, relaxing breath, hold it for a moment, and then exhale. Allow yourself to think of the number one. You
see a number one in your mind. And as you see the number one, you
are feeling relaxed, so very, very relaxed. Allow this feeling to spread over
your entire body, from the top of your head to the tips of your toes. Take
a few moments to enjoy this sensation . . . the sensation of being totally
relaxed. Just focus on how very good you feel. Now, in a moment, count
upward from one to five. One . . . slowly becoming awake and aware.
Two . . . even more awake and aware. Three . . . as you count upward
you are feeling more and more awake. Four, you are feeling aware and
awake. Five, you are now wide awake and feeling refreshed!

That was a very short and simple meditation exercise. How did you do? We were aiming for a feeling of relaxation, so if you were relaxed, you did just fine. You got where you needed to go.

Still, people worry about whether or not they "got" there. When someone first works with meditation, they expect to feel different. In classes I hear comments such as, "It can't be that simple." Well, yes, it can . . . and yes, it is. But because a meditative state is so familiar to our mind, it can be difficult to recognize and label as such.

When I teach beginner meditation classes, my students and I have *slightly* different goals. They want to know how to reach a meditative state so they can use it. My purpose is to teach them to get there when they want, and then to hold and control that state so they can use it. Teaching them to reach it is the easiest part. Once we've done an exercise or two, I rarely have to spend time convincing them that they were "there."

HOW DO I KNOW
IF I DID IT RIGHT?

The next big concern is "Did I do it right?" A common statement is, "I'm sure I didn't do it right. I could hear everything going on around me. I could hear the dogs barking next door and the grandfather clock downstairs." Or, "I listened to the meditation tape, but I could still hear every word that was said."

That's quite true, you can hear noises. You are still aware of what is going on around you. You hear and understand things that are said to you. You are not in a zombielike state. Have you ever been daydreaming and the telephone rang? You were aware of that fact. You may have wondered for a moment or two if the telephone was ringing in the daydream or ringing in the present time. However, you were able to hear it. During meditation your senses are still intact; you can smell, hear, and feel. You also can think and make decisions.

It is true that the deeper the meditative state you attain, the less you are concerned with what is going on around you. However, very few people reach such a deep meditative state as to be unaware.

When people reach a very deep state they just do not pay attention to normal noises and distractions.

The mind is always aware of what is going on, even if it's not at the forefront of conscious thought. It's one of our basic instincts for survival. Should something occur that your mind perceived as a possible danger, you would quickly be alert to that possibility. Even when we are sound asleep we have some awareness of our surroundings. We all know people that we jokingly say could sleep through a bomb blast. While they may sleep extremely deeply, you can bet they'd wake up for a real bomb.

You can use noise to your advantage. I like to add to my scripts comments about noises such as this: "The traffic noises will not disturb me, in fact, they will help me reach a deeper, more relaxed state. With each passing truck, with each passing car I will feel more and more relaxed."

BY CAR, BOAT,
PLANE, OR TRAIN?

Do you have a favorite place you like to go to? Perhaps you have a good friend that you enjoy visiting. Getting there is fairly easy because you know the way. Maybe it took a little longer the first time you went because you didn't know the route. But after that, finding it again was easier. Or have you ever ridden along with someone to the same place several times but found you had to think about the route the first time you drove there yourself? Going into a meditative state is much like that; you've been there before. It also gets easier to return there with just a bit of practice.

Let's think about the analogy of your friend's house a bit more. There might be several ways to travel to her house. Most of the time you probably take a certain route, but once in a while you may take an alternate road. Maybe the fastest way is by highway, but there are days when you prefer a more rural route. Both will get you there; only the scenery is different.

The most important thing to remember is that there is no one way to "get" there. We are all individuals with different tastes and our own likes and dislikes. We have different moods. There are many routes we can take to the meditative state. So don't allow yourself to get caught up thinking that there is a right way because that also implies that there is a wrong way. Whatever works for you at the time is the right way.

Below are some different ways to "get" there. You can use them just to relax or as a deepening method for any meditation you want to do. Feel free to experiment by trying them with some of the scripts and techniques in this book or with your own scripts.

Counting: The Beautiful Horse

Of course you can simply count either up or down. One ... two ... three ... and so forth. What you are trying to do is make the mind get from "here" to "there." Now technically there is no here or there, it's just a brain wave pattern. But the mind is accustomed to having a way. Counting can work quite well. Although simply counting can be a bit dull, there are ways to spice it up.

> Imagine a beautiful horse, tall and majestic. See how he prances about, looking proud and strong. He's in a wide, open pasture, standing beside a fence. This fence extends as far as the eye can see. It's a warm, sunny and breezy day, just the right kind of day to make a horse feel exhilarated, free, and happy to be alive. Notice how he starts running alongside the fence and how his long mane and tail flow out behind him. As he runs, each fence post passes by. As the horse stretches his legs, mane and tail flying . . . and runs . . . you see the first fence post as he passes by it. The horse is feeling free and happy and runs past the next fence post . . . two . . . see his mane and tail extending behind him as he passes the next fence post . . . three . . . notice how free the horse feels as he passes the next fence post . . . four . . . see how his hooves move in rhythm as he passes the next fence post . . . five . . . feeling so free and happy . . . as the next fence post goes by . . . six . . . feeling relaxed and wonderful . . . seven . . . so very happy to be alive . . . eight . . . more and more free and relaxed . . . nine . . . feeling more free and relaxed than he has ever felt before . . . ten.

Feeling: The Beach

You can make use of your senses, such as feelings and touch, to help you reach a meditative state. The more senses you use, the more real your meditation will be. And that will help make it more effective.

> Imagine yourself at the beach. It's a lovely day, the air is fresh and clean, and the temperature is just right. See yourself walk down to the water's edge. You are feeling very happy, safe, and secure. The sand feels wonderful between your toes. Feel how cool and refreshing the sand is as you sit down near the water. Stretch your legs so the waves touch your feet and gently cover your ankles. See and feel as the first wave flows over your feet and ankles and then retreats. Allow yourself to relax as each wave gently washes over your feet and ankles and then slowly retreats. The waves come in and out . . . in and out . . . And with each wave that flows over your feet and ankles, any tension in your body and mind just washes away.

ANATOMY OF A SCRIPT

An easy way to start practicing meditation is by using a script. In fact, for novices it's probably the best way to get used to holding a meditative state. Scripts can help you to keep your focus. Especially in the beginning, the mind can easily wander. As you listen to the words and phrases, the words help keep you on track. A script is simply a list of phrases that will help you achieve meditation and focus on what to do once you are there.

These are the basic elements and characteristics of a script:

A *deepening method*

Positive, reinforcing statements

Statements for focus, such as imagery

Statements for an action, i.e., relaxation, behavior modification, self-improvement

Repetition

A method for returning to full consciousness

A Deepening Method

The purpose of a deepening method is to shift your awareness from the outside world to your inner world. There are many methods that can be used, such as counting, using stairs, eye fixation, or breathing. There are a few in this chapter, as well as different styles throughout this book.

Studies show that we tend to have one sense that is our predominant mode of learning, thinking, and perceiving. Just as people do things differently, they have different methods of thinking and of processing and using information. However, that doesn't mean this is the only way we can do those things. It means that is how we tend to do them in most cases. This predominant sense will have much to do with the deepening methods that work best for you in meditation, and even the ones you prefer.

Positive, Reinforcing Statements

These are such statements as "you feel very relaxed," "you feel comfortable," or "you feel safe and secure." Phrases such as these help to reinforce feelings that will enhance relaxation. Other statements are suggestive in nature so that you can do the action: "It is very easy for you to relax." "You are a confident and positive person." Meditation exercises have a purpose. They bring about a feeling of relaxation or aim for improvement of a behavior, or both.

Statements for Focus

Meditation involves being able to focus. Thoughts, sounds, feelings, and visualizations all can be used toward this end. A large number of scripts utilize guided imagery, which is simply a series of phrases that will help evoke not only pictures in our minds but feelings and thoughts as well. The point of guided imagery is to help us use as many of our senses as fully as possible.

Other methods certainly can be used. Visualization is not the only method. We can focus on a sound by using a mantra. Concentrating on feelings, especially pleasant ones, work quite well. Even focusing on the sensation of touch can be very conducive to achievement of a meditative state.

Statements for an Action

These statements could be simply relaxing. However, meditation can be used for a wide range of purposes beyond relaxation: improvement of self-confidence, ridding oneself of bad habits, goal setting, memory improvement, and more. A statement such as, "Now you see yourself full of confidence, sure of your abilities" allows your mind to see this as an accomplished feat. This helps motivate you to make that mental picture a reality in your day-to-day life.

Repetition

When we are in a meditative state, we are highly suggestible. The more repetitive a script is, the more likely it is that our subconscious will take those suggestions. Repetition strengthens those suggestions because the mind has heard them before. It builds familiarity. Think about how commercials work; they repeat phrases throughout the script. It's also no accident that companies frequently pay to have their commercials repeated within minutes. Again, repetition builds familiarity.

Method for Returning

You will usually find a phrase similar to "you will be wide awake" at the end of scripts and meditation exercises. Now, you never were asleep. Well, maybe you were, as people have been known to fall asleep while meditating. However, that's different. The meditative state itself is not sleep. It may feel similar to sleep as we may recall that daydreamy state we are in when we first wake up. If you watch someone meditating, it may even look like the subject is asleep.

A phrase like that is used not to wake us up, but rather to create a shift of awareness. Just as we wanted to pay attention to our inner world while in meditation, we now want to pay attention to our outer world once again.

FLYING WITHOUT A SCRIPT

I call these free-form meditations. In a free-form meditation you take an idea or a concept and then "go with it." You use a deepening method of your choice, or simply close your eyes and start imagining and thinking. For example, you might want to work on your self-confidence. You would then imagine yourself in situations, picturing yourself as already having self-confidence. It helps to have people around you in your visualization, for instance, seeing a friend of yours coming into the "scene" of your meditation. Be creative. Add as much detail as you can, making up the scenario as you go along.

I use the free-form method a lot. Before I actually do the meditation, I figure out exactly what I want to accomplish. Am I looking for relaxation? Do I need to work on a habit I'd like to eliminate? Do I just want to allow my mind to be creative and see what happens? Free-form meditation takes a little more focus, so new meditators may want to start out using scripts or meditation tapes. However, I certainly encourage you to try it out even if you are new to meditation. The worst thing that will happen is that your mind will wander a bit or you'll fall asleep.

Below are some ideas for free-form types of meditation. Use the deepening method you prefer.

Picture or imagine yourself having lost weight

Picture or imagine yourself as a nonsmoker

Picture or imagine going on a vacation

"Practice" an event that will soon take place, such as an upcoming job interview, or a talk that you plan to have with a friend, boss, or co-worker

YOU TAKE
MY BREATH AWAY

Breathing is an important function for sustaining life. As we breathe we take oxygen into our lungs. It's an involuntary act, which we do instinctively and rarely think about. The trouble is, a great number of us do it in an inefficient way. We tend to breathe while pulling our stomachs in, thereby breathing with our chest muscles. The proper way to breathe is to allow your abdomen to expand as you take a breath. Have you heard the expression "Use your diaphragm"? The diaphragm is a large muscle located at the bottom of the chest cavity, right below the lungs. When you take a breath, your diaphragm tightens and flattens, allowing the lungs to fill with oxygen.

Not sure whether you breathe efficiently? Take a moment now to focus on your breathing and how you do it. Is it your chest or your stomach that is expanding? Do this a few times over the next three or four days. Note whether you are chest breathing or abdomen breathing.

Another not very healthy habit is that of holding our breath. This is common during times of stress. This only serves to keep stress in our bodies.

We also breathe too shallowly. That isn't the same thing as working hard to breathe. It has to do with the amount of oxygen we take in. We don't have to breathe hard to take in more oxygen. Actually, the slower we breathe, the more oxygen we take in.

Proper breathing allows us to maximize the amount of oxygen we take into our bodies. When we breathe, oxygen purifies our blood, removing toxins and wastes.

HOW TO PRACTICE
PROPER BREATHING

Lie down on the floor. Place a small pillow under your knees for support

Place one hand on your chest and one hand on your lower abdomen

Take a slow, deep and comfortable breath, breathing through your nose and allowing your abdomen to rise

Exhale slowly and deeply through your mouth, allowing your abdomen to lower

Repeat several times, allowing a few moments between each cycle of breathing

When doing this exercise properly, you should feel your hand on your abdomen (stomach area) rise. If the hand that is placed on your chest rises instead, then you are not using your diaphragm to breathe. Notice that breathing in should be comfortable. Do not breathe so hard that you feel uncomfortable or dizzy.

A breathing meditation is a wonderful way to learn how to focus. By thinking solely of your breathing cycle—that is each set of breaths in and out—you are doing exactly what brings about a meditative state. You are focusing. It is also extremely relaxing, as well as being healthy.

Breathing Exercise

Find a comfortable place to lie or sit. If you are lying down, place a pillow under your knees for support. Place your hands loosely at your sides. If you prefer to sit, sit with your feet flat and touching the floor, without crossing your legs. Place your hands comfortably on your legs, palms up, or palms down, whichever is most comfortable for you.

Now close your eyes and as you do so, take a deep, slow breath, inhaling to a count of four. Feel your belly gently rise. Allow yourself to think only of that breath. If other thoughts come into your mind, just allow them to drift away. Gently hold your breath for a count of four, and then exhale to a count of five. Feel your belly gently lower. Allow yourself to think only of that breath. Now take another deep, slow breath, inhaling to a count of four. Feel your belly gently rise. Allow yourself to think only of that breath. Gently hold your breath for a count of four, and then exhale to a count of five. Feel your belly gently lower. Allow yourself to think only of that breath. Now, take a deep, slow breath, inhaling to a count of four. Feel your belly gently rise. Allow yourself to think only of that breath. Gently hold your breath for a count of four, and then exhale to a count of five. Allow yourself to think only of that breath. Now take another deep, slow breath, inhaling to a count of four. Feel your belly gently rise. Allow yourself to think only of that breath. Gently hold your breath for a count of four, and then exhale to a count of five. Feel your belly gently lower.

Keep repeating this pattern, allowing your thoughts to be only on each and every breath. For each breath you inhale, think only of that breath. For each breath you hold, think only of the breath you gently hold. For each breath you exhale, think only of that breath.

FOCUS

Meditation is the ability to focus on one thing or just a few things at a time. It is easy to reach a meditative state, but more challenging to hold it. Stray thoughts creep in and interfere with what we were focusing on. You can improve your ability to focus, and as you do so, you'll find that holding a meditative state becomes easier.

This candle flame exercise works well, not only in helping with practicing and retaining focus, but also aids in improving visualization skills. This exercise is best done in a draft-free room.

Candle Flame Exercise

Sit in a chair at a table, or sit on the floor. Place a candle on a flame-proof surface such as a stoneware plate. Take a few moments to allow yourself to relax, such as a breathing exercise. Now, light the candle. Watch as the flame bursts into life. Look at the flame and focus your attention on that flame. Think only of that flame, how it looks . . . the way it flickers in the slightest of breezes. Notice the color of the flame . . . how it appears to be one color near its center, and another at its tip. Focus your attention . . . your awareness on all the colors of the flame. Watch as it slowly moves . . . just as if it were a living, breathing thing. Think only of the candle flame, how it looks, how it acts. If a stray thought comes into your mind, simply brush it away. You can come back to it later, but for now your thoughts enjoy being on the candle flame. Notice how it moves as though it were dancing just for you. Notice everything about the candle flame . . . how it looks . . . how it moves . . . how it smells.

Now, close your eyes and see the candle flame in your mind. Focus your attention on that flame. Think only of that flame, how it looks . . . the way it flickers in the slightest breeze. Notice the color of the flame . . . how it appears to be one color near its center and another at its tip. Focus your attention . . . your awareness on all the colors of the flame. Watch as it slowly moves . . . just as though it were a living, breathing thing. See only that candle flame, how it looks, how it acts. If a stray thought or another picture comes into your mind, simply brush it away. You can come back to these thoughts or pictures later, but for now your thoughts enjoy being on the candle flame. Notice how it moves as though it were dancing just for you. Notice everything about the candle flame . . . how it looks . . . how it moves . . . how it smells.

If you need to remember what the candle flame looks like, you can simply open your eyes and look at it for a moment. Then close your eyes and picture the candle flame in your mind. See it, sense it, know it; yes, you can see the candle flame perfectly.

Spot on the Wall Exercise

Find a spot on the wall at a comfortable eye level. You could choose a picture hanging on the wall or even a design in the wallpaper. Sit comfortably in a chair, preferably one with back support. Then, just stare at the spot on the wall.

As I look at the spot I have chosen, I place all my attention and all my awareness on that spot. As I continue to stare at that spot, I notice that as I do so, it becomes easier and easier to focus on the spot. It becomes clearer and easier to focus on the spot. Even if it appears to move a little, I am still easily able to stare at that spot. Even if it doesn't move at all, it is so very easy for me to keep looking at that spot. I allow myself to think only of that spot, I am focused on that spot, and it is easy for me to do this. If another thought comes into my mind, I can simply brush it away, knowing I can return to that thought later. For now, my awareness and my focus is on the spot I have chosen.

I'm going to close my eyes for a moment and allow my thoughts to remain on that spot. And as I close my eyes, I can easily think of the spot, and only the spot I have chosen. Now I reopen my eyes, and as I do so, there is the spot I have chosen right before me. It is easy for me to focus my thoughts on this spot. Now, I close my eyes again and allow my thoughts to remain on the spot I have chosen. And as I have my eyes closed I know that my awareness and my focus are on that spot. I can lift up my hand and point to the spot I have chosen. It is as though I can touch that spot . . . as though I can feel it. If any other thoughts come into my mind, I can simply brush them away, knowing I can think about those thoughts later. For now, my awareness and my focus are on the spot I have chosen.

And now I take a deep gentle breath, hold it for a moment, and then slowly open my eyes. I may now return my awareness to the things around me. I can stretch my arms, fingers, neck and head, legs and feet, and my awareness returns to the chair I am sitting on . . . the room I am sitting in. I feel very relaxed, comfortable, and aware.

THE SENSES

The meditational world is not one-dimensional. We have the ability to use all of our senses, such as sight, hearing, touch, and even taste. Our meditations become more realistic and effective if we can bring as many of our senses as possible into them. Both styles of meditation utilize the senses. Active meditation tends to use them more purposefully. However, passive meditation isn't "nothingness." It just means we are mentally less active.

WHY EYES CLOSED?

Near the beginning, almost every meditation tape or exercise has the statement, "close your eyes." Why? The reason is stimuli from visual sources. There are literally hundreds of thousands of data that the eye takes in all within seconds. If you close your eyes, you've just made it easier to focus because you have shut out quite a large number of distractions. Quite simply, for most people, especially those new to meditation, it's easier.

However, you *can* meditate with your eyes open! We usually daydream with our eyes open and do it quite well. Hopefully, highway hypnosis occurs when our eyes are open. I've even seen some people who are able to attain sleep with their eyes open.

The major reason for bringing up this point is because I am so often asked, "If I open my eyes, am I going to ruin it?" When we see a picture of someone meditating, typically we see a person with his or her eyes closed. It is easy to assume that it is a requirement, that it won't "work" if we have our eyes open. Especially while in meditation groups, we may want to check our surroundings. "Am I safe?" "What are the people around me doing?" "Did someone new come into the room?" "What is the source of that sound?"

This is a good time to also bring up the fact that you can move while in meditation. If you have an itch, by all means scratch it. You will not ruin a meditation by moving a leg or an arm. In fact, if you find yourself thinking, "I really am uncomfortable, and want to move my leg," just go ahead and move it. If you don't, soon that is all you will be focusing on, the fact that you are uncomfortable.

VISUALIZATON

Let's talk about visualization. I'd like to help you get past the misconceptions people have. I hear all too often, "I don't visualize well. I probably can't meditate because of that." You don't have to visualize well in order to meditate effectively. When we daydream, we can visualize well enough. But we aren't thinking about how well we visualize.

In meditation we don't have to see things crystal clear. It's not quite the same thing as actually seeing, as we do when our eyes are open. It's more of an "inner seeing." Visual people tend to see more complete visualizations. They may see complete movielike images, and their visualizations also often involve symbols.

My friend Phylameana Désy of Spiral Visions is primarily a visual person. She described to me how the process of visualization works for her: "When I first worked with meditation and visualization, I noticed that I saw simple symbols. One of the first symbols that came to me was that of a spiral. I just saw it in my mind's eye, sort of like an inner seeing. A few years later when I started my own business, I decided to incorporate that symbol into the name of my business."

If you are not highly visual, your ability to see more clearly can and will improve over time. I'm an auditory person, and when I first started, I had difficulty sustaining pictures in my head. I could see flashes of a picture, and then it would quickly disappear. Then a new picture would come into my mind. Since I am so highly auditory, I can hear a running commentary in the background. I may see a picture, but I am verbalizing the action in my mind. My daydreams, and dream state are very much the same.

Those who are more kinesthetic may "sense" what they are seeing more than actually seeing complete visualizations. They may feel the action, or even relate it verbally to themselves as, "I can feel myself walking." It can be more like a "knowing" rather than a physical seeing.

EXERCISES TO IMPROVE VISUALIZATION SKILLS

You can improve your ability to visualize. By practicing visualization with exercises such as the ones listed below, your ability to see and hold an image will get stronger.

Not all the exercises below require you to be meditating. For the ones that do, just use the deepening method you prefer. Just as with physical exercise, meditation exercises don't have to be drudgery. They can be fun and entertaining! Some may even seem a bit silly, but that's okay. You want your mind to have fun so it won't be bored and drift off elsewhere.

Visual Recall

I find this one of the best exercises to improve visualization skills. First, it's easy to do. You just recall a place you already know well. Second, it is an exercise you can do almost anywhere whenever you have a few spare minutes. You do not have to be in a meditative state.

To do one of these exercises, defocus your eyes as you do when you daydream or close your eyes if you prefer. A quick way to defocus your eyes is to think about something that happened yesterday. You will probably notice that your eyes tend to move to the side. Some people will look off to the side and slightly down, others off to the side and slightly up.

Imagine in your mind where you live. As you imagine your house or apartment, "see" it in your mind. If you are not already inside, go inside. As you do this, move around the room you are in. Stop to examine things . . . pictures on the wall, furniture, even the materials of the walls and the floor. Take the time to remember . . . and to see . . . every single object in that room. Go from room to room in your house or apartment and do the same thing in each and every room.

The more you practice this exercise, the more you will be able to see visual detail. Please note that when I use the word *see*, it is likely to be an inner seeing rather than an actual physical seeing. Using the place in which you live is a good example, for we know our home well in the real world. That makes it easier to see it in our inner world. I highly recommend using it as your first example for visual recall exercises. Then, as you go along, it's beneficial to add other places. This will give you greater flexibility; it will stretch your visual muscles. I also encourage you to have fun with these exercises so you'll enjoy them a lot more and they won't feel like boring practice.

Here are other examples for this exercise:

Use a friend or a relative's house

Use the home of one of your favorite TV characters

Go to your closet and examine each article of clothing. Notice the colors, fabrics, textures in as much detail as possible

Meet a Tree

Imagine yourself to be standing in a forest. See yourself in the forest. See the trees . . . how their trunks look, the colors of their leaves. Pick a tree that you would like to use for this exercise. Feel yourself walk over to that tree, and see yourself standing right in front of it. See how the breeze gently moves the leaves at the top of the tree. Smell how fresh and clean the air is.

Notice how the leaves on the ground smell as you walk around the tree. Hear the rustling of the leaves under your feet. Hear how the leaves sound when the breeze blows them. Feel how good it is to be in this forest, in front of this tree. It's very peaceful here. It sounds peaceful and it feels peaceful. Now see and feel yourself walking closer to the tree and touching it. Feel the bark against the palm of your hand. Notice how it feels on the tips of your fingers. Watch your hand as it gently touches the tree. Look closely at the bark, the texture it has. Feel the texture of the bark with your hand. Now hear yourself saying hello to the tree. Hear yourself talking to the tree.

SMELL

Don't discount the importance of the sense of smell in meditation! Smells can bring back memories and feelings. How about the smell of fresh apple pie baking? A lawn freshly cut? A baby fresh out of a bath? Certain fragrances can bring feelings of peace and calm, thereby enhancing meditations.

Incense is one way to utilize the sense of smell. However, there are those who do not like such a heavy scent or the smokiness it creates when burned. Essential oils, which are less heavy and smoky, are a wonderful way to introduce smell into your meditations. Essential oils are the liquids taken from the roots, stems, bark, flowers, or seeds of plants. They can be diffused into the air. The chapter in this book on Aromatherapy and Meditation will cover their use in greater detail.

Fresh, clean air helps in the meditative process. If we cannot breathe well because the air is stuffy, it will be distracting. You probably don't want to sit in a heavy draft however.

HEARING AND SOUND

Sounds can assist you in retaining focus, especially using a repetitive sound such as a mantra. Mantras are words or wordless sounds. Most mantras are one syllable, but a phrase can be used effectively.

Quite honestly, you can use any sound or word as long as it is reasonably pleasing to you. Some sounds just have a nice resonant tone. The sounds, *ohm* or *aum* are such tonal sounds. Auditory people do well using mantras or sounds to enhance their meditations.

Some modalities do use special sounds and words, but you do not have to use them if you have any concerns about them. You can substitute any word or sound you want. There are no magic words in meditation.

Perhaps you have seen a list of mantras in a book, but you aren't sure what the words really mean and that bothers you. Those words may have significance and meaning in a particular modality, but they center only on those specific beliefs. Those words or sounds have no special powers to make meditation work "correctly." Know that you can use any word or sound *you* feel comfortable with. Obviously, you want it to be a pleasing sound. Discordant sounds aren't conducive to a meditative state, but otherwise the actual sound or word makes absolutely no difference. If you wished, you could use the scales: *do, re, me, fa, so, la, ti, do.*

One meditation group I was in chanted the word *money* over and over. It was quite an interesting experience. We basically sang the word *money*—it came out much like, *muun—neeee.* We also used lines from pop songs, such as *sha na nah nah, hey, hey, hey.*

I'm sure that sounds a little ludicrous, but a mantra's purpose is to help you focus. It doesn't matter what you use. If you were meditating with a religious or spiritually-based group, it would be a different matter. But for basic meditation, the mantra's use is solely for focus. Words like *love, joy, smiles* could all be very good mantras.

There are two ways a mantra can be used: to keep focus by bringing one's attention back to the sound itself, or as a vehicle to see what visualizations it brings up.

Let the mantra come deep and rich from the back of your throat in a deep pitch. Think James Earl Jones, not Mariah Carey. Be sure to breathe, and don't hold a sound for so long it makes you dizzy or your throat hurt. Comfort is important. Take a breath and then sound out the word as you exhale. Slowly inhale again, and then sound the mantra while exhaling. If you need to, take a break between sounding the mantra to have a few quiet breaths.

Music

Music can be inspiring, mood elevating, soothing, and so much more. It is my feeling that the ability to make—and appreciate—music has been with us from the very beginning of time. Do certain pieces of music call up memories or create certain moods? There's no doubt about it, music is a powerful force.

You can use music to help achieve a meditative state. I often do this by playing pieces softly in the background that move me. Instrumental music works well because there are no lyrics to distract you. This is not a hard and fast rule, however. Sounds in nature, such as waterfalls, rainstorms, and thunderstorms, can be very soothing and relaxing. It's definitely your individual preference, for what relaxes me may not do the same for you.

Select a piece of music you like and play it softly. Close your eyes and really listen as though *you* were the music.

TOUCH AND MOVEMENT

Had a rough day? Massage can be a totally relaxing way to meditate. If you can't schedule a massage, get together with a friend and give each other a massage. Add some positive affirmations while giving the massage to make it extra special. Your friend doesn't have to be as good as a massage therapist for you to enjoy it. Just get some massage oil, such as almond oil, or add some essential oil mixed into unscented massage oil, and enjoy.

Movement such as dancing or rocking in a rocking chair can bring about a meditative state. You don't always have to be sitting or lying down to meditate. Go find a nice rocking chair on a porch—preferably one with a great view—and allow yourself to relax as you rock.

What's Your Position?

Some of us cannot attain a half or full lotus position. It's either uncomfortable or physically impossible. But does body position really matter? In some modalities that use meditation as part of their practices, yes, it does matter. But it has nothing to do with the ability to meditate successfully. It has more to do with energy flow and the way in which meditation is utilized in a particular belief system. It's the same with hand positions. For those who are interested, I will talk about this in the chapter on religion, spirituality, and modalities.

Hand or body positions, however, don't have much of an impact on basic meditation. That is not the same as saying they do not matter at all. What matters is having a common sense approach. You may not be interested in or believe in energy flow such as *Ki* in the body. But sitting or lying in a position in which circulation is not hampered is important. Muscle strain and fatigue are just as important a consideration.

With basic meditation we are concerned with comfort and health, as well as what is likely to work best for you. The first area to cover is the "sit or lie down" question. Which is better?

Neither one is "better" than the other. There are advantages and disadvantages to both. Ultimately, your decision will be based on what you prefer and what you find easiest for you. There are times when I sit, and other times when I prefer to lie down. Mood and tiredness play a big role in my decision-making process, and will probably do so in yours.

Lying Down

New meditators soon find that when they lie down they too easily fall asleep. You're in a recumbent position, just as you are when you go to bed. It's easy to slide right down into sleep. Mr. Sandman lies in wait for brand-new meditators (and some not-so-new ones as well)!

However, it's a very comfortable position and is unlikely to cause muscle strain. Lie down on a bed or on a padded mat. It is helpful to place a small pillow under your knees for support. Place your hands on the mat or on the bed beside you, or rest them lightly on your stomach.

Sitting

You can still fall asleep while sitting, but it's less likely that you will fall asleep as easily as you do lying down. Using a mat, pillow, or a chair is fine. Good back support can be very helpful, so a chair might be more comfortable. It is best to keep reasonably good posture, as it's easier to breathe, less of a strain on the muscles, and much healthier. The problem lies in posture, especially if you are sitting on a mat on the floor or using a pillow. Your neck and shoulders can get sore because your head can hang forward.

DIET . . .
DOES IT MATTER?

"Do I have to become a vegetarian to meditate?" No, it's a misconception that all people who meditate are vegetarians. Also they don't all wear turbans, have flowers in their hair, or wear long flowing robes.

Good nutrition and proper diet are important for health. A poor diet can put stress on the body and affect our ability to think. However, the decision to become a vegetarian is purely personal. I don't happen to be a vegetarian and I meditate.

A very full stomach can make you sleepy. Just think about how you feel after having a huge meal. Meditating when you are so lethargic is bound to put you to sleep. If you are going to eat before meditating, it's best to eat something light. But you *can* eat; you do not have to fast in order to meditate!

Caffeine can hinder meditation, so it helps if you don't drink coffee or soda just before meditating. I was talking with my brother Michael about this recently. I joked that whenever we went to meditation conferences everyone seemed conveniently to forget about the effects of caffeine. The first thing in the morning we would line up to go into the conference room with large cups of coffee in hand, and at lunchtime we would go have sodas. Oh well, it just proves that we're not perfect.

BITS AND PIECES

Here are some little tidbits about meditation:

Your body temperature falls when you meditate, so you might want to have a light blanket if you get cold. I always place one nearby, just in case. If you get cold and uncomfortable, soon that is all you will be thinking about. You'll be focused . . . but not on what you planned.

Cats love meditators! Now you might think it's because you are sitting and you've made a nice, comfy lap for them. Or, if you are lying down, that your stomach looks *just* as comfy. That may well be true, but the bigger reason is that you are in an alpha brain wave pattern. Cats are predominately in an alpha level, so they are attracted to you. It's as if they can sense it. Think this sounds a little farfetched? Ask any cat owner who meditates, or see if this happens to you when you meditate around your cat.

Chapter Five

Stumbling Blocks Along the Way

The scene is set. You are sitting in a quiet, comfortable place. You close your eyes, breathing in and out gently but deeply. As you let feelings of peace and serenity wash over you, a face appears. It's your boss reminding you that the report is due at 9:00 A.M. sharp and it better be good! Then your mother gets into the act, asking why you haven't changed the cat litter today and why are there dust bunnies under the bed.

You open your eyes, take a few deep breaths, and start again. This time as you drift into serenity, you remember that you forgot to pick up the dry cleaning.

Do you want to know the remark I hear most often when I discuss meditation? It's "I can't meditate." If you read the chapter on language you'll realize the other implications of that statement. But now, for the purposes of this chapter, we'll discuss its relation to stumbling blocks.

That statement is usually followed by explanations like these: "My mind wanders whenever I try to meditate," "I can't sit still," or "I can't visualize."

I'M PERFECT . . . NOT!

I've used meditation in my daily life for years. You might think I never have any problem meditating, right? Wrong! There are many days when I find myself easily distracted or have great difficulty staying focused. Stress rears its ugly head from time to time. These are very common occurrences, and I can pretty much guarantee that it happens, or will happen, to almost everyone.

In a perfect world we would all be able to meditate any time we choose. Distractions would not bother us, we would be able to shut out our problems, and stray thoughts would never come into our mind. We'd always have plenty of time. We'd never be too stressed out; after all, isn't that one of the reasons to meditate? But this is not a perfect world; the reality is that most of us will meet stumbling blocks somewhere along the way.

What are the likely culprits for causing problems and those stumbling blocks? Basically, they are

- Distractions and stray thoughts
- Stress
- Procrastination
- Fear

It can be one of these things, a combination of them, or all of them at once. The good news is that there are ways around them—and that's exactly what this chapter is about. Don't be afraid or discouraged, we'll take it step-by-step. It's time to pull out the artillery, and we have more than enough.

STRAY THOUGHTS, PUPPIES, AND MEMORIES

I wanted this book to include not only what people wanted to know but also what they needed to know about meditation. I spent a great deal of time talking with people and found that one of their biggest fears was not being able to do it "correctly." An overwhelming number of people felt they were doing it "wrong" because they couldn't keep stray thoughts from interfering.

Stray thoughts rank right up at the top of the list of stumbling blocks. Don't be discouraged; in fact, I am here to tell you to be *encouraged*! It's proof that you are a normal human being and your brain is working and functioning exactly as it should. It is a rare person who can consistently hold a meditative state time after time with no distraction ever creeping into their thoughts.

An interesting experiment to try is to write down every single thought that crosses your mind in a short period of time. I mean *each* and *every* thought. Doing this for only five minutes can fill up sheets and sheets of paper. Go ahead, try it; it's nearly impossible to do. By the time you have written down one thought, six others may have occurred to you. As soon as you have noticed that, you realize that realization is a thought in itself.

No, I am not trying to scare or discourage you. I'm merely pointing out what you are working with—a mean, lean thought machine! After all, that is what our mind does best: think. And, wow, can it ever produce thoughts in rapid-fire succession! My point is that a few stray thoughts, or even more than a few, should not be something to criticize yourself for.

Think of the mind as a wayward puppy. Left to its own devices, it will do what it wants, how it wants, when it wants. This is especially true for those who are new to the world of meditation. Your mind is merely acting like a puppy. It has been used to running its own show, and suddenly you are doing something different. It will try to take over again and produce stray thoughts to get your attention. It wants to be the boss!

Since it wants to be the boss, your mind feels what it's trying to tell you is more important. After all, you are just sitting there daydreaming. Of course the dry-cleaning is more important. How dare you try to run your own mind!

Another factor comes into play here. When you quiet your mind and reach a meditative state, memory comes into play. There are fewer thoughts to compete with, and all of a sudden you remember things. How many times have you been somewhere and tried to recall a person's name? At the time, no matter how hard you tried, you just couldn't remember it. Then of course, later on as you are drifting to sleep or even daydreaming at work, it will hit you. Peter! That's the name. While this tendency is wonderful when you need to remember something, it can be a distraction while meditating.

Reiki Master Lacy Ann Struve, from Wilmington, North Carolina, has an interesting way to deal with distracting thoughts while meditating. She told me, "I imagine having a corral right next to me when I meditate. Whenever a distracting or stray thought interferes, I simply imagine opening the gate to the corral. I usher in the thought, close the gate, and go back to my meditation. In that way, I know right where those thoughts are and I can give them attention later."

It will get easier with a bit of practice. The greatest difficulty for most people is not producing the meditative state but holding it. Again, it's like that puppy. It can be easy to get a puppy, but to make it do what you want takes a bit of effort. It squirms and struggles because it wants to run and play. It just takes a little discipline.

Ugh, *discipline* and *practice,* what ugly words! We often equate anything that takes effort as not being very much fun. Practice does not have to be drudgery. Much of your success can be measured by your attitude. Is meditating work or play? Is it enjoyable?

When you read some of the exercises in this book that are designed to help you practice, learn to focus, or enhance visualization skills, you might think some of them are silly. You are quite right. A few are rather silly. I did that on purpose. Why? Because boredom is a major reason for failure, loss of focus, procrastination, and even the "I just don't want to do it" scenario.

It reminds me of piano lessons. Like many children, I took them when I was a young girl. I really hated them; they were boring. I didn't think that repeatedly practicing the scales was much fun. I didn't take many lessons before I quit. Today I realize the importance of those exercises—the necessity of learning the basics. Since then, I've met a few piano teachers who have figured out ways of putting fun into those basics. They realize the importance of injecting fun into the process. I bet their students appreciate it; I know I would have.

MEDITATION OLYMPICS

Let's face it, our ego also can have a lot to do with our success. It's human nature to want to do things well. Many of us are highly competitive, especially with ourselves. We want to be perfect! It becomes a matter of how fast we can learn something, do it, and then excel at it. Go easy on yourself.

It's like a baby taking his first steps. Usually a baby will take a step or two and then fall down flat on his little behind! Rarely have

I seen a baby who just gets up and starts walking perfectly from the start. Babies achieve results from practice and more practice. Still, do not be discouraged if there are times when your ability to concentrate flags. I learned to walk like most babies, but even as an adult I still fall down occasionally. I know how to walk; I just don't do it perfectly one hundred percent of the time.

STRESS—THE CATCH-22

Meditation is wonderful for reducing stress. Yet stress can be a large stumbling block. The very same stresses in our lives we want to use meditation for, can be the very same things that make it difficult to meditate!

If you are heavily stressed, take the time to do a long physical *and* mental relaxation technique, such as the ones in the Relaxation chapter. Then work with meditations that help with focus, as that's usually a problem area when highly stressed. The One-Minute Vacation technique, which is listed below in this chapter, is also an excellent way to practice when you are too stressed or distracted to easily meditate. That way you can chip away at a heavy stress level bit by bit. I would recommend doing it several times during the day. That will help your stress level become more manageable.

PROCRASTINATION
REARS IT'S UGLY HEAD

Why would we procrastinate when it comes to meditation? After all, it's good for us, and it can make us feel better. But why do we procrastinate when it comes to anything? It's because we have "reasons." Now, reasons can be real or they can be excuses masquerading as reasons. I call these the "I'm-too-ers."

"I've been busy" and "I don't have time" are probably two of the most common excuses on the face of the planet. Not just for meditation either. If you think about it, I'm sure you've used them a lot; I know I have.

Question: "Why haven't you called?"

Answer: I've been busy.

Question: "Why didn't you read that report?

Answer: I've been busy.

It's one of those one-answer-fits-all statements. It works in a multitude of situations. I've often felt that we all own a book called, *How to Survive Life and Get Away with It*. It's an imaginary book of course, but I know we have it just the same. It's filled with all kinds of information and details: how to handle sticky situations, stock answers to trick questions, and lines that work for every occasion. Take for example the question, "Do I look fat in this dress." Correct answer: "No, of course not." Exactly how and when to use the line "I've been busy" *must* be in that book!

There are times when it's not an excuse, and we have been busy. Taking time out during the day to meditate might be a near-impossible dream. If you were that busy, it certainly would be good for you to take the time. Meditation can relax and rejuvenate you. That doesn't mean you can easily take the time, however.

The One-Minute Vacation

In the chapter on relaxation, there is a technique called the Mental Vacation. It's a great technique, and I hope you experiment with it. The really good thing is that it has a side benefit. Once you've done it once and have a special mental vacation place, you can easily picture yourself there in a matter of seconds.

So on really busy days when you have precious little time, use this technique:

Take a deep breath, mentally say the word *relaxing* to yourself, and as you exhale, picture yourself in your special vacation place.

It's as simple as that. You don't have to be in a deep meditative state. You don't even have to be in a meditative state at all! You can do it as a short meditation for as little as a minute or two. Chances are, you can sneak a minute or two out of your schedule no matter how busy the day is. When I was in the nine-to-five work force, and things got hectic, I used to do this technique during a short powder room break. No one will ever notice because it can be done so quickly and you don't have to be gone for any length of time.

Since you quickly go to an alpha state, that minute is a very restful one. It is believed that our bodies regenerate while in alpha. The alpha brain wave pattern is the same brain wave pattern we are in while meditating. So a minute in the meditative state is far more restful than a minute in a non-meditative state.

Yes, you can produce alpha that quickly! At the end of the exercise in the chapter on relaxation, you give yourself a post-hypnotic suggestion. You tell yourself that from now on whenever you take a deep breath and mentally say "relaxing" to yourself while exhaling you will quickly be relaxed. Then while you are picturing yourself at your special vacation spot, you are both physically and mentally relaxed in just a minute.

I say this phrase at the end of most of the meditations I do: "Whenever I take a deep breath and say 'relaxing' to myself mentally while exhaling, I will become relaxed both mentally and physically." It continually reinforces that post-hypnotic suggestion, and therefore, it is very easy for me to relax quickly.

Another time and place that is perfect to meditate is just before going to sleep. You're in bed anyway, so if you fall asleep while meditating it won't be a problem. It is a blessing for insomniacs because it can help you get *to* sleep. Insomnia at times is caused by having too much to think about and rehashing of the problems of the day. By meditating instead you could do three things at once: stop obsessing about the day, *do* something about it, and fall asleep.

I'm Too Tired

This is another all-time great excuse for a multitude of situations. Consider, however, that meditation can help you feel less tired. Using the One-Minute Vacation technique described above, or one very similar, is rejuvenating. Sometimes we are tired because we don't sleep well at night. Meditation can help you sleep better and wake up rested. Utilizing a short meditation, such as the one below, just before going to sleep can help you have a more restful night.

Sleep Better Meditation

Lie on your back or side, whichever is the most comfortable position for you. Take a few moments to do some gentle breathing. Take slow breaths in, hold for a few moments, and then gently exhale. Allow your body to stretch . . . luxuriate in the feeling of being able to stretch in the bed. Stretch out any kinks in your body . . . stretch your hands and fingers . . . stretch legs, feet, and toes. Now that you are comfortably stretched and feeling relaxed, allow your body to take a comfortable position. And as you become comfortable, you know that this feeling of comfort will last for the entire night, for the entire time you sleep. Your body will easily find a position that is comfortable at any time during the night. It will be so easy for your body to do this, you won't even notice if you change positions. Isn't it wonderful that this feeling of being stretched, relaxed, and comfortable will be with you during the entire time you sleep.

Now that you are comfortably in bed and ready to drift off to sleep for the night, you know it will be easy and effortless to allow your thoughts to be restful and peaceful. Any problems you had during the day just fade lightly away . . . just like a dream . . . like a pleasant dream. And as you relax even more, you find that you are ready to dream . . . wonderful dreams . . . and you know that your dreams will be pleasant.. . . and that when you wake up in the morning you will wake up feeling refreshed. You will wake up at just the right time . . . the time you need to wake up . . . easily and gently . . . ready to start a brand-new day. You will feel wonderful when you wake up . . . for you will have had a whole night's sleep . . . a whole night of comfortable sleep. You will be as comfortable as you are now . . . and feel just as you do right now . . . comfortable and peaceful and ready to rest. So now . . . just allow your thoughts to drift into those pleasant dreams of restful sleep.

FEAR

Fear can be a stumbling block for those who are new to meditation. They wonder what the experience is going to be like. Information is the key, for having information and knowledge about meditation beforehand will reduce fear. There are a lot of myths about meditation. Let's look at some of the more common ones:

> *Myth*: You can get stuck in meditation.
> *Fact*: No, you can't get stuck. Meditation is a brain wave pattern, and the brain regularly cycles in and out of these patterns. It would be impossible to hold a meditative state forever. The most that will happen is that your brain wave pattern will slow down and you will fall asleep.

> *Myth*: I don't visualize well, therefore, I can't meditate.
> *Fact*: We all are able to visualize, we just have different ways of "seeing." Visualization is more of an inner seeing, rather than seeing with our eyes.

> *Myth*: I can't empty my mind, therefore, I'll never be able to meditate.
> *Fact*: Meditation does not require an empty mind. There are two forms of meditation: active and passive. Even passive meditation doesn't require that you have an empty mind.

> *Myth*: I might miss something important, like my children calling me or a fire in the room.
> *Fact*: You are still aware while in a meditative state. If something happened that required your immediate attention, you would come out of the meditative state.

BRING IN ALL THE ARTILLERY

There are days when I have difficulty reaching a meditative state. My mind may wander, or I'm easily distracted. Sometimes I'm just not in the mood because I have a lot on my mind. I use aids such as scented candles, incense, or essential oils to make the room smell pleasant. I put on soothing music in the background. I turn off the bright lights and use candles instead. I create a mood—one that's relaxing and soothing.

I am primarily an auditory person, therefore, music is one of the best aids for me. Whenever I am too distracted or stressed to meditate easily, putting on a soothing CD makes a world of difference. Never mind just for meditating, I find music to be very relaxing at anytime. Actually, I'd like to thank Kenny G., Enya, Loreena McKennitt, and Yanni for helping me stay relaxed while writing this book.

Use a gentle light source such as candles if you are primarily visual. If you are able, create a pleasing space in which to meditate. Use colors that are pleasing to you. Find paintings and posters that you find aesthetic and place them on the walls.

If you are kinesthetic, try filling up the tub and soak for a while. Go ahead and add the other senses, use scented oils in the water, play music in the background, and light candles. Again, make a whole mood—one that is relaxing and enjoyable. It's time for you, go ahead and take it!

Chapter Six

Religion and Meditation

A monk lies prostrate on a cold stone floor oblivious to his world around him. The bells toll in the background, yet he is focused on his thoughts.

A priest sits at the bedside of a comatose patient. He takes the person's hand and sits in deep contemplative thought.

A young Indian warrior goes on a vision quest: He fasts, climbs to the top of a mountain, and sits quietly awaiting a vision.

When I told a colleague that I was writing a book on meditation, he asked, "Isn't meditation part of one of those strange religions?" While meditation is part of many religions, meditation itself is not a religion. They are two completely different things. True, in some religions meditation is such an integral part of their practices and philosophies that it is difficult to separate the two. However, meditation is a distinct and separate practice from religion.

Throughout history, meditation has been a part of religion. Shamans, medicine men, priests, and spiritual leaders all have used meditation in some form. Prayer is very similar to meditation. While praying you are focusing on the prayer or on the act of praying. This focus brings about a meditative state.

You can meditate and not be part of any particular religious creed. You can also meditate and not go against the tenets of your religion. The practice of pure meditation does not go against religious practices. The ends to which you *use* it could well do so, in some cases. For example, meditating for relaxation is a common use. I doubt any religion on this planet would be against relaxation or stress reduction. Using meditation to communicate with spirit guides, however, may be considered a suspect practice by some religions. For others, it would not be a part of their belief system. A member of those religions simply would not use meditation for those purposes.

Meditation, as practiced by the large majority of people who use it, is completely separate from religion. It's simply focusing on fewer thoughts or images. It's a natural process of the brain. Interestingly, I am repeatedly asked to explain the correlation between meditation and religion. Because religious beliefs are such an integral part of our core belief system, I certainly understand why.

In this book, I use meditation techniques that are as pure as possible, without any religious slant one way or another. The same principle applies for the purposes for which meditation can be used. Should any of them run counter to your beliefs, simply disregard them. Please feel free to discuss the methods in this book with your priest, rabbi, or spiritual counselor.

Because each religion or modality that uses meditation has its own doctrines, it *is* possible to meditate incorrectly. For example, some practices require the practitioner to sit in either a full or half lotus position. In others, certain hand positions are necessary. Meditation itself has no such requirements. Body or hand positions are more a matter of what is comfortable and will not restrict circulation. There are groups and practices that have the singular goal of reaching a very passive meditation or of silencing the mind. However, meditation has both active and passive modes.

BUT IS IT A CULT THING?

Many people feel uncomfortable telling others that they meditate for fear of being thought weird or a member of a cult. This is magnified by the media's tendency to portray meditation as part of New Age beliefs. Meditation is not a New Age practice; however, some people who believe in New Age ideals practice it. There is a big difference. While many people who meditate also use astrology or tarot, meditation stands on its own. There are cults that have used meditation as part of their group activities. But it is important to realize that the cult's beliefs have nothing to do with meditation itself.

A short while ago I was facilitating a meditation class. A gentleman who happened to be walking past the room stopped and asked me what I was teaching. I told him that I was teaching meditation techniques for stress reduction. He looked at me with a horrified expression on his face and asked what my religion was. I asked him what teaching stress reduction and my religion had to do with each other. He said that stress reduction wasn't the problem, but he had been told that meditation was a cult religion. Once I understood what his concerns were, I was able to explain exactly what meditation is . . . and isn't.

There are groups that use the word *meditation* in their name. Because of that, it would be easy for people to associate meditation solely with that particular group. One such group I am constantly asked about is Transcendental Meditation, or TM. This group has come under fire for concealing the fact that their views and practices may be religious in nature.

It is not within the scope of this book, nor is it my intention, to prove or disprove that there are religious beliefs behind Transcendental Meditation. Perhaps it is because of the publicity, but whenever the words *cult* and *meditation* are linked together, someone will undoubtedly bring up TM. Since I am writing a book on meditation and this is a question I am often asked, I feel I should talk about this issue.

There are legions of supporters who feel that TM practices are extremely beneficial and nonreligious in nature. In the book *Happiness, The TM Program, Psychiatry and Enlightenment,* authors Harold H. Bloomfield, M.D., and Robert B. Kory say this: "In fact, the TM technique is easy, works immediately, requires no special postures, and does not involve a change in religion, belief, or lifestyle." However, large numbers of people vehemently disagree with that statement.

TM uses a series of mantras, sounds that are repeated to help create focus for a meditative state. The controversy lies not in the fact that mantras are used, but in the presence or absence of religious meaning behind those mantras. Additionally, there is controversy about the failure to disclose the religious meaning of a mantra to members. The mantras that are given are considered to be sounds sacred to Hindu gods or Vedic deities, yet members of TM are told that mantras are individually chosen by a "secret code" and that they have no special meaning.

Some claim that even the teachers of TM are not told that the mantras have religious significance. John M. Knapp, the executive director and editor of *Trancenet Journal,* was a TM instructor for twenty-two years. He told me, "We were told in TM teacher training—and throughout our TM career—that the TM mantras had no special meaning. But most of us knew this wasn't true, especially once we were told to add 'namah' and 'shri' to lengthen our original mantra. Even with the little bit of Sanskrit we were taught, we knew this translated as 'I bow down to the illustrious (god).'"

Some have qualms about showing respect for Hindu gods, for Hinduism is one of the world's major religions. There are many religions in this world, and each has a fundamental right to exist and to have its own beliefs. Some proponents of TM feel that merely repeating Sanskrit mantras does not betray their own religious beliefs, that these are just words. But others feel that it is contrary to their religious beliefs and that it is unethical to teach a method and not disclose the philosophy behind it.

Meditation in and of itself is not a cult, nor is it dangerous. There are many groups that use meditation in ways of their own that are far from the purposes of basic meditation. Whether these groups are cults or not is difficult to determine.

Various groups have strict requirements with respect to meditation. Groups whose original intention was far from any cultlike purpose have transformed themselves into bona fide cults. Some groups have been accused of cult activity although there is no real basis for the allegation. How can we tell the difference? The chapter on group meditation will cover this in greater detail.

OTHER MODALITIES

Many modalities and practices utilize meditation in some fashion, including yoga, reiki, and massage. For some, it's an integral part of the system; for others, it's a complementary companion.

Yoga

The practice of hatha yoga in the United States is increasing in popularity. Instruction is given in gyms, local YMCAs, and even in adult education classes. Hatha is but one branch of yoga. Yoga, an ancient religious philosophy with its roots in India, is well over five thousand years old. There are six branches of yoga: raja, karma, bhakti, jnana, tantra, and hatha.

The word *yoga* itself is Sanskrit. Mara Carrico in *Yoga Basics* says "It comes from the root *yug* and originally meant 'to hitch up,' as in attaching horses to a vehicle. Another definition for yoga is 'to put to active and purposeful use.'"

The way hatha, the physical branch of yoga, is used and taught in the western world is nonreligious in nature. The purpose of this branch of yoga is to prepare the body for meditation. Hatha yoga concentrates on postures and breathing. The postures, called *asanas,* build flexibility, strength, and stamina. The breathing techniques taught in hatha yoga enhance the postures. In yoga, the breath is known as *pranayama.* Actually, pranayama is much more than breath; it's a total way of breathing.

There are various traditions within hatha yoga. Ananda yoga, developed by Kriyananda, concentrates on an inner focus for meditation. Certain forms are done in a pattern that flows in order to enhance the meditative state.

Affirmations, which students mentally recite while stretching, are a large part of ananda yoga. This style of yoga is taught as a preparation for meditation, or *dhyana,* the state of pure consciousness.

The goal of integral, another form of hatha yoga, is ultimately preparation for meditation. Developed by Satchidananda, it is a blend of styles focusing on the total body and mind. It's a very challenging yet gentle form.

Yoga is thought to teach concentration and relaxation in order to enhance one's ability to meditate. In yogic meditation, the aim is mental stillness, or a quiet mind. The goal is to detach from the ego in order to achieve objectivity. Dhyana is thought to be a state of pure consciousness.

Massage

It is easy to understand how one can enter the meditative state while having a massage. After all, you are lying comfortably and someone is gently stroking and rubbing the muscles in your body. It's usually performed in a quiet, serene place, and massage therapists play soothing music to heighten the relaxed mood. As you are being massaged, your focus is only on how relaxed you feel mentally and physically. It's difficult *not* to enter a meditative state.

If you have ever had a relaxation type of massage, you will know what I am talking about. If you haven't, my suggestion is to try one in the near future; it can be absolute heaven.

Reiki

Reiki, which comes from Japan, was founded by Dr. Mikao Usui. Its roots are undeniably religious in nature. There are conflicting opinions about whether those roots are from Buddhism, Hinduism, Christianity, or a blend of all three. Students of reiki are taught the history or at least the theories of its origins.

Reiki as it is usually practiced, however, has no religious implications. It has as its basis the supposition that there is energy inherent in the universe. Reiki practitioners are encouraged to have their own beliefs as to the source of this energy, whether that source be God, a god force, or the physical nature of the universe.

This energy flows throughout all living things—plants, animals, and human beings. Reiki practitioners are not giving away their energy, nor taking any from their clients. They merely function as a channel for this universally abundant energy.

With reiki, the practitioner utilizes hand positions to direct this flow of energy, called *ki* or *chi*. Practices such as reiki and yoga help that energy flow more smoothly.

A practitioner is not a healer but only a facilitator for that energy. Only God or the god force (depending on one's religious views) does healing. For the client, it can be a wonderfully relaxing sensation. Comforting, nonthreatening touch is sadly lacking in our world today. Hospitals across the nation are incorporating reiki treatments in their offerings to patients.

Clients who are having reiki sessions often slip easily into a meditative state of mind. Like massage, it feels good and it's difficult not to relax. Since reiki is a very gentle, nonmanipulative technique, the practitioner can relax as well. Both client and practitioner are often in a relaxed meditative state!

Chapter Seven

Guided Imagery and Audio Tapes

Go to any New Age store or browse through a metaphysical catalogue. You will see hundreds and maybe even thousands of audio tapes. The topics will be rather diverse, from tapes to help you gain self-confidence to those that improve your memory. You name it . . . you'll probably find a tape for it.

Audio tapes, for the most part, utilize what is known as guided imagery. The narrator on the tape speaks words and sentences designed to evoke images and visualizations. The use and involvement of all the listener's senses are encouraged. Music or nature sounds are frequently used in the background.

Guided imagery works well because it directs the focus on visualizations. The scripts for the tapes are also designed to help listeners keep their focus. Remember that meditation is the ability to focus on one thing or fewer things. It's like watching a movie or reading a book. Once you get involved in the story or the pictures you go easily into a meditative state. Tapes help us get there and stay there.

Tapes are an inexpensive introduction to meditation. Experienced meditators may find that tapes are both useful and enjoyable. High quality tapes can be bought for less than $15. They are designed for repeated use—for a small investment you can get hundreds of hours of use from a single tape. I doubt you will find a tape that is meant for one-time use. It's not like a book or video where once you know the plot listening a second time is not as enjoyable.

An incredible variety of tapes are available. You will find tapes that are lyrical, poetic, and a delight to listen to. If those aren't to your liking, there are tapes done in a more matter-of-fact style. Every person's likes and dislikes are highly individual; therefore, your preference is a matter of your own taste. With the choices available, you'll most likely find many tapes that would be enjoyable.

Audio tapes allow you to try out different techniques and styles. For example, I dislike counting down. For some reason it bores me, so I tend to avoid it. Perhaps certain types of music bother you. If so, you can choose tapes without music or tapes with only music you like.

DIFFERENT STROKES FOR DIFFERENT FOLKS

How and where do you find great meditation tapes? It may be difficult to decide which tapes are worth buying when the choices are so staggering. It's not like popular music, which you can hear on the radio before deciding to buy the CD or tape. I have stacks and stacks of tapes I've bought, listened to once, and then realized they weren't for me. Yet, I have also found some of my favorite tapes by taking a chance and buying blindly from a catalogue, or a music or new age store.

Still, who wants stacks of dusty tapes lying around? Word of mouth can be a good way to find out about interesting tapes. Ask your friends what tapes they use and enjoy. But beware what one person thinks is wonderful, someone else may not. It is somewhat like recommending a restaurant. One person may think a particular restaurant has the best food and service imaginable and recommends it to his friends. Then those friends go there for dinner and think it is the worst restaurant they've ever been in. Still, recommendation can be a guide to help narrow down the choices.

You can ask to borrow a tape so you can decide if it's something you'd like to buy. If someone asks to borrow a tape that's one of my favorites, I let them come over and listen to it rather than lending it out. This is just a thought for those of you who have lent favorite books and tapes and have never seen them again.

I have found a use for those dusty tapes sitting around in a pile, tapes that are *not* my favorites: tape-trading groups. Tastes differ, and one person's garbage is another's treasure. Recycle audio tapes by trading them with friends and fellow meditators. Who knows, maybe the tape with the gongs and xylophones will find a good home.

People react differently to tapes, and at times the reactions can be far removed from the purpose of the tape. One of my favorites is a tape on prosperity. It's designed to help unblock negative thoughts about prosperity. Who wouldn't want prosperity in their life? I'd heard about it from friends who raved about how great a tape it was. It was inexpensive, so I went out and bought a copy.

This particular tape is slightly subliminal. Subliminal means that words or phrases are recorded so they cannot consciously be heard. On this tape, there are words that are softly repeated in the background, at a much lower level of volume than the narrator's voice. It isn't totally subliminal because the voices can be heard.

When I listen to this tape, however, all it does is make me laugh. The narrator does a good job, but the voices in the background whisper earnestly, "money is good, money is good" over and over. For some reason, the sound of the voices and their inflection just cracks me up. Now, I know this particular tape is supposed to be serious and not comical. It's just my reaction to it. Whenever I am in a bad mood, I simply pop in the tape and soon I am howling with laughter! It has turned out to be one of my favorite tapes.

Your tastes and preferences will have much to do with whether a tape works well for you, or if you even like it.

STAYING ON TARGET

Tapes can be good for those who have difficulty staying focused. The preset dialogue of the script will keep you on track and focused on the meditation. Your mind can wander while listening to tapes; I certainly have found this to be true. But, since you are listening to a set script, there is less room to wander off track.

MAKING YOUR OWN TAPES

Making your own meditation tapes is easy and has the following advantages over commercial tapes:

Your own voice

You design the deepening method

You design the script—style and words

Timing, pauses, and cadence

Music and background of your choosing

Tapes you make yourself are often more effective than ones you purchase because the brain recognizes your own voice. There is built-in trust, so your brain is more comfortable with what you are telling it to do.

You can use the deepening method you like best. For instance, I dislike counting down as a technique to reach a meditative state. I find it boring and have a tendency to mentally substitute another method while listening to commercial tapes. When I make my own tapes, I can use any method I want. You may even find that you don't need a deepening method. Just start with a script and go from there. As you listen to the tape you are building focus, and you will enter a meditative state.

You design the script and choose the words. Use positive language and words you understand well. You are actually giving yourself suggestions. Are you going to use the tape at bedtime or during the day? If you are going to use it at bedtime, you can give a suggestion that you fall asleep peacefully. If you are going to use it only during the day, you should give suggestions that you wake up feeling refreshed.

When you make your own tape, timing and blank spots can be suited to your needs. On a prerecorded tape, the producer or narrator determines how long blank spots last. If the spot is too long, it gives an opportunity for the mind to wander. If it is too short, the mind can't easily follow.

Modulate your voice to your preference. If you have used audio tapes before, you should know whether you prefer a melodic type of voice or one without inflection. One of the things I like to do is to sound out the instructions. For instance, if I say "take a deep breath," I audibly take a breath myself. I like to "act" the tape, putting voice inflection, emotion, and mood into the script I am reading.

You can select music you like. I have several tapes where I enjoy the text but do not like the music, or vice versa. When you make your own tapes, you are in control. You may not even like music in the background; it's up to you.

TIPS FOR MAKING
YOUR OWN TAPES

Write out in advance what you are going to say. Speak slowly and clearly. Set the volume control and test the level in advance. It's worth spending a few extra dollars for a high quality tape. The hissing from a lower quality tape can be distracting. The best length tapes are either sixty- or thirty-minute tapes. Sixty-minute tapes have thirty minutes on each side, a good length for most meditation exercises.

DO SUBLIMINAL TAPES WORK?

I'm often asked, "Do subliminal tapes really work?" And the answer is, maybe.

The truth is I could fill this entire chapter, or even a whole book, with "proof" either way. Advocates on both sides claim to have well-documented "scientific proof." I found reams and reams of material on the subject when I did some research.

First of all, what does *subliminal* mean? In relation to audiotapes or videos, it means that messages or statements are recorded just below the threshold of awareness. In other words, the human ear cannot hear those statements. Music or sounds are used to mask these statements, or they are recorded at such a low volume that they cannot be heard.

Supporters and manufacturers of subliminals claim that the statements on the tapes are able to bypass the conscious mind and go straight to the subconscious. It is felt that this enables the suggestions to be readily accepted by the listener. Critics of subliminals claim that there is no evidence to support the assertion that this method works better than direct suggestions.

The question remains, "Do subliminal tapes work?" I believe we have to define clearly what is meant by "work." Are we asking if they work, or are we asking if they are effective? I believe that they will be effective for some people, and ineffective for others. One size does not fit all.

There are other considerations as well. Some people are uncomfortable with subliminal tapes because they want to know exactly what is being said to them. Subliminal tapes aren't likely to be effective for those people. We aren't likely to accept suggestions we are unsure about, even if they are "good for us." Tape manufacturers may argue otherwise, claiming that the tapes will work anyway. I suspect those types of people aren't likely to buy subliminal tapes in the first place, so it might be a moot point.

There are people for whom the subliminal tape's promise alone can be an effective suggestion. Using a tape to achieve weight loss may help by making a project out of it and putting their focus on the goal. For those people, subliminals can be quite effective.

An even more difficult question to answer is whether subliminals work. The majority of subliminal tapes require that you work with them for a period of time, usually at least once a day for thirty days. People easily lose interest, and most will not dutifully listen to a tape the required number of times.

You'll find that most tapes carry a thirty-day money back guarantee. Of course, this is a great selling point. Why would they offer a product that didn't work if people could get their money back if it failed? One reason could be that many people do not follow through. It's too much work to go through getting your ten or twenty dollars back. Also, if the specified time to work with the tape was thirty days, how would you know if it worked before the thirty-day money back guarantee expired?

I know I haven't really answered the question of whether these tapes work. I believe that they work for some people and not for others. I have no proof one way or the other. That is, in large part, because I haven't worked with them to any great extent. My personal preference is to use tapes on which I can hear what is being said. You'll have to make up your own mind as to whether you want to try them and whether you believe they are effective.

Chapter Eight

Meditation Groups

Meditation is often thought of as a solitary experience, yet that does not have to be the case. Working with a group can be a powerful, informative, and fun experience. There are many interesting, as well as creative, meditation exercises that need more than one person, some of which I'll include at the end of this chapter. But can groups ever be dangerous? I'm often asked about brainwashing and cults. Is this something we need to be aware of?

Well, yes, we do need to be aware of what or with whom we are getting involved. Maybe not from an alarmist point of view, but more from a common sense approach. Would you join *any* kind of group without giving it some thought? There are many factors that should go into the decision-making process whenever you have an opportunity to join or work with a group, no matter for what purpose. Even joining a bowling league or a tennis group requires some thought.

True, I doubt there are many bowling leagues that could be accused of being a cult. But it's just as true that the majority of meditation groups are as far from being a cult as any bowling league. Yet, it can happen. Therefore, I feel it's best to discuss what might be warning signs.

Actually, the word *cult* doesn't automatically mean its members are bad or evil. For most people, though, the word does have a negative connotation. Quite honestly, not all cults have some horrible, nasty motive. The meaning of *cult* is "obsession with an item or ideal." Collectors of Beanie Babies become members of a cult in that sense! They may be quite fanatical in their quest for those little creatures. But are they dangerous? I hardly think so.

Still, it is understandable that we think about the more negative connotation, especially since the tragedies of Jonestown, Waco, and Heaven's Gate. There has been an increasing concern about such cults and sects. At the time of writing this book, we are not very far from the millennium. History has shown that the turn of a century has always brought out cults and fanatical groups with a wide range of platforms.

It is also understandable that people might be leery of groups who use meditation. Meditation is a mental process, and they are fearful that these groups might aim at mind control. That is indeed the purpose of some groups, however, they employ far more drastic methods than meditation. Much has been written about cults and brainwashing, and the consensus is that the majority tend to use drastic lifestyle-immersion techniques, as well as total separation of group members from peers and family. These groups have aims far greater than using basic meditation.

The purpose of this book is not to help you decide whether to join a religious or political group. The rest of this chapter will focus on groups whose sole purpose is meditation. There are many such groups: some groups consist of a few friends; others are part of a larger community or even a worldwide sect. Discussion groups, such as Internet e-mail groups or news groups, don't meditate together; they exist solely for sharing experiences and knowledge. There are even temporary groups that meditate at the same time for goals such as world peace, the end of a war, or good health.

CHOOSING A MEDITATION GROUP

Whether it is a small group of a few friends or a larger group, you should ask questions. In that way you can decide if there are things with which you would be uncomfortable.

Here are some good questions to ask:

What is the purpose of the group?

Who runs the group?

How often and where does the group meet?

Are there fees or donations?

Are there rules and policies?

If problems arise, what is the procedure for resolution?

Warning signals:

Insistence upon rigid beliefs

Lack of freedom to express opinions or ideas

Insistence that the group's ideals become your entire focus

Insistence Upon Rigid Beliefs

As stated earlier, it is possible in some modalities to meditate incorrectly. In most cases, that isn't really a problem, for some have fascinating concepts behind their particular beliefs. Be warned, however, if a group totally denounces any option other than its own. This is what I would call the "our way is the only right way, everyone else is wrong and therefore doomed" syndrome.

Let's face it, in many things, we all think our own way is best. But that is a far cry from denouncing the validity of another method or denying someone else's right to exist.

Lack of Freedom to Express Opinions or Ideas

Everyone should have the freedom to express ideas, opinions, or concerns in a group situation. You should be wary of any group that proclaims, "Don't worry about it, it just is," or "Don't question it, just accept it." If you are repeatedly told your opinions don't matter or aren't valid, that is another warning signal. Any time you have two or more people, there is likely to be a difference of opinion.

However, that does not mean that individuals forfeit the right to a different view.

If you aren't even allowed to ask questions, that would be a signal to run, not walk, away from that group as quickly as possible.

Insistence that the Group's Ideals Become Your Entire Focus

It's easy for groups to become enthusiastic. The trouble lies in expecting a member's whole existence to center on the group's ideals. A group that asks you to drastically change your lifestyle or to give up friends and family is suspect.

Other Pitfalls

It is best to find out beforehand what a class or group will entail. Is it hands-on or mostly lecture? Is discussion encouraged? Is there a live instructor or facilitator? I remember all too well my first experience with a meditation class. I had heard of a class where meditation would be used to explore one's "inner self."

Perfect, just what I was looking for! I had tried meditation by myself several times, but felt sure I was not doing it correctly. I wasn't sure how to recognize when I "got there" and what to do if I did. Finding one's "inner self" sounded like a good goal.

So I sent off my registration fee and excitedly waited for the big day. I arrived the night of the class with pillow in hand. The advertisement for the class suggested that we wear loose, comfortable clothing and bring a floor pillow. It sounded easy and uncomplicated. All was going well until I looked at the other participants and listened to their conversations. It seemed like everyone else but me knew how to meditate. I felt intimidated, but I was determined to do it right. So I just pretended that I knew what I was doing.

Finally the instructor came into the room, collected the balance of our class fee, turned on a tape, and left the room. I was totally dismayed to find that the class was simply listening to a prerecorded tape. I could have done that at home. That's when I learned to ask if a class was taught by the instructor or depended upon tapes or videos.

THE PLUS SIDE OF
WORKING WITH GROUPS

Meditating with a group can be a wonderful experience, especially if you find a group of people you really like and enjoy. Friendships can be made. My friends and I meet at a different house each time and do a potluck dinner. We make a social event out of it, which makes it even more enjoyable.

It can be fun to explore meditation exercises that need more than one person. It's easy to get into a rut, even with meditation. Everyone has different methods of doing things, and by working with a group, you can find new and interesting ways to meditate. Creativity can be increased exponentially by group brainstorming. I'm sure you have heard it said that "two heads are better than one."

These are some of the advantages in working with a group:

Sharing of experiences, knowledge, and feedback

Discipline and motivation

Focus

Fun and creative group meditations

Sharing Experiences and Knowledge

Perhaps one of the biggest advantages of a group is the opportunity to share your experiences with other people. By taking time to talk with others about your experiences you can pick up helpful tips and hints. You can share methods of getting around stumbling blocks. Others may have found that their mind had a tendency to wander, but have discovered ways to bring it back into focus. Actually, just the realization that you are not alone in wrestling with this tendency can do wonders for your confidence in your ability to meditate.

Another person notices that her shoulders are a bit sore after a meditation exercise. You can tell your friend that it's because that is where she is holding stress in her body. When we meditate, we relax our body as well as our mind. Stress seems to find a place in the body to reside. For some of us, it's our shoulders. For others, it's the small of our back. The part of our body where stress lodges is now dramatically more noticeable because the rest of our body is so relaxed.

I have a vivid imagination, so I personify stress as though it were a little creature looking for a nice, comfy place on my body to reside. For me, it's my neck and shoulders. *"Ah, Holly's shoulders look like such a good place to land, let's go visit there."* When it's physically noticeable, it is a clue that I need to work with a long body-relaxation meditation. I will take extra time on that area of my body adding suggestions and imagery:

> *Feel your neck and shoulders relaxing. If you would like, imagine a pair of massaging hands softly soothing away any tension or stress that lives in your neck and shoulders. Feel the relaxation spreading down your neck and over your shoulders. Feel relaxation flowing, flowing through your neck and shoulders.*

With a group, one person can recite a long, slow body relaxation script. It's easier at times to simply sit back and listen as opposed to free-forming your own script as you go along. The advantage over a prerecorded tape is that extra time can be given to various areas of the body. The group can get together and decide which areas need the most attention.

Feedback from other group members can be instrumental in helping you write your own meditation scripts. You can try out a script you've written on others. They can tell you, "That was a particularly nice analogy you wrote: *'And your creative mind opens and eagerly unfolds just as the petals of a rose do in the sunshine,'* it worked very well for me."

Discipline and Motivation

Discipline and motivation are two distinct advantages of working with a group. By setting aside a specific time and a place to meditate, you are more likely to follow through. It's like a weekly card game or a softball game. You go there each week specifically to do that activity. It becomes part of your schedule. There is also the added enjoyment of having others to do it with you.

A tool that can make our lives better can lie around unused. Sometimes we just need a reminder that we have it at our disposal. For instance, do you have any exercise equipment in your home? I used to have an exercise bicycle. Before I sold it, it made a fantastic clothes rack. Some people find that a gym inspires them to exercise. Meditation is no different. By working with a meditation group, you have the motivation to use it.

Focus

Meditation classes can help people get past common stumbling blocks, such as learning to keep focused. Also, many are caught up in the "I don't know how to meditate" syndrome. Knowing how to meditate is not the problem. The problem really is how to do it when you want to and how to keep focused. A facilitator can help you produce the meditative state more easily and keep it once there.

When I teach classes, I joke with my students that I am really just a sheep dog. My purpose is to guide people. I know almost intuitively when some of the participants' minds are wandering. My job is to herd them back on track. Remember the analogy I drew between the mind and a wayward puppy? Have you ever watched a puppy explore a new place? You can almost hear the puppy's thoughts: "Wow, what a great rock. Hey, what's that leaf doing there? Oh, and what's that over there?" Our mind wants to explore and often jumps from place to place.

I can often tell from people's body positions and facial expressions that they might be elsewhere. As a group facilitator, I have the advantage of being live and able to ad-lib. I can add focusing statements from time to time, such as, *"and now as you focus on being confident . . ."*

A disadvantage of tapes or solitary meditation is loss of focus. There have been countless times when I've listened to a tape, for example on self-confidence, and found myself dutifully listening to the tape one minute, and somewhere completely different the next minute. I'll have gone from focusing on positive suggestions for confidence to thinking about being on a desert island with George Clooney. How did I get there from thinking about self-confidence? It's quite easy.

Of course, with a group, that can still happen, but it is useful to have someone to help you keep focus. When you are in a group, you are cognizant of the other people in the room, and that can help with focus by keeping you in a state of greater awareness.

Fun and Creative Group Meditations

Can there be group connectiveness? Meditating with a group can make you feel more powerful. People who do group meditations often report feeling powerfully connected with everyone else in the room. It's also quite an interesting experience to meditate at the same time as a large group of people, even if they aren't in the room with you.

Below are some meditations and meditative exercises to do with another person or a group. Enjoy!

Double-Sided Meditation

This meditation exercise requires three people. One person sits facing forward in a chair. The other two sit on either side of the person in the chair, facing the opposite direction. They sit so that they can speak at about the ear level of the person in the chair. Then each of these two people reads a meditation script, speaking into the ear of the person in the chair. This exercise can be done in two ways, either using the same script or two different scripts.

If the same script is used, one person starts, and the second reader starts his script about a minute or so later. If you choose to use different scripts, they should be of a similar nature. For instance, a script for self-confidence would work very well with a script on motivation. The exercise will work best if the scripts are highly repetitive.

Although the person sitting in the chair will not be able to listen consciously to both scripts, this exercise demonstrates that the subconscious mind does hear them, especially the key phrases and suggestions.

Finding Each Other Meditation

This exercise works best with at least six people. There needs to be an even number of people for this to work. In a large room with open space, gather in a circle and hold hands. An opening meditation or affirmation prayer is a nice touch and enhances the feeling of togetherness.

Have everyone close their eyes and let go of each other's hands. Breathe in and out for a few moments. Then, at a signal from the group leader, each person should *slowly* walk forward with arms and hands extended. Touch the hands of any person you come in contact with. Do not talk during this process; communicate solely by touching hands. How do different hands feel to you? Walk around the room slowly, keeping your eyes closed. Keep walking around and touching hands until you come to a pair of hands that "feels" right to you, and vice versa.

Slowly lower yourselves until you are sitting on the ground. Keep your eyes closed and do not talk. Simply hold hands and meditate. Concentrate on the experience, how it feels, and how the other person feels. Do you feel a connection between the two of you? How does that feel? What thoughts are going through your mind? After about five minutes or so, slowly open your eyes and look at the person you picked to be your partner. It's nice at this time to talk and share your perceptions and experiences.

Two-Person Mirror

Sit down facing a partner. Stare into the eyes and face of the other person without saying a word. Do this for at least ten to fifteen minutes. Keep your eyes open and focused on each person's face and eyes. Notice the thoughts that come into your mind, and allow them to come naturally. What are you thinking and feeling? After this exercise, discuss the experience.

Group Meditation Experiments

These types of meditations can be done in several ways: A group can get together in the same room, or all members of a group can meditate at an agreed time. I belong to several discussion groups on the Internet, and we regularly hold different kinds of meditations in this fashion.

GROUP MEDITATION FOR
HEALTH AND WELL-BEING

A powerful group experience is a meditation to send healing energy to those who need it. This may or may not be directed at specific persons; it depends upon what the members of the group decide they wish to do. Does this work? There are people who certainly believe that it does, or at least can help. One such personal experience has given me a very open mind about the possibility.

In mid-August 1987 a planetary lineup occurred called the Harmonic Convergence. It was thought to be a time of great power, and many groups all over the world convened together to meditate. I attended a conference of about two thousand people, where we did a healing meditation. We were told to picture or think about people we knew who were sick. If we didn't know anyone, we were to picture the healing energy finding someone who needed it. We then imagined ourselves sending healing energy into the universe. The hope was that the sheer number of people meditating at the same time would increase the power of our meditations.

At that time, one of my relatives had recently been diagnosed with terminal cancer. During the meditation I pictured her as I meditated. My relative went into remission and lived for another ten years. Now, I don't claim that this meditation caused her remission, but I have always wondered if it played a part.

OTHER IDEAS FOR GROUP EXERCISES

A meditation for prosperity for everyone in the group

A meditation where one person thinks of an object and the rest of the group meditates and works to guess what the object is

A meditation to send energy to a group project

Examples: The group I work with writes out a "list of intentions" once a month similar to the Scribe and Vibe It method in the chapter on positive thinking. We all then meditate to send group energy to the list.

Part Two

The Relaxation Response

Chapter Nine

Relaxation

Is *stress* a bad word? Should we say it in hushed, whispered tones? Not all stress is bad; I certainly don't mean to insinuate that it is. Some stress we actually enjoy, such as anticipation and excitement. Remember waiting for Santa Claus or a birthday party? Going on a much-anticipated date with someone special? Accepting an award from your peers? These are all stress-producing situations.

STRESS AND TENSION

Having *no* stress in our lives would not be a good thing. Almost any event in our world will produce some stress. Almost every reaction that we have is in some sense stress-related. The complete and total absence of stress would probably mean that we weren't alive.

We do talk about stress as a bad and an almost evil thing. If I asked you to draw stress as a person or character, I doubt very much that you'd draw it as a nice one. I bet it would be dark, ominous, and perhaps threatening-looking. I've done this very thing as an experiment in several workshops. Never have I seen anyone draw stress and have it come out looking anything but nasty.

Stress has a dual nature: a good side and a bad side. It is the side of stress that is detrimental to our health and well-being that we are referring to when we talk about stress management, stress reduction, and relaxation.

Yes, there are two chapters in this book that are incredibly similar—this one on relaxation and another one on stress management. There isn't a great deal of difference between using meditation for stress management and using it for relaxation. The aim of both is to reduce the level of stress and its effect on our health.

There are, however, different perceptions of what the two terms mean. It's not uncommon to associate the word _relaxation_ with lazy. I have had people tell me that the only time they felt they were allowed to relax was on vacation. Imagine thinking that the only time you are allowed to relax is during one or two weeks of the year? Preposterous! Yet that is exactly the view numerous people have toward relaxation.

We not only deserve relaxation in our lives, we need it! Relaxing is not wasting time but rather saving time. Think of all the time you waste being worried or, worse yet, being ill because of stress. If you knew how much time you wasted that way, it would amaze you. If you want to have a realistic idea of how much time, keep track of the time you spend worrying for one week. Be sure to write down the times that you spend thinking about stressful situations as opposed to actually doing something about them. If you look at stress that way, taking ten or fifteen minutes a day to meditate for relaxation is hardly wasting time, comparatively speaking. Yet those few minutes can do a world of good for your physical and mental well-being.

We don't have to be business executives to have stress in our lives. Just about every profession has stressful aspects. Stress is not confined to just our jobs either. Our home lives are full of situations that are difficult to cope with: the children, the neighbors, the bills. All the ingredients are there to make a boiling pot of stress stew.

Nor is stress just an adult problem. Students and very young children aren't immune to its effects. Parents who fight, problems in school, and peer pressure are just a few of the things children have to cope with every day. It's not unheard of for a teenager to have ulcers. High blood pressure is affecting younger and younger people each year.

There are many different ways to manage and reduce stress. Some of these are quite healthy and productive, such as physical exercise, talking out problems with friends and family, and taking positive steps to change the situation. But it's the other things we do to manage stress that can get us into trouble: things like drinking, illegal drugs, overeating, and dependence upon prescription medicines.

These two chapters, and this whole book actually, are dedicated to helping you find positive ways to deal with stress and tension. I've said it elsewhere in this book: You deserve it and you are worth it!

PHYSICAL RELAXATION

Take a deep breath, hold it for a few moments, and then gently exhale. Throughout this exercise, just breathe in and out naturally. I'm going to ask you to focus your attention, your awareness, on certain areas of your body. As you do so, notice that part of the body and how it feels. If you don't know the feeling of relaxation, just for a moment I want you to take your hand and ball it into a tight fist. That's right, make it very, very tight. Now just let go and open your hand. That feeling of letting go is the feeling of relaxation.

Now place your attention on your head and scalp. You might even notice a slight sensation of warmth. As you continue to breathe in and out gently, allow your head and scalp to relax. Even if you do not feel like your head and scalp are relaxed, don't worry. As we continue this exercise your body will become relaxed.

Now place your awareness, your attention on your forehead. Notice and feel the skin covering your forehead. As you do so, just allow your forehead to become relaxed. Now your forehead is completely and totally relaxed.

Now place your attention on your eyelids. Gently allow your eyelids to relax. That's right . . . you don't have to hold them tightly closed. Just allow them to be comfortably closed and relaxed.

Now place your awareness on your cheekbones and jaw. And if it is comfortable for you to do so, allow your jaw to open slightly. Continue breathing in and out naturally and gently. And as you do so, your cheekbones and jaw become completely and totally relaxed.

Now place your attention on your neck. Allow all the muscles, ligaments, and tendons in your neck to become completely and totally relaxed. Notice how your neck just naturally supports your head. It is easy to allow your neck to relax. And now your neck is completely relaxed.

Now, if you will, place your awareness on your shoulders. If you would like, you can imagine a pair of soothing hands gently massaging your shoulders. Feel all the muscles, ligaments and tendons in your shoulders relaxing. It feels so very good and relaxing.

Now place your awareness and attention on your arms. Feel your arms from your shoulders, down your forearm, down to your wrist, down to your hands, and all the way down to your fingertips. Feel all the muscles, ligaments, and tendons relaxing. Just allow the soothing relaxation to flow all the way down through your fingertips. And now your arms and hands are completely and totally relaxed.

Now, if you will, place your attention on the top of your back. Feel all the muscles, ligaments, and tendons in your back. Allow soothing relaxation to spread gently over your back. Continue to breathe in and out gently and naturally. As you become more relaxed, you notice your spinal column. The feeling of relaxation continues to flow down your spinal column right down to the small of your back. It feels so very good and relaxing. The top of your back and your spinal column all the way down to the small of your back become completely and totally relaxed.

Now place your attention on your chest area. As you do so, know that all the cells, tissues, and organs within are functioning together harmoniously to create perfect health and a feeling of relaxation. And as you place your awareness on your chest area, it becomes completely and totally relaxed.

Now, if you will, place your awareness on your abdomen. As you place your attention on your stomach area, know that all the cells, tissues, and organs within are functioning together harmoniously to create perfect health and a feeling of relaxation. And as you place your awareness on your abdomen, it becomes completely and totally relaxed.

*Now place your attention on your hips. As you place your awareness
on your hip area, you notice the relaxing feeling spreading throughout
your hips. And it feels so very good and relaxing. Your hips are now
completely and totally relaxed.*

*Now, if you will, place your awareness on your legs. Notice your
upper legs, your thighs, and your knees, all the way down to your
ankles. Know that all the muscles, ligaments, and tendons are feeling
relaxed. And as you place your attention on your legs, they become
totally relaxed.*

*Now, place your awareness on your feet. Notice your heels, the tops of
your feet, the bottoms of your feet, and all the way down to your toes.
And as you do so, your feet become completely and totally relaxed. Now
take a deep breath and hold it for a moment. As you exhale, any linger-
ing tension in your body just fades away. Your whole body is now completely and totally relaxed.*

THE MENTAL VACATION

Throughout this exercise, allow yourself to breathe in and out gently and naturally. Close your eyes and imagine you are going on a
vacation. Neither time nor money is important. You may go wherever you wish. It can be any place real or imagined: a place you have
visited before or somewhere you would like to go someday. Someday is here and now. You are free to go. You can even invent a place
you would like to visit.

*We are going to count from ten to one, and at the count of one, you
will be where you wish to be.*

Ten: Allow yourself to breathe in and out naturally and gently.

Nine: Feel yourself relaxing.

Eight: Your body is becoming limp and loose.

Seven: *Even more relaxed.*

Six: *And as you continue to breathe, you are so very relaxed.*

Five: *Deeper and deeper, you become deeply relaxed.*

Four: *That's right, down you go into relaxation.*

Three: *It feels so good to be this relaxed.*

Two: *Take a deep breath, hold it for a moment and then exhale.*

One: *Now you are there . . . at the place of relaxation, the place you want to be.*

You are now in this wonderful place. It's a special place; it's your place. You have all the time in the world to be here. There is nothing you need to do; there is nowhere else you need to go, there is no rush. You have plenty of time to take in your surroundings. Feel the air, smell the wonderful scents. Immerse yourself in this feeling of peace, joy, and serenity. Breathe deeply of the air of relaxation that is here. Take time, take a lot of time to be here . . . to do anything you wish to do . . . or even nothing at all. Just being here is exactly what you need. Remember that this is your place, your wonderful place. You can choose to be here alone, or if you wish, you may have a special person with you. You may come here any time you wish simply by thinking yourself here.

THE MOVIE THEATER

Have you ever noticed that a large part of stress is caused not by what has happened, but rather by what you *expect* to happen? You receive a note on your desk from your boss telling you that he wants to see you as soon as possible. You have a meeting next week with a very important client. These situations cause stress, even though they haven't yet happened. The stress comes from anticipating what might happen. And, as we all know, often what we anticipate will happen is far worse than the reality.

Instead of taking up time envisioning horrible scenarios, why not take that time to visualize positive ones? Such a technique has the added benefit of allowing you to mentally rehearse situations in advance. We actually do that very thing when we worry, but we rarely give those scenarios positive outcomes.

Imagine that you are standing in the lobby of a movie theater. It's a brand-new building, built with comfort in mind. It's a state-of-the-art theater, designed for the comfort of those who come here. It's also a very special theater: you control the action in the movie, just like a movie director! You control the lighting, the dialogue, and even the scenery.

See yourself walking into the theater. Look at how wonderfully large the theater is. All the seats are spaced wide apart. Even the space between each row is wide and comfortable. There is plenty of room to stretch out your legs. See yourself walking down the aisles to pick a seat that you would like. Walk down past the first row, feeling very relaxed. Continue down past the second row . . . feeling even more relaxed. Continue down row after row until you come to the row you most want to sit in. That's right . . . see yourself selecting the row you want. Now select the seat you want and see yourself sitting down. Notice how comfortable the seat is. What a wonderful theater! No one is sitting in front of you; you have a perfect view of the screen. On the arm of your seat is a remote control. This remote control allows you to control the action and all the parts of the movie. Now allow yourself to sit comfortably, holding the remote in your hand, and wait for the movie to begin.

As the movie begins, you see that it is a movie about the situation you are in. Allow the movie to play out for a bit. Notice if there are people in the scene with you. If so, notice what they look like, who they are, and the things they are doing. Allow the scene to go on for a little bit. Now, if you'd like, take the remote control and rewind the movie. This is a very special theater so you can talk to the actors playing you and the people with you. See yourself instructing the actors, telling them how you'd like them to play the scene. They are very happy to try it different ways. Play out the scene for a little bit. Allow yourself to keep using the remote to rewind the scene as many times as you'd like. Each time you can give exactly the directions and instructions you want to the actors. Keep doing this until you get just the right movie, just the right way of playing the scene.

When you have the scene exactly the way you like, allow yourself to view this movie from beginning to end. Immerse yourself in this movie, the feelings, the smells, the sounds, and the sensations. It's a wonderful movie, and it's all yours.

Chapter Ten

Stress Management

What is the difference between using meditation for stress management and using it for relaxation? There is no difference really, it's just semantics. For some people, especially those in the business world, stress management sounds better. Perhaps it's the perception of the word *relaxation*. Pictures of sitting around and doing nothing spring to mind. Yet label it "stress management," and *voila*, it implies taking action. Stress management sounds efficient. It makes a better marketing package!

When corporations realized that stressed-out employees were less productive, they started offering seminars in stress management utilizing meditation. Today stress management programs have grown up and matured. Companies are recognizing that a comprehensive program should include proper diet, exercise, and rest, along with other stress-reduction techniques. Stress management programs are now being offered with a balanced approach.

Nearly everything in life requires balance. Meditation on its own is a good step toward a healthy lifestyle. However, as individuals it is important to realize that we need to work on our body as well as our mind. We are a total package. We can consider ourselves a corporation and design our own comprehensive stress management programs.

Interestingly, we can use meditation not only as part of a program to reduce stress, but also as a way to assist in attaining other goals. We can use meditation to help motivate us to exercise, maintain a proper diet, and sleep better.

HOW DO I MANAGE STRESS?

Let's start with the basics. First, don't deny that you have stress. Events and situations happen to us that cause it. Our bosses and coworkers do things that make our jobs difficult. Relationships cause stress. The children, the dog, the bills, you name it. It's all out there waiting to get us ... if we let it.

Nor should you deny that you have less than positive emotions at times. There are those who feel that having negative emotions is a sign of weakness. However, life throws all kinds of events and situations at us, and reacting to them is normal. It is much worse to deny or ignore those feelings than to admit to them. Built-up stress is often the result of ignored feelings.

James has a reputation at the office as a real go-getter. When projects are given to him at the last minute, he miraculously completes them on time. Because of this, more and more projects are assigned to him. James likes the attention this brings him from his superiors. Sooner or later, though, James will likely experience a breaking point, where he just can't do it all. If he ignores it when it does happen, his stress level will become unbearable. His work will suffer and so will his health. True, there are some people who seem to thrive on stress. But even they have a breaking point.

Mary has a client who schedules meetings and then often cancels them on short notice or, worse, on no notice at all. Mary never admits to herself that this upsets her. She tells her coworkers, "It doesn't bother me, it goes with the business." Soon, whenever her client calls to schedule a meeting, Mary starts getting a stomachache or a headache.

It would be better for both James and Mary to admit to their feelings of stress and then work to find ways to alleviate or reduce it. That may not change the situation they are in, but it will help them cope with it better. Dealing with stressful situations from a point of stress isn't productive. We don't think as clearly when we are under heavy stress.

Second, don't dwell on things. Either you can do something about it or you can't. Yes, you should admit that you have stress in your life. But that is not the same thing as dwelling on it. Once you realize that you are stressed, you are in a position to deal with it. Dwelling on it merely keeps you trapped in a stress cycle

With stress, there are generally three scenarios: It's a situation you can actively do something to change, or it's a situation over which you have no control, or stress has magnified a situation out of all proportion.

James and Mary have real situational stress in their lives. But stress can be imaginary. Imagined stress? Yes, that can happen! When we have a niggling feeling or doubt, our thinking and imagination can amplify it. For example, your boss frowns just as you happen to walk by one afternoon.

Now, anything could be going on. Maybe her checkbook is overdrawn or her spouse is cheating on her. It hasn't anything to do with you. Back at your desk, however, you dwell on the implications of that frown. You wonder what you have done or, worse, what you haven't done. Soon you are worried that you are about to be fired.

That may sound a little contrived, but it isn't. Our imagination can run away with us and go down a road that reality would never take. How many times have you imagined dramatic scenarios from just one little word or action? We all get a little paranoid from time to time and blow things out of proportion.

The stress produced by that type of situation, though, is just as real to your body! The body is not able to differentiate where stress is coming from; it just reacts. Remember the example of the lemon? Just imagining biting into a lemon can produce the actual physical sensation of salivating. Don't discount the very real effect of such stress. As far as our body is concerned, stress is stress no matter the source.

Knowing the reason for our stress can help us select the right technique to reduce it. Here are two very helpful questions to ask:

Is it real or imagined (amplified)?

Can I do something about it?

In the case of stress resulting from our imaginings, we can utilize meditation techniques that enable us to distance ourselves and be objective. We can use visualization to replay the situation without our emotions being involved. This allows us to judge whether our feelings are based on a situation or an emotion.

We all are individuals, and we react differently to stress. We respond differently to situations at different times as well. Something that may not have bothered us one day might feel overwhelming the next. This too can amplify the amount of stress we feel in relation to a problem. Using the same type of visualization technique to replay the situation can help us be objective about the magnitude of our problem.

There are situations we can't do anything to change. Death is one of the most stressful events in life, yet we can't change it. Divorce sometimes is inevitable. We can't change the events, but we still need to do something about the stress those situations create. There might be situations too difficult to cope with by yourself. Seeking out therapy or just talking it out with a friend or a family member may be what is needed. Having stress in your life isn't a sign of weakness; it's a sign that you are human.

Sometimes just talking to someone can make a big difference. But what if there is no one to talk to? Using a technique where you visualize a friend, a counselor, or even a guardian angel can be emotionally helpful.

The Counselor

Use the deepening technique you prefer. In this meditation, you may choose whoever you would like for the counselor. It could be a mentor, a teacher, or a professor you had in school. It could also be an actor or actress you admire or a historical figure that you feel is wise and compassionate. It could be an angel. It can be anyone you wish—only in this situation they have very special powers and talents. They have the ability to be totally objective, and they are more than happy to listen to you.

Imagine yourself sitting down on a bench in a garden. You are all alone. Perhaps you are feeling a little sad or unhappy because things have been difficult for you. Just allow yourself to sit on the bench in this garden. Take a few minutes to look around. Notice the landscaping, the flowers that are planted here and there. Look, there are several of your favorite ones right over there to your left. As you sit on the bench and look at your surroundings, take a few minutes to take a few deep, slow, satisfying breaths in and out. You are feeling a little better already.

As you sit there comfortably on the bench, you notice a path to your right. And as you notice this path, you see someone slowly walking up the path toward you. Around them is a gentle golden light . . . you know that this person comes only from the light of truth and goodness. And as this person comes closer, they come close enough to sit next to you. They smile at you and take your hand. They ask you what is bothering you, and they tell you that they have plenty of time to listen. Imagine yourself telling this special person exactly what is bothering you. Don't be afraid, and don't hold anything back. Anything you tell them is in strict confidence, you know you can trust them. Take all the time you need to talk with this special person. Tell them how you feel, what you think, and what you know. Know that you have plenty of time to talk, and that this special person is there just for you. They are there to listen.

Sometimes we can do something about our situation. Let's take the case of two men, John and Todd, who are both experiencing stress-related headaches. Both have worked for a company for several years, slowly rising through the ranks. John, however, feels stuck in his job. He's not likely to gain a promotion unless one of the executives above him leaves. John has done his job diligently, yet he feels he is no longer receiving adequate compensation. Life at home is not too good either. John's wife complains about their income and makes him feel inadequate.

Todd, on the other hand, works for a company where he feels appreciated both financially and creatively. Yet, there is one coworker, Ralph, who casts a pall on all the positives. Ralph criticizes everyone around him and blames his shortcomings on others' work.

Todd could change jobs, but he is happy except for having to deal with Ralph.

John could use techniques for change or goal setting, whereas Todd might benefit from a shielding technique.

Shielding

Do you know someone who just seems to spread negativity? Using a shielding technique can help this negativity to bounce right off. Depending upon your views, it's a psychological tool or one that is metaphysical in nature. Maybe it's a bit of both. It does have psychological merit, for we are building ourselves up mentally to be strong enough to reject negative statements and actions thrown at us. We are deciding what we will and will not let affect us.

There are those who feel this technique is also metaphysical, in that we are strengthening our energy and are, in fact, creating an energy force field around us that deflects negative energy.

Imagine yourself standing upright, straight and tall. As you stand there, see a special light surround your entire body. This light spreads around you and conforms to the shape and size of your body, just like a force field. This force field repels negative energy directed at you and allows positive energy to be absorbed. Negative energy simply bounces harmlessly off and away from you. Negativity just cannot penetrate.

The Collection Box

I keep a box on my desk where I place stressful events and circumstances. If I don't have time to deal with the situation right now, I write it down on a piece of paper and place it in my collection box. Then I can deal with it later. This is not denying a stressful situation, but rather putting it off until a time when I can devote my attention and energy toward resolving it.

Left, Right, Left . . .

I've worked with several corporation executives, and it would be inaccurate to stereotype all of them as analytical left-brain types. Yet, in my practice, I have noticed that a large percentage have that mode of thinking. A different approach may be required, especially with deepening techniques. In some cases, I've found guided imagery types of deepening methods to be ineffective.

We need left-brain types in this world; without them things wouldn't get done. Yet sometimes that efficiency causes stress. Analytical types tend to plan every aspect of their lives. They like to schedule things: "I'm going to meditate for exactly seven minutes, then I must leave for my meeting with clients." Active meditation fits busy people like a glove. They get to "do" something, yet they receive all the benefits of passive meditation.

An analytical mind can have its drawbacks when it comes to some deepening and meditation techniques. One client I worked with critiqued each phrase or sentence I used. He'd say things like, "That is interesting, I can understand why that would be effective," or "I can understand that using stairs is a much healthier approach, but wouldn't an elevator save time?" His profession required him to sort through large amounts of data quickly and figure out how to apply it. He couldn't keep from doing the same thing in a meditation. At first I was a bit frustrated, and wondered how I could help him to relax if I couldn't get him past examining the process.

I knew that he was extremely analytical from his language patterns and from his use of phrases like "I can understand" rather than "I can see" or "I feel." I needed to bypass that mode of thinking, so I changed my tack and had him focus on an action that required thought and precision. I told him to close his eyes and imagine that he now had a piece of graph paper in front of him. I then directed him to mentally color in every third square. I gave him ample time to become totally involved in this project, and I then directed positive statements at him. Consciously, he never noticed them because he was too busy coloring squares. That was fine with me, it was his subconscious mind I wanted to reach!

Chapter Eleven

Daily Meditations and Affirmations

Here is what numerous people associate with meditation: daily meditations. Look in a bookstore and you will find a large selection of books dedicated to "nice little thoughts for the day." I have to admit I like them a lot.

Taking time out to reflect upon something positive and inspirational—what a joyous way to start the day! I wonder what the world would be like if everyone did that? Okay, it's not likely to happen, but it sure would be nice.

What is your morning like? Do you rush out the door after hastily drinking a couple of cups of coffee and, of course, without any breakfast? What is your mind-set like when each morning is like that? I'll bet you are harried, stressed, and mentally tired. But what if you took five minutes each morning to meditate and reflect upon an inspirational message?

It's easy to feel we don't have five extra minutes in the morning. I know full well how it feels; I'm not a morning person. Think about it—we set our alarms each morning for the latest possible hour that will give us enough time to make it to work. Oh, and the importance of snooze buttons. Trust me, I know the feeling of wanting that extra nine minutes. Actually, it's not that we want those extra nine minutes, we have to have them. Am I right?

But what if you got up five minutes earlier each day and meditated? I know, you are thinking, "I'd lose five whole minutes when I could be sleeping." You wouldn't be losing five minutes of sleep. You'd be gaining five glorious minutes to devote entirely to yourself, five minutes in which you can pamper yourself. You deserve it! Does that remind you of the L'Oreal commercial where Heather Locklear says, "I'm worth it"? Maybe you don't need to color your hair, but that sure is a healthy attitude, "I'm worth it!"

Not quite convinced yet? Then, if I may, let me ask you a question. Do you recall a day when you woke up feeling wonderful? Didn't the rest of the day go better than usual for you?

Well, taking five minutes each morning for an inspirational meditation helps you start out the day feeling that way. If you ask me, it sure beats being crabby and feeling like it's just another day with nothing to look forward to. True, rose petals won't suddenly be strewn across your path. Yet remember the days when you started out feeling positive. Chances are that you found it much easier to handle irritations and life's little bumps. Why not start out your day positively, on purpose?

HOW TO USE DAILY MEDITATIONS

You can do this type of meditation each morning by itself, or you can take a few moments just before you do the count up/return to consciousness part of your meditation. Use the deepening method of your choice and then mentally recite the daily affirmation meditation to yourself. It is really nice to reflect upon what it means, rather than just saying it.

And, for those of you who really do desperately want those nine minutes from the snooze button—here is a golden opportunity to use them in a wonderful manner! Just place a piece of paper with the daily affirmation meditation on your nightstand. Then when the alarm goes off in the morning, go ahead and hit the snooze button. Then repeat the daily meditation to yourself and think about that for those remaining few minutes.

Daily affirmation meditations can be positive verses and poetry, or very simple statements. They can come from classic literature, famous quotes, the Bible, meditation books, or simply write them yourself.

Support groups realize the positive effect and potential of daily inspirational meditations. Alcoholics' Anonymous has several books and booklets with daily meditations and inspirational sayings. And, by the way, you don't have to relegate them to just mornings!

SOME AFFIRMATION MEDITATIONS FOR YOU
WHO IS WORTH IT!

We once thought that we would never reach the stars, but we have. Is there something you think you can't reach. Never fear; you can.

Each time I take a breath today, I will be one step closer to reaching my goals and aspirations.

Life is a quest. Learn to live each day discovering what it holds.

The birth of the sun each day gives us the opportunity to start fresh everyday—it's the dawning of a brand-new day.

Celebrate the joys of each day and the sorrows will seem less.

Life is not a dress rehearsal; it's the real thing, so act accordingly. Set the stage and be a participant, not a member of the audience.

I am thankful for all living things, and most of all, I am thankful to be living.

I thank God for the air that I breathe, the birds that sing, the leaves on the trees, the flowers that grow, and I thank God for the ability to appreciate these things.

We wonder what this day will be like, when we should like this day of wonder.

Chapter Twelve

Health and Well-Being

Our thoughts can have a direct impact upon how we feel emotionally. When we feel sad or unhappy, our thoughts tend to follow that pattern. It's like a snowball, and soon we can easily find even more reasons to justify why we feel that way. It can be a vicious trap. The more we think about how we feel, the more we actually *feel* that way. We are caught up in our own emotions and thoughts, and they become a real part of our actual experience.

It's just as true that our thoughts can affect us physically. Our thoughts *can* and do have an impact on our health! Now to suggest that we would never be ill if we only thought positive, healthy thoughts would be untrue and very misleading. It would be unethical to state that every disease or ailment could be eradicated or cured simply through meditation. Conversely, just *thinking* about a disease will not make us come down with that malady.

Yet the mind is a powerful force. Can our thoughts affect our health? The answer is yes. They can and do evoke direct physical responses. For example, close your eyes and imagine that you are biting into a tart, juicy lemon. Most of us will find that we salivate. Our thoughts produce a physical response. The lemon may have been imaginary, but the reaction is not.

We all have negative thoughts occasionally about our health. In this day and age it's an almost impossible situation to avoid. We are constantly bombarded with input. There are television shows that center on illness. Read the newspaper or turn on the evening news. There is usually at least one story about the latest theory of what causes illness, such as the air we breathe, the foods we eat, the materials in our homes, even the fibers in our clothing. We are surrounded by negative and alarming health news. Is it any wonder we worry or ask ourselves if is it something that could happen to us?

For the most part, we learn to filter out much of this so that it does not affect us. Still, we are very suggestible. Consider the very different scenarios that follow:

You are at work. The morning has started out fairly well, nothing unusual has happened, and you go about your regular routine. One of your coworkers walks past you and stops to say, "Are you feeling okay? You look a little pale." At that point, you might not take it too seriously. Then a few minutes later another coworker stops by and says, "You really don't look well today. Are you getting the flu that is going around?"

Soon you begin to wonder if you really do feel well! Now that you think about it, your stomach *is* queasy and you feel a bit feverish.

You are at work. The morning has started out fairly well, nothing unusual has happened, and you go about your regular routine. One of your coworkers walks past you and stops to say, "You look fantastic today! Is that a new dress?" You probably smile and feel good. Then a few minutes later another coworker stops by and says, "Have you lost weight? You look like a million dollars!"

The more you think about it, you realize that yes, you *do* look nice today. You stand up straighter and feel absolutely wonderful!

The effect is often much more than just physical. Emotions, such as happiness, sadness, anger, and even fear, can be triggered by thoughts.

Imagine yourself walking down a dark, deserted street. It's late at night and you are alone. There are no streetlights, and all the buildings around you are empty or closed. There are a few straggly bushes here and there along the uneven sidewalk. You can smell the decaying food in the battered garbage cans.

As you walk along, you hear a sound behind you. You quickly look to see if something is there, but you do not see anything. You take another step, and there it is again. There is a definite rustling sound in the bushes! Fear knots in the middle of your stomach and your breathing becomes shallow. Could there be a mugger in the bush? All of a sudden, the bush moves and something jumps right out at you!

It's Just a Stray Kitten!

Now, there never was a mugger in that bush, your imagination invented that possibility. Yet your body reacted with a rush of adrenaline, you broke out in a cold sweat, and you were ready to scream and run. Your body had a real response to an imagined situation.

There has always been a fine line between too much information and too little. When it comes to health issues and concerns, that line is even harder to tread. Through information, we can learn how to stay healthy and increase our chances of longevity. But how often have you heard a report about a particular disease and found yourself wondering if you just might have some of the symptoms?

One or two thoughts are not going to make us victims of a serious disease. If that were true, there would not be a person left alive on this planet. Fortunately, studies indicate that it's a much more complicated process. Our thinking is but a part of it. It is probably a combination of many things, including nutrition, hygiene, environmental and heredity factors, and our own actions. The good news is that we can control some of these factors.

Most noninfectious diseases probably do not appear overnight, but rather develop over time. We put ourselves at risk by the way we live, the things we do, and how we treat our bodies. We can take steps to reduce our susceptibility to infections and even hereditary diseases by taking better care of ourselves. We can work on improving our health, step-by-step, day-by-day. Meditation can be a powerful tool to assist us in this respect by reinforcing a healthy mindset.

What about people who are already suffering from an illness or a disease? Can meditation help them? It can help reduce pain and discomfort. It can help them cope with mental and emotional difficulties. And, yes, in some cases, miracles have happened. There are many documented cases where alternative health measures such as meditative techniques have been used successfully. There are stories of cancer patients and others with life-threatening diseases who have gone into remission. But I do not feel that anyone can in good conscience guarantee a cure.

Used as an adjunct to an existing health care treatment plan, meditation is a safe and inexpensive tool. But it's just that—a tool. It would be unethical to suggest that any method, be it meditation, herbs, or medicine can cure everyone everytime. Yet the mind *is* a powerful force.

We can find examples of how our thinking directly affects our physical health. Many illnesses, both minor and major, are thought to be psychosomatic in nature. The *American Medical Association Family Medical Guide*, states, "Almost every physical disorder has some connection with emotional factors." But do not be misled into thinking that means that ailments are merely in our heads. By psychosomatic, it is not meant that those illnesses are just in our imagination. These disorders have transformed into real illnesses. What it does mean is that the root cause can often be traced to our thoughts as well as our emotions. Stress and worry generally are the biggest culprits. .

It is a well-known fact that ulcers can be caused as a result of high level of stress on a continuing basis. Headaches, insomnia, and muscle pains are often the result of stress in our lives, as are anxiety, hypertension, and high blood pressure.

At times it seems we almost *expect* to become ill! Let's take the common cold for example. Someone in your household or your workplace has come down with a cold. Have you ever thought, "Oh, boy, I *know* I'm going to get that cold"? You start noticing your body even more. "Is that a sniffle coming on?" Or "I know my throat is feeling a bit scratchy." It's almost as though you talk yourself into getting that cold!

Even our goals, hopes, wishes, and desires can have an impact on our health. Our thoughts make an impression upon our subconscious. The mind takes these thoughts seriously as well as literally and works to help us achieve those goals.

For many years I knew I wanted to pursue my own business full-time. I knew deep down inside that was the direction I wanted to go and needed to take. For me, this was not just a hope; it was something I truly wanted and planned to do. However, I was a single parent and felt I needed the security that working for an employer could provide. A weekly paycheck and benefits were not a luxury;

they were a very real need. Starting my own business was just too much of a chance for me to take at the time, and I was not willing to run the risk.

I found that my work experience and education kept leading me to jobs which made more demands on my time and energy than I wanted. I kept finding jobs which required almost round-the-clock involvement. I wanted to be able to spend time with my son, as well as fit in a social life somewhere in my schedule.

I used the meditation techniques that I taught to others. I sat down and wrote my long-term goals in life, as well as my short-term goals and requirements. I knew what was important to me in the interim before pursuing my long-range plans: I wanted a job where my every waking moment was not dedicated to the job. I also wanted to work at a place where, as long as I did my work well, I would be treated fairly and with respect.

I took a job at a local law firm. At the time, I thought it would be a good match. It was a basic nine-to-five job. I could go to work in the morning and leave at a decent hour. I didn't have to work nights or weekends. It was located near my home, so I didn't have a long commute. I didn't have to bring work home with me or think about it when I wasn't there. I thought to myself, "Finally, I can just go do my job, and then when the time is right, I can pursue my real goals and interests."

What I didn't envision was how wonderful that job would turn out to be. I ended up loving my job. The people I worked with were friendly and everyone went out of their way to help each other. Our employer treated us like family members. The pay was exceptional. Every bad thing you hear about lawyers was *not* true in this firm. They were ethical, honest, and caring.

Every day brought some new adventure. The firm was involved in local and national politics. Now, I've never been deeply interested in politics, but what fascinating people I met! Imagine answering the telephone and finding the White House on the line? I was even able to shake the hand of the president of the United States.

I still wanted to have my own business, but kept putting off doing anything about it.

Then it happened: carpal tunnel syndrome struck. At first it affected only my right hand. My employers were very accommodating. They allowed me to answer the telephone and do tasks where I did not need to use my right hand. Being ambidextrous, I used my left hand as much as possible. Then I developed carpal tunnel in that hand too.

My world was thrown into turmoil. I could no longer physically do my job. Looking back, that time was one of the most difficult in my life. I became depressed because I felt useless. I went on disability and felt guilty because I was not productive. I was not used to sitting around doing nothing while earning money.

All the other areas of my life suffered as well and deepened my depression. The simplest of tasks were now major undertakings. My hand motor skills were practically nonexistent. I dropped things constantly. I probably broke at least two sets of dishes and numerous glasses. Cooking was a challenge, and I soon learned to make very simple casseroles that required very little work. I remember one time when I just sat down and cried because I'd gone to take dinner out of the oven and dropped it. There was our dinner all over the kitchen floor. I think my son felt worse for me than I did!

I had been used to being independent and self-reliant, but now I had to rely on the help of others to do many tasks that I took for granted. I felt even guiltier because my son had to take over many of the household tasks while he was studying for final exams.

I found it painful to drive any distance, and soon found myself becoming a hermit. I didn't want to go out and socialize because I felt self-conscious about having to wear two splints. I felt that everyone was looking at me and talking about me.

As difficult as that time was it did spur me into action to pursue my original goal of having my own business. I continued my education and worked to establish a full-time practice. A very negative event did, in fact, have a positive side.

Now, it is difficult to prove that an illness is spearheaded by psychological factors. As I look back, I can understand how large a part those factors can play. I might never have left my job and attempted to fulfill the goal I kept reinforcing to my subconscious if I had not gotten ill. I know I would not consciously have wished carpal tunnel syndrome upon myself, but I never wavered from my original goal. Did my subconscious take action?

I have not allowed this to stop me from setting and meditating upon goals I wish to achieve. I have learned by trial and error to add suggestions at the end of my meditations such as, "I will accomplish my goals in the healthiest way and the best possible manner."

SECONDARY GAIN

Illness can be further complicated by what is known as "secondary gain," that is, something gained by that illness. The reasoning behind the gain may not seem logical to our conscious mind, but it does to our subconscious.

Yes, it is true that some people consciously and purposely fake an illness in order to gain something in their lives. Perhaps they are looking for attention, or wish to be able to collect money from an accident, or to stop working. There can be many reasons.

However, secondary gain as being discussed here is a much deeper subconscious cause and effect. The person usually is not consciously aware of it. Therefore, it can be very difficult to ferret out the underlying reasons for it to occur.

We are comprised of different "parts." Our personalities are multifaceted. All of our separate parts contribute to our whole personality. This is not the same as having a multiple personality disorder which is an entirely different matter. A multiple personality disorder is having separate and distinct whole personalities. "Parts" in relation to ourselves is merely recognizing that we have many shades to our personalities. We react differently to situations, as well as feeling different ways about them. To better understand this concept, let's take the following example:

You are invited somewhere by a friend, for instance a beach party. Now, "part" of you wants to go. It sounds like a very fun event. Your friend has told you that a lot of people are planning to go. The weather forecast predicts warm, sunny weather. You are ready for some fun! You want some fun.

Yet, there is another "part" of you that doesn't want to go. You have a project due at work. It's a very important project, one that could earn you a promotion and a raise. You want that raise.

Here you can see a case scenario of two different parts of yourself. The social side of you wants to go. The responsible side of you doesn't want to go. Each one has its own feelings toward the same event.

Let's say that the social part of you is seemingly winning and you plan to go to the party. Yet, the responsible part of you is very strong. You might find that the day of the beach party you wake up finding yourself not feeling well enough to go to the party. So, you stay home thinking, "I might as well work on that project."

The above example isn't too complicated, but many secondary gain issues are.

In his audio series, *The Miracles of Hypnosis,* Dr. Kevin Hogan recounted the following case:

A young woman contacted him because she was suffering from environmental illness. Quite simply, she was allergic to almost everything in her environment. Dr. Hogan had to go to her home since she was too ill to come to his office. In fact, she never left her house except to go to the hospital whenever she required medical intervention.

When he arrived there, he found her house almost completely stripped bare. There were no carpets on the floor because she was allergic to the glue commonly used for carpeting. The walls were lined with tin foil, and there was no wallpaper or paint on them. She wore a surgical mask on her face because dust caused a severe allergic reaction. She weighed less than ninety pounds. Most foods caused allergic reactions. There were very few things that she could eat. She literally was dying.

Dr. Hogan did an intensive, hours-long hypnosis session to find out the underlying reasons for her illness. After the session she was able to take off her surgical mask and breathe without an allergic reaction. Both she and Dr. Hogan felt they had been successful. She was able to leave her house and start to resume a normal life.

Several months had passed when the doctor received a telephone call from the woman. She reported that the environmental illness had started to return. This time, Dr. Hogan added "parts" therapy to his session to find out if any part of her personality had a reason for needing the illness.

He discovered that during her illness her husband was often home or nearby because she frequently had to be rushed to the hospital. When she recovered and was able to function, he took a job that required an hour commute each way.

"Part" of her had grown to depend upon her husband being close by at all times. When that changed, that "part" was not having its needs met. Her illness started to return. The woman was intelligent and mature. This was not something she would do on purpose. However, it is important to remember that the subconscious mind is very childlike.

In the therapy session Dr. Hogan had a dialogue with that "part of her personality—the psyche" to find out what would fulfill its need while still allowing the woman to live a life free from the environmental illness.

Using a contemplative meditation technique similar to the one at the end of this chapter can help you identify the part or parts of your personality that have an investment in secondary gain. However, this can be a complicated and involved issue, and it may be best for some people to work with a counselor or hypnotist trained in parts therapy.

THE COLORS OF YOUR LIFE

Using colors is a wonderful and easy way to meditate. Colors can be soothing and refreshing or vitalizing and energizing. Have you ever noticed how certain colors make you feel? Some colors make you feel wonderful, while others make you feel drained or tired.

Take a close look at your wardrobe. Do you find that many of your garments are in a few favorite colors? How about your home? We tend to decorate our home in colors and patterns that make us feel comfortable. We even buy cars in colors we like.

Even if you do not feel able to visualize easily, using colors generally works well. It does not matter if you cannot see clear pictures or scenes; most of us can at least sense colors. We can imagine how those colors would make us feel.

We often associate certain colors with moods and emotions. Think about some of the expressions we use: "He was so angry he saw red," or "She was feeling sad and blue."

The following meditation is one of my favorites. I use whatever color I "feel" I want to use that day. Some days I need energizing and I use a vibrant color like red. On other days, I need to relax and pick a soothing shade of blue. If I am feeling sad or depressed, I pick a sunny yellow.

For the following meditation, just substitute whatever color you wish to use.

Color Meditation

Sit or lie down in a comfortable place. Allow yourself to breathe in and out naturally. Close your eyes and imagine that you have a bucket of water in front of you. Now this is a very special and magic bucket of water.

The water is incredibly beautiful and is your favorite shade of green. Notice how clear and wonderful the water in the bucket is. It's just the right temperature, not too cold or too warm. Now, imagine lifting the bucket over your head and slowly letting the water gently pour over your body. Feel how wonderful it feels on your body. You can feel it flow over your skin. Feel the water soak into your skin, bringing its color energy within your body.

INSOMNIA: SLEEPING BEAUTY

I think most of us have been hit with insomnia at one time or another. I know I have. At one time in my life it was a serious problem. I used to get hit with what I call the "but did you consider this" syndrome. It seemed that my mind just wouldn't turn off. It kept thinking . . . and thinking. I'd get to the point where I was *just* about to fall asleep, when I'd think, "Well, did you consider this?" Then, of course, I'd have to think about that for a while. It's a rather common problem and a major cause of insomnia.

Occasionally, insomnia can strike when we are excited or worried. Maybe we are excited about something we have planned for the next day or are dreading what will happen. We could be worried about something and have a lot on our mind. So, we hash and rehash it all night long.

Years ago I used the supposedly tried-and-true method of counting sheep. I know I've mentioned it before, but I tend to have a creative mind. I'd start out counting sheep, and soon the sheep would be making faces at me, or their faces would totally change. Next the sheep might turn into dragons jumping over the fence. Then, of course, the dragons would say things to me, or they'd end up doing a song and dance number. Entertaining, but hardly conducive to sleep.

Counting sheep is supposed to be boring. Then you'll go off to sleep because your mind would rather do anything but count those darn sheep. It works well for some people. Creative people, though, just find ways to make it less boring—which doesn't help them fall asleep.

I finally found a technique that works for me. I didn't start out using it for insomnia, but I soon found that I always fell asleep while doing it. I still do, every time. I mentally build my dream house. I get right into every minute detail. For some reason, *that* must bore my mind, for I can never stay awake very long doing it. It might suit you if techniques like counting sheep don't work. Plan a project that requires attention to a lot of little details and has little or no emotion attached to it.

Meditation for Those Who Think Too Much

What you need to do is reason with your mind just as you would with a child. It wants you to think about your problem. You need sleep. Remember, you are the adult here.

With this technique, use the deepening method you prefer. A counting method might work well and may even put you to sleep.

Instead of counting from ten to one, count from one hundred or even higher down to one. If you visualize the numbers, make them as dull and as colorless as possible. If you are still awake after your deepening method, then simply announce to your subconscious that you are more than willing to think about your problem . . . tomorrow. Right now you need sleep so you can have the energy and vitality to deal with it. Tell your mind that you will give the problem its due attention . . . tomorrow.

Tapes for Sleeping

If you have a collection of meditation audio tapes, find the longest or the most passive one you have. It helps if you have one that's very boring. That may not be too difficult. Quite honestly, many meditation tapes are rather dull. But in this instance that's a positive. Put the cassette player on your nightstand so it's near enough for you to hear the tape. Don't play it too loudly. Preferably it should be at a level you can just barely hear without straining.

Nature tapes are also wonderful to listen to when going to sleep. Waterfalls, ocean waves, and rain are especially good when you are having difficulty sleeping.

DEPRESSION

About seventeen million Americans suffer from depression in some form. Depression is a badly misunderstood condition. There are people who feel that someone who is depressed can simply "cheer up" and things will get better. However, feeling depressed is very different from suffering depression. It's not always a matter of cheering up.

There are three kinds of depression: chronic/major depression, situational depression, and chemical depression. Meditation can help with all three. However, with chronic/major depression, or depression that is chemically caused, seeing a health care professional is vitally important. It's not just a matter of feeling blue. A health care professional may suggest or use meditation as part of the treatment plan. But meditation alone is not enough. Chronic/major depression interferes with work, school, and social life. Situational depression is common following divorce, death, change of residence or jobs, and any event that causes a major change in lifestyle. Chemical depression is physiological in nature. Manic depressive disorder and bipolar disorders are examples of chemical depression. In this type of depression the chemicals in the brain that communicate with the body's cells via neurotransmitters don't function correctly.

We all get the blues from time to time. It's probably impossible to be happy all the time, even for the most upbeat person. However, when someone is depressed more often than not it is a warning of a deeper depression. Psychologists feel that depression that lasts for more than two weeks could be a sign of major/chronic depression.

What are some of the signs of depression?

Sudden and dramatic changes in behavior

Sudden changes in appetite, either loss of appetite or overeating

Insomnia and difficulty sleeping

Trouble with concentration

Excessive fatigue

Loss of interest in friends and/or family

Increased drug and/or alcohol use

Constant feelings of worthlessness or self-hatred

Preoccupation with death, dying, or suicide

There are more signs, but these are some of the more common ones. If you or someone you know is suffering from depression, try to get help. It may not be easy. Some people who suffer from depression are not aware of the fact. Others feel they cannot be helped.

Short-term depression can be helped by meditation. We may just have had a bad day, and positive meditation can help us see things in a better and clearer light.

Situational depression, such as occurs following a death, can also be helped by positive meditation. The below meditations are useful for short-term depression.

Planting a Garden

Use the deepening method you prefer.

> *Imagine yourself in a large field that you have carefully tilled. It's ready for planting. You can plant whatever you choose . . . vegetables . . . flowers . . . fruit trees . . . or all of them. Whatever you'd like to plant. See yourself planting them . . . very carefully placing each tender plant into the rich soil. See yourself watering each and every plant. Know that each plant, flower, and tree is part of you. As you plant each one, you are giving it life and the opportunity to grow . . . the opportunity to grow strong, beautiful, and full of vitality. See yourself in each and every plant.*
>
> *And every day take a few moments to visit your garden and watch as it grows. Carefully tend each flower, plant, or tree. Give each tender plant water whenever it needs it. Know that each and every plant is part of you. It's like watching yourself growing strong, vital, and healthy. And if weeds ever pop up, simply pluck them and pull them out of the soil. You do not need weeds in your garden. Simply remove them. Know that this garden is yours . . . and is you. Visit it for a little while each day. Tend it well each day. Give it fresh air, sunshine, water, and love.*

The Comedy Channel

Laughter can be a great help in getting out of a depressed and sad mood. I highly recommend going to the movies or renting a comedy video as a way to lighten your mood. It has been said, "Laughter is the best medicine."

The meditation that follows is similar in nature to watching a comedy on television. Put yourself in the show. That makes it more personal. Use the deepening method you prefer. For a variation, choose one of your favorite sitcoms, and put yourself in the starring role.

Imagine that you have been cast in a new comedy show. You are also the writer and the director— what a talented person you are! Remember a day when you did something very funny and enjoyed doing it . . . something that made people laugh. See yourself doing silly and funny things. People are having a wonderful time; you are making them so happy. It's nice to see people laugh . . . everyone needs laughter. Now look, here comes a new scene. Look, there you are . . . dressed as a clown. See the bright, colorful makeup you have on. You have a big bright colorful smile painted on your face. And what big shoes you have on! You are so funny, even YOU are laughing. Feel yourself laughing . . . see everyone else laugh. It feels good to make people laugh . . . it's important to be able to laugh. You are doing a good and wonderful thing. See yourself prance around, doing silly things . . . pretending to fall over your big feet. Oh, look, you have a flower. Look at it closely. Oops, it squirted you with water. See everyone laugh at the silly and fun things you are doing. Feel yourself laughing and enjoying yourself. Oh, it's so much fun to be silly just like a clown.

GOOD HEALTH MEDITATION

Close your eyes and picture yourself standing in a ray of sunshine. You are feeling wonderful, feeling full of vitality and healthy energy. Feel the ray of sunshine wash over and through you. As it does so . . . it infuses you with even more healthy energy. Feel yourself bask and glow in this ray of light . . . this golden light of health . . . spreading through your entire body. Feel how this light makes you feel even better . . . even healthier . . . even more vitally alive.

What if you already have an illness or a disease? Can meditation help? There are reports and research that show that, in many cases, a positive attitude has made a difference. Meditations like the ones below when added to your existing treatment plan might well be effective. However, it is essential to continue to work with your health care practitioner.

If you can, work with meditations like the ones below two or three times a day. Morning, noon, and at night before bedtime are good times to practice them. You also can take a few minutes here and there throughout the day to quickly visualize a scene from one of these meditations. It's just like daydreaming with a purpose. Simply envision the scene for a moment or two, and then you can go back to whatever you need to do.

The Paintbrush

Imagine that you have a bucket and a paintbrush in front of you. Go ahead . . . look inside the bucket. You will notice that the paint is very special. It glitters and glows and is all sparkly. Perhaps it is a silver color . . . perhaps it is a golden color. Whatever color you like is perfect for you. When you dip the paintbrush into the bucket and spread some of the paint, you notice that it glows just like a million stars in the sky. How beautiful it is . . . how very special and magical. It's a healing energy paint, a very special paint. This paint is sent from the heavens and is so very special. Take the paintbrush and spread the paint all over your body . . . just as though you were a canvas. See yourself as you glow and sparkle and shimmer. Feel it as each brush stroke covers your skin . . . your body. Notice how it feels as it glides over each part of your body, infusing its special magic into each and every pore of your body. Go ahead and cover your entire body . . . it feels wonderful! And when you finish painting your body with this special paint, just stand back . . . it's as though you were looking at yourself. See how your body glimmers and glows with health and vitality. See yourself turning around . . . arms outstretched. See the smile on your face. See the glow you have . . . that glow that is coming from both inside and outside. Take a deep satisfying breath and breathe in this feeling of health and vitality.

The Game

Imagine your body as a playing field for a game . . . a video game.
Imagine yourself standing upright or lying down . . . whichever is most
comfortable for you. See the little game pieces . . . they look just like
those little PacMan characters. See them as they go through your body,
searching for any illness that might be there. If they find any . . . they
simply remove it bit by bit. See as these little characters go through your
entire body, cleansing it of any illness. Feel how much stronger and
healthier you feel as the little characters move through your body . . .
and they find each and every spot of illness and remove it. They completely cleanse your whole body. As they continue throughout your body
. . . you feel healthier . . . stronger . . . more vitally alive and healthy.

Part Three

The Next Step

Chapter Thirteen

Positive Thinking

We all want the best in life, or at least that is what we *think* we want. Oftentimes, we actually limit ourselves by thinking the exact opposite. "I'd like a new job, but I could never get one; I can't compete in today's market." Or, "I'd like to have a relationship, but no one could love me; I'm too fat and ugly." That mode of thinking sends a strong message to your brain that you believe the goal to be impossible to achieve. You have unknowingly placed a huge obstacle in your path.

Our brain dutifully attempts to do what we tell it, and often in a very literal manner. Most of us don't pay much attention to our patterns of thinking. We just go along on automatic pilot, so to speak. When we tell ourselves we'll not be able to remember, do, or achieve something, the brain attempts to comply.

On the other hand, if you believe you are able to succeed, the brain also attempts to comply. Does this sound a lot like psychobabble drivel? Not when you realize that what you are actually doing is, in effect, giving yourself hypnotic suggestions.

Now, you aren't going to get anything and everything you desire just by "thinking." But you will give yourself a tool that will help you achieve what you want, and a powerful tool at that. Have you ever heard the saying, "It's all in the power of the mind"?

Yes, there *are* some impossibilities in this world. There is a difference between what is possible and what is fantasy or wishful thinking. My favorite movie actor is *Desperado* star, Joaquim de Almeida. No matter how hard I try, I'm probably not ever going to marry him. I've never even met the man! Nor will I ever become a famous singer. Quite honestly, I can't sing a note. One does have to be realistic.

However, much of what we perceive as impossible to achieve or receive is not! Read the stories of those who have succeeded in their field, and you will find that they believed in their ability to succeed. They worked hard and strove to attain their goals. Most important, they didn't give up, even when they failed.

There are just as many stories of people who have not succeeded. What makes them different from those who did? Perhaps they were told that it took "too much" to rise to the top, that very few people have what it takes. Maybe they felt they didn't deserve it, that only special people can make it.

We complicate matters further by feeling it is bad or selfish to want material things, again limiting ourselves. Wanting a better life, a better job, love, or a more comfortable lifestyle is not selfish.

It's really a matter of what we "tell" our brains—our minds— what we want and believe we can have or are "allowed" to have. We are, in effect, programming ourselves, be it for negative . . . or positive.

If we keep thinking negatively about the very things we want, we are really saying we don't think we can . . . or should have them. Perhaps we fear what it would be like if we achieved that goal. Things often come with a price. Are we willing to pay that price?

Many times it's because we are afraid to fail. Then we hide behind saying we will try. The word *try* in itself is indicative of a high probability of failure. When we say we will try to do something, we really mean we doubt our ability or desire to do so.

Usually things will not just fall out of the sky or suddenly appear on your doorstep. This is not magic, although in many instances things will seem to happen effortlessly. Lady Luck may appear to be on your side for a change. You may find lots of lucky "coincidences" happening to you.

Major goals still require work and dedication. However, there are techniques you can use to focus your energies and activities in order to succeed. Instead of sitting around wishing you could do something or have something, you'll find yourself taking positive steps toward that end. Add some of those "coincidences," and you have a very powerful technique in your repertoire.

HOW TO STAY POSITIVE
IN A NEGATIVE WORLD

Television, radio, newsprint, and now the Internet bombard us with negative messages. With all of the negativity that abounds, how can we stay positive? Is it even possible? And if we strive to keep a positive outlook, are we just seeing the world through the proverbial rose-colored glasses?

There *is* a difference between blindly ignoring reality and seeing things as they are and still looking for the positives. The world *can* be a cruel place, blighted with crime, unhappiness, and disease. The world *can* be a wonderful place, full of love, compassion, and joy. Both scenarios exist and affect our lives. Which do we want to be as the prominent emphasis in our lives? Quite honestly, attitude is a major factor. It is the difference between optimism and pessimism. Is the glass half full or half empty?

I cannot tell you that it is easy to remain positive at all times. Some disciplines of New Age thought seem to suggest that a truly enlightened and spiritual person is able to welcome all events and view them as a positive: "Oh great, another learning experience." Intellectually, that can be easy to grasp. But what happens when a "learning experience" hits home and comes crashing into our lives?

Although we might be studying and moving forward on an enlightened spiritual path, we still live in the real world. We may be on the path, but that path is somewhere on planet Earth—New Jersey, Oklahoma, New York—wherever! When a negative event happens—perhaps a death of a loved one, or a rape or murder—it is difficult to be enlightened. It is not easy to see this as just another learning experience.

This sounds like I'm being a bit negative, doesn't it? What I'm trying to say is that we are not perfect. Most of us cannot maintain a positive outlook all the time. We are human. Negative things can and will happen to us. The glass is half empty. By the same token, *positive* things can and will happen to us. A positive person will strive to emphasize good and positive things. The glass is half full. Well, maybe it's not full yet. But it just might be on the way to becoming full!

It comes right back to attitude and what we allow to be the major emphasis in our lives. By having a positive outlook, we are not ignoring reality or denying our emotions. When we are hurt or unhappy with events, we should admit it. Negativity is being caught in a rut and dwelling on those hurts. Being positive means allowing time to heal and then moving forward.

If we really think about it, some of the worst things that have happened to us have put us in a position to receive wonderful things. At the time we weren't very happy. But with the passage of time, we can accept those seemingly negative things as having a positive outcome.

Don't criticize yourself if you are not enlightened enough to be positive and happy all the time. That is unrealistic for most of us. The important thing is to strive for a positive perspective.

I believe we are more likely to find positives and attract positives to us if we have a positive outlook. First, we attract like energy, therefore, if we think positively, we will tend to attract positives. Second, a positive outlook will help make us aware and ready to receive!

May the sum of the negatives in your life always be outweighed by the positives.

DARE TO DREAM

A nearly impossible thing to explain is the difference between fantasy and a real possibility. Hundreds of medical and technological advancements have been made because someone dared to dream. At the time, they must have sounded like pipe dreams. If we had been living in the late 1400s, many of us might have thought Christopher Columbus was crazy. Imagine the mold on a piece of bread becoming the basis for a wonder drug or flying like a bird in something called the airplane. The list could go on and on: the telephone, a flight to the moon, a cure for polio.

Unfortunately, there is the flip side of the coin. Too many lives have been lost because someone thought God told them to commit mass murders. Hitler's dream that the Aryan race should be supreme resulted in the deaths of thousands and thousands of innocent people.

In light of events like these, it is difficult to stay positive. Nevertheless, I have always hoped that the positives will ultimately outweigh the negatives. I hope people will still dare to dream. Perhaps someone's pipe dream will lead to a cure for cancer or AIDS.

It's apparent that we need to have realistic goals and aspirations. Living completely in a world of fantasy is neither healthy nor productive. But how do we tell the difference? It is helpful to ask ourselves questions. Is what we want or envision truly logical? Will it hurt us or someone else? Are we willing to accept the results if we do achieve it?

LEMONADE, ANYONE?

One of my favorite expressions is, "When life hands you lemons, make lemonade." I admit, years ago when someone said that, I'd roll my eyes and snicker. It just reeked of too much pop psychology mumbo jumbo for my tastes. Now I find the ability to be that positive one of the better goals in life to strive for. Have no doubts about it, I can whine with the best of them! It's been suggested that we should view negatives as opportunities for a learning experience. When I am hit with one of life's hard knocks, I find myself thinking, "Oh, no . . . here comes another learning experience. Haven't I learned enough already? Aren't there Cliff Notes for this?"

It occurred to me, though, that it takes as much work to complain about something as it does to make the most of the situation. Positive thinking does not mean lying down and cheerfully accept every hard knock life throws at us. Nor does it mean denial of reality. Positive thinking means working to find a way to get the most positive result out of a negative occurrence.

This is the area where I use meditation the most. It helps me to move past the melodrama and go forward. What can I do? Where can I go from here? What have I got to use?

FANTASY AND
WISHFUL THINKING VERSUS REALITY

There are many books about positive thinking on the market. Think positive and you will get what you want. However, there remains that nagging question: how to tell the difference between wishful thinking and cold, hard reality. How do you know whether what you want is something truly attainable or just a pipe dream?

First, you need to take the time to get to know yourself. A good first step is to sit down and list your talents and abilities. Be honest, but do not be afraid to be your own fan club. What do you have to work with?

The next step is to list what you are willing to do to further those talents and abilities. Are you willing to continue your education? Practice more? Then list what you feel holds you back. Do you need to work on becoming more self-confident?

You may want to find the cure for cancer, but if you have no scientific or medical background and no plans to work toward that profession, that goal is unrealistic.

Decide what you are willing to work for. You may want to do many things, but may not have the motivation to accomplish those things. For instance, I said I knew I'd never be a famous singer. I don't have the talent or abilities. I could take training, but I'm not willing to work that hard.

CAN'T I HAVE A BAD MOOD?

Well, of course you can. Positive thinking does not mean denying that we have feelings and emotions. Moods are a part of life. We have good moods, we have bad moods, and we have moods that lie somewhere in between. They are a natural and normal part of daily existence.

"It's my mood, I own it, and I'm going to enjoy it, gosh darn it!"

It's not healthy to hold in our emotions. Many studies have shown that this can lead to illness. Expressing our emotions is healthy. True, it can be the better part of valor to quiet our temper before verbally attacking another person. Sometimes we can't express our emotions to that person. Meditation can help here.

We need an outlet for those emotions. In some cases, it's easy to find ways to express emotions without being threatening or hurtful to another person. We can find ways to get our emotions out. For instance, I talk to inanimate objects, like my car: "Oh, please, please start. If you don't, see if I ever give you a coat of wax again!" Lately I find that I talk to the grammar check in my word processing program: "Who cares about subject-verb agreement, I *want* to use that phrase. And gosh darn it, I'm *going* to use that phrase!"

DON'T TAKE LIFE SO SERIOUSLY!

I consider humor to be more than a coping strategy; I consider it to be a survival technique. Humor is a great stress reliever. It'd be unrealistic for me to tell you to laugh at everything that happens in your life. There are things that just aren't very humorous. However, the more humor we *can* find in situations, the easier those situations are to deal with.

I use as much humor as possible in my personal meditations. Using humor in meditations, especially visualizations, is extremely effective. The brain notices humor. It's like putting an exclamation point at the end of a sentence. It makes a statement. It goes back to the analogy I made earlier comparing our subconscious mind to a puppy. Puppies like to have fun!

We need balance in our lives. Our mind has a sense of humor. Use humor as often as possible in your meditation scripts. It's less boring. Your mind appreciates humor.

WHAT THEY ARE REALLY THINKING . . .

I hope you have some fun with this! The statements in brackets are what these people *really* think.

Meditation teacher to students:

> And now, I'm going to stop talking for a while. Just let your thoughts carry you away for while.
> [Good, now I can go make a sandwich!]

Yoga teacher to students:

> Now hold that position for a count of ten.
> [Ha! Let's see them try that one!]

Brain to dreamer:

> Here's a nice dream for you.
> [Just try and make sense out of that dream, sucker!]

Nature spiritualist to tree:

> I honor your existence. I thank you for sharing your beauty with the creatures of the earth. I thank you . . .
> [and on and on and on]

Tree to nature spiritualist:

> This airy-fairy stuff makes me cringe. Just wait until the fall.
> [I'll be laughing my bark off when you have to rake up all my leaves!]

IF ONLY . . .

You've done it, I've done it, and presidents have done it. How many times have you thought or said, "If only I had not done that." "If only I had told my father I loved him." "If only I had not said that."

I've certainly done things in the past that I regret. Some I might excuse more easily because I was a child and I didn't know any better. With others I was an adult; I knew better and yet I did it.

It's a rare person who does not have at least one or two skeletons in the closet. But dwelling on past mistakes is counterproductive. It simply summons up an emotional state such as regret or guilt. Such emotions can allow us to be caught up in a vicious cycle of thinking: "I should not have done that. I am a bad person." This type of thinking goes around and around with no way out.

"If onlys" are good for future reference. They help keep us from making the same mistakes over and over again. But dwelling on "if onlys" is a waste of time. What's done is done. It's the present and the future that we have to work with.

We can't change past actions, but we can use meditation to change our perception of them and the degree to which they affect our ability to progress. This does not absolve us of responsibility for our actions. But it does allow us to practice a more positive behavior in the here and now, as well as the future. Meditation is instrumental in achieving this end.

It is also wise to remember that recall is often inaccurate. Our memory of events may be far different from what actually occurred. Our past actions may not be as bad as we think. However, they pack an emotional punch and that is what affects us in our present life.

Pay attention to your "if onlys." When you find yourself thinking "if only," take the time to notice why you are using it. Patterns of behavior and actions can emerge. We can utilize meditation to help break that pattern and those actions.

First, we can break the emotional hold those thoughts have on us. Second, we can eliminate nonproductive self-criticism, such as "I am a bad person." Third, we can work toward changing our behavior.

With meditation, we can find patterns to our actions.

Do we hurt people because we speak without thinking?

Do we criticize ourselves constantly?

Do we procrastinate if we think something is too hard?

Do we avoid new people or situations because of past events?

THE PURSUIT OF PERFECTION

I feel the most important part of the journey toward perfection lies in realizing that we will never reach it. To reach it would mean an end. That would be anticlimatic and, in all honesty, rather boring.

It is easy to get caught up in the perfection trap. We think that we must be perfect in all we do. Other people can be normal, but we have to be superhuman. We don't cut ourselves any slack! Being positive does not mean being unrealistic. Expecting perfection from ourselves is just that—unrealistic. Be sure to set goals for yourself that are humanly possible. *That* is thinking positively.

SCRIBE AND VIBE IT!

Most of us think we know what we want, when in fact we know only vague generalities. A technique I share with clients and friends helps to do just that—identify what we want.

For this exercise you need a notebook or a steno pad. You can use a computer if you wish. Sit down and make a list of everything you think you want. Don't show your list to anyone because you will tend to censor it. For example, you may put down what you *think* you should put down, such as, "I want world peace." Now, you may want world peace, it's a worthy goal. But it might not be something that is uppermost in your life.

You will also be more honest if you don't think anyone will be judging your list. If you write down something that might seem trivial to someone else, you might not list it, even if it's something you really want. You may, for example, want a gold bracelet. There is nothing wrong with that, but you might feel guilty for wanting something that isn't a lofty goal.

For instance:

I want a new job.

I want a good relationship.

I want to lose ten pounds.

I want to have a house.

The first time we make our list it looks very much like the one above. It's very vague and general. That is fine for now. This exercise will help you become more specific as you go along.

Now that you have written your list, review it at least once a day. As you do so, you will most likely find that you want to change items slightly. For example, if you put down "I want a new job," you may realize that you want "a new job that is closer to home." As you review the list, you may find that you have received or achieved an item on it.

When you find something that requires changing because you've done it or you need to be more specific, rewrite the entire list. This part is important, for rewriting the list helps cement it in your subconscious mind. If you are using a computer, retype the entire list. Don't use cut and paste!

After a while your list will become more and more specific. You will realize exactly what you want to do.

I like to keep my lists and date them. Then months later I look back at what I've written. It's interesting to see the difference between what I thought I wanted and what I really want.

AFFIRM IT!

When we think positively, our thoughts and words can have a strong impact upon us.

Affirmations are a good way to reinforce positive thinking in our daily lives. Taking a few minutes each morning to state our goals can be an effective tool.

You do not have to meditate to use affirmations. Use them when you are standing in front of the mirror shaving or doing your hair. Simply look at yourself and repeat one or two affirmations. You can do them mentally or out loud, it makes no difference.

Positive-Thinking Meditation

Use the deepening method you prefer. A long body relax is especially nice with this type of meditation.

Imagine that you are at a waterfall with a large pond of water at the bottom. In this pond are flat rocks scattered here and there . . . just perfect for sitting on. It is a beautiful warm day; the sun is shining and the air is fresh and clean. The temperature is warm . . . just right. The sky is pleasantly blue, with puffy white clouds scattered here and there. You are dressed comfortably and are barefoot. You can dabble your toes in the water. It is cool and refreshing. Pick one of the rocks to sit on. Notice how warm the rock feels from the sun. You feel very rested . . . perhaps a little lazy. That's fine . . . this is a time to relax and feel fine. You have plenty of time . . . there is nowhere that you have to be . . . nothing that you have to do except sit on this sunny rock and relax. As you sit on this rock you can hear the sound of the waterfall. Hear how relaxing and soothing the sound is. Once in a while you can even feel a bit of the water's spray on your face. It's clear and fresh.

As you sit at the bottom of this waterfall, you realize just how much you have to offer the world . . . how wonderful you really are. You can think clearly and positively. You have achieved much in your life and have much to share with those in your life. Life is good . . . you are good . . . and you are enjoying this day . . . this time . . . you know that you deserve it. And as you continue to sit on this warm, sunny rock, you know that you can always find the positive in things, that you know how to look at things in the best way possible.

You know that you are a positive person. You know how to get the most out of life. You know that the more positive you feel and think, the more you find to enjoy in life. Now take a deep breath, hold it for a moment, and gently exhale. Know that from this moment forward, for each breath you take, you will be able to find the most positive part of any event or situation. You are a positive person.

SAYING GOOD-BYE TO THOSE WHO HAVE LEFT

It has been said that "Death is hardest on those who have been left behind." Death is one of the most emotionally wrenching experiences we have to face. All too often we regret not having said good-bye to loved ones or told them how much we love them.

You notice that you are in a place of light and golden mists. There is a source of light illuminating this place, although you cannot physically see that source of light.

Know that you have come to a special place that lies beyond time and space. It is the place of all time and being, where all things are possible. Everything that has ever been is here in this place; everyone who has ever been is here in this place. Because you come with love in your heart, you are allowed to enter this special place and talk with those you have loved. Take the time to see, feel, and sense your surroundings. Feel the joy and wonder and the power of this place. Allow yourself to wander around until you see a spot slightly off in the distance. This spot has a resting place, with a wondrous garden and benches placed here and there. There are paths leading from all directions to this place. As you look down one of the paths, you notice a figure coming toward you. As the figure comes close to you, you are able to see that this is [fill in the name of the deceased person]. They slowly come closer and closer, and now they are standing directly in front of you. And as they are standing in front of you, you look at them with joy upon your face, and you see that same joy reflected in their face. The two of you embrace and smile at each other. How good it feels to be able to embrace each other. See the two of you embracing, feel it, sense it, know it.

Now, see the two of you sitting down in the resting place. Take all the time you wish just to gaze upon your loved one's face. You are allowed plenty of time in this place; take all the time you wish. Allow yourself to look at your loved one. How wonderful it feels to be able to look upon their face!

Now see the two of you talking together. Listen, you can hear what you are saying to each other. Listen as you share the memories and events of your lives together. One, by one, the events of your lives together unfold. See them, sense them, hear them, and know them. [Pause]

And as you finish your conversation, hear yourself say, "I have so many regrets. I wish I could have said good-bye to you." And as you say those words, you can hear your loved one reply to you: "Good-bye is merely a phrase. I am in a place where knowing-ness is a part of my existence, my being. And as for love, it never dies, love lives on. I know that you loved me as I loved you. I know that you love me as I love you. Love always remains alive. I know what you have in your heart. Trust that I know this, for it will bring you peace. I am at peace and wish the same for you. There were things in our earthly life together that we did or said to each other that brought sadness, anger, or hurt. But those are just passing memories, like the sands blowing across a desert. For there were things in our earthly lives together that we did or said to each other that brought about happiness, joy, and pleasure. It is those things that I hold near me. I wish for you the same: to hold the dear memories close and let all others pass away. Hold the dear memories close to you. I love you as you love me."

And now, see yourself and your loved one embracing once again. Know it, feel it, sense it, and see it.

Now take a deep breath and allow the feelings of love and serenity to wash over you, and take those feelings with you into your daily life from this day forward.

Chapter Fourteen

Memory Improvement

A major reason to improve memory is for purposes of study and learning. The need to learn is no longer relegated to those under twenty-five. People of all ages are going to college. Numerous companies have training programs and in-house courses for employees. We need to be able to learn and remember what we learn.

Meditation can be used to improve memory. First of all, we have better recall when we are relaxed. How many times have you been in a situation where you needed to remember someone's name and couldn't do it? However, later on—perhaps when you were daydreaming—you suddenly remembered the name. Second, during meditation we can give ourselves positive suggestions that will aid in recall. And last, we can use visualization techniques to strengthen recall of events and information.

Experts disagree as to whether memory is elicited from alpha or theta. Since few of us hook ourselves up to an EEG while meditating, we're unlikely to know which. But, since memory can be accessed while meditating, for most of us it won't matter. We just need to recall people, places, things, and events.

You, no doubt, have heard of short-term memory and long-term memory. We don't need to remember everything we see or do. Short-term memory is fairly limited. We can recall only about five to seven names or numbers before we lose our ability to recall. Long-term memory probably contains everything we have ever learned from the world around us. Information that makes it from short-term to long-term memory is probably what our brain deems most important.

Have you ever noticed that some people learn easily and others don't? Why do we have trouble learning and recalling information? Here are some of the reasons:

- Stress
- Fear
- Lack of attention
- Lack of motivation
- Poor skills
- Disease, drugs, diet

STRESS

When we are stressed we don't have as strong an ability to recall information as we do when we are relaxed. Have you ever crammed for a test at the last minute? First, you are too stressed to take in the information. Second, you are trying to place too much information into memory at once. Using relaxation techniques while studying can and will give you a distinct edge in memory recall.

FEAR

Were you ever called upon to answer a question in school but found you couldn't come up with the answer under pressure? All your friends were looking at you. You just knew the teacher was thinking that you were stupid. Fear combined with a lack of self-confidence is the culprit in situations like this. We become physically fearful, our blood pressure rises, and our breathing becomes quick and shallow. No wonder we don't recall things easily.

LACK OF ATTENTION

We don't recall some people's names because we aren't paying attention. The next time a friend introduces you to someone new, notice exactly what you do. Or watch another person when they meet someone new. If you observe yourself closely, you may notice that you look away slightly when you are introduced. This is a common occurrence. I don't really know why, but there could be a huge list of reasons from fear to indifference.

In a manner of speaking, we aren't paying attention. To better recall names, pay attention when you are introduced to someone. Don't turn away.

When you meet someone new, mentally give yourself a suggestion that you will recall their name. Mentally repeat their name while looking at them. Later on, you will more than likely be able to visualize their face and "hear" their name.

LACK OF MOTIVATION

Do you recall the entire Gettysburg address? How about the Preamble to the Constitution? But I bet you remember vividly the first time you were kissed or your first car. It's a matter of what is important to us. Our minds "feel" the same way. Information has to be considered important to have some meaning. If there is no motivation to remember a list of items, most likely you will not.

Language can play a big part in motivation. How many times have you said, "I can't remember this"? This was discussed in great detail in the chapter on language, "What We Say Isn't What We Mean." Consider that a statement such as, "I'll never remember all those formulas" gives your mind no reason to remember.

POOR SKILLS

It is sad to see the lack of proper study habits in our culture. We procrastinate and then try to cram for exams at the last minute. It is impossible for the brain to take in that much information that quickly and learn to assimilate it, especially when we are anxious. If you are a student or a person who has to commit large amounts of data to memory for business, you need to develop proper study habits. Meditation can help, but not if you wait until the night before a test or a presentation. Meditation is not a magic pill.

DISEASE, DRUGS, AND DIET

There are many prescription drugs that affect the ability to remember. Obviously, if it's a prescription that is medically necessary, it is important for you to continue taking it. However, recreational drugs like cocaine aren't necessary. They can mess up your ability to think and recall.

A disease such as Alzheimer's can be a factor. Although it is most common in people over the age of sixty-five, it can affect much younger persons. Alzheimer's disease severely affects memory.

The brain consumes more energy than any other organ in the body. A poor diet definitely affects our ability to think. Our brain needs fuel to function, and we receive our fuel from the foods we eat. The brain functions poorly when the diet is lacking in vitamins, minerals, and amino acids. Feed your body . . . feed your brain!

Book Meditation

When you need to study material from a textbook, first find a quiet and comfortable place in which to study. It really is not a good idea to have the television or the stereo blasting, not if you want to make good use of your studying time. If you study correctly, you will spend far less time studying. Then you will have more time for other things, like listening to music or watching television. That having been said, sit down in a comfortable chair with good light. Put the book you need to read in your lap. Close your eyes and take a deep satisfying breath, hold it for a moment, and then gently exhale. Take a few breaths in and out. If you are feeling stressed, add a long body relax, such as the one in the chapter on relaxation.

After you have relaxed mentally and physically, tell yourself that you are about to read a book and state its title. Then tell yourself that you will be able to remember and *understand* the material in the book, and use that information when necessary. Then open your eyes and start reading the chapter or chapters you need to read.

If you notice at any time that you are no longer relaxed, stop and put down the book. Close your eyes and do some breathing exercises. Then go through the process above of stating the name of the book and telling yourself that you will be able to recall what you read. You may need to do this several times.

The purpose of this exercise is to bring your brain wave patterns as close to alpha and theta as possible. You will be relaxed when reading the material, so you will be in a better position to recall it.

This is also a good technique to use when preparing for a test. At home, before going to class, do a relaxation technique. Then, before bringing yourself out of meditation, tell yourself that you are about to take a test. Tell yourself that when you take the test you will be able to recall all you read in the book, as well as what you learned in class

If you feel yourself becoming stressed out during the test, use the technique from the chapter on relaxation: take a deep breath and mentally repeat the word *relaxing*. That will help you feel less anxious. When you are less anxious and stressed, you will find it easier to take a test and recall material. You can adapt this method for business meetings and presentations as well.

Lecture Meditation

Use a slight variation of the preceding technique when you have to attend a seminar or lecture and recall the material presented. This technique is done before you leave for the lecture. I recommend that you do this technique as close as possible to the time of the lecture. That may not be possible if you have to leave early in the morning and the lecture is later in the day.

Find a comfortable spot and sit or lie down. Use a deepening method you like. A breathing or long body relax is excellent. After you have relaxed sufficiently, tell yourself that you are going to attend a lecture. State the day and time of the lecture, and the name of the person who is giving it if you have that information. Tell yourself that you will be able to recall every word that is said in the lecture. Tell yourself that you will

*remain relaxed throughout the entire lecture. If at any time you feel
yourself becoming less relaxed, all you need to do is take a satisfying
breath, hold it for a moment, and then mentally repeat the word **relaxing**. Then your body and mind will become relaxed. You will be able to
listen to the entire lecture relaxed but alert. Then at any time in the
future, you will be able to recall the information presented in the lecture,
understand that material, and use it.*

Test Rehearsal

Another good technique is a test "rehearsal." The mere mention of
the word *test* is enough to make the most confident of us quake.
We get nervous and anxious. How many times have you known the
material, only to forget it during the test? Of course, the minute
you leave the exam room, it all floods back. If you take the test when
you are relaxed, that is not likely to happen.

Years ago, when I taught college classes, I used to lead my students
in a short relaxation meditation just before tests. As a teacher, I wanted
them to succeed. Seeing a student holding his pencil so tightly that
his knuckles turned white wasn't something I enjoyed. I knew from
experience that if students could relax while taking a test, they would
do better. Of course, if they hadn't studied, relaxing wouldn't help.
I couldn't study for them, but I could help them to relax.

Use any deepening method you like. This technique can be modified to rehearse a business proposal or presentation.

*Imagine you are already in the classroom taking the test. See your-
self successfully answering the questions on the test paper. See yourself
looking calm, relaxed, and confident. See yourself going through each
question, one by one, and successfully answering each and every one of
them. See yourself smiling. You are smiling because you know the material, and you know you are going to receive a very high grade. You are
able to answer all the questions easily and well within the time limit
given for the test. After you have watched yourself answer all the questions, see yourself place the test on the professor's desk and leave the
room feeling confident.*

Memory Improvement Meditation

This is an affirmation type of meditation that should be done daily for a period of time. Do it for thirty days, then once a month as a follow-up. Use the deepening method you prefer.

> I know that my memory improves each day. My memory for all things is improving each day. I remember names well . . . I remember faces well . . . I can remember facts and numbers very well. Each day, I find that my capacity to recall information, faces, and data becomes stronger. And each day I find that my enjoyment of learning increases, along with my ability to recall the things I learn. I am good at learning and remembering. I enjoy learning and remembering. My abilities make me feel confident and successful.

Chapter Fifteen

Creativity and Problem Solving
SETTING THE STAGE
FOR CREATIVITY

The quickest way to kill creativity is to demand it. You're not to-tally sure about that? Okay, I want you to come up with a new idea for a movie, a book, or a television show. You have exactly five min-utes to do it, starting right now; no excuses allowed.

It's a little hard, isn't it? It's difficult to force creativity. We have to create the right atmosphere to allow it to develop.

There are times when creativity wasn't our intention; it just hap-pened. Those flashes of insight just hit us. Those flashes most likely came at a time when we were in a daydream, a meditation, or a dream state.

The same thing often happens just before we fall asleep. I can't tell you how many times I had been drifting off to sleep when a thought occurred to me that I wanted to include in this book. I'd get up, fire up the computer, and write it down. Soon I learned to give myself suggestions to remember what I was thinking about the next morning. I wanted sleep!

At times like these we tend to produce alpha or theta brain waves. It's as though we free our brain from the everyday type of think-ing. What do I mean by everyday thinking? We think about what we are doing, where we have to go, and how we need to do it. We are thinking analytically, and we are aware of our thoughts as well as our actions.

But when you take a shower, you don't concentrate much on what you are doing. You've done it countless times; it's a mind-less, mechanical action. I doubt many of you consciously think, "First I'll stand under the water spray and get wet, and then I'll reach for the bar of soap." You just do it. And while you are doing it, your brain is free to do other things, like being creative.

It's the same for other actions that don't require conscious thought. Runners, for instance, have been known to experience what is known as a "runner's high." Once they get involved with the pattern of running, they no longer think about the physical steps they are taking. The brain starts producing predominantly alpha or theta brain waves, and the athlete is in a meditative state while running. Many runners have told me that they do their best thinking while running.

What about someone who has a project they have to get done. They are responsible. They buckle down, concentrate, and just do it. Aren't they forcing creativity? That is a good point, however, there is a difference. What those people do is concentrate on getting the project done. They focus on the project itself, not the emotion. Focus and concentration can produce the meditative state. Their focus brings about the correct atmosphere for creativity.

Focusing on an emotion doesn't have the same result. It only serves to magnify those feelings. In this case, those are usually feelings of anxiety: "I know I'll never be able to do this project; I'll never get any ideas." This is hardly a creative atmosphere.

Room for Creativity

Find a comfortable place and sit or lie down. Take a deep satisfying breath, hold it for a moment, and then gently exhale. Now, just imagine yourself in a bathroom with a large clean shower. The tiles and faucets are gleaming. The towels are thick, soft, and abundant. The floor is carpeted so thickly that your toes sink right into it. Go ahead and wiggle your toes. See how good that feels! There is music playing softly in the background . . . one of your favorite relaxing songs by an artist you like. Hear how soothing it sounds . . . hear it as it plays softly in the background.

Now, see yourself step into the shower and turn on the faucet. The water temperature is perfect. It's just right . . . not too hot . . . and not too cold. It's just right . . . warm and inviting. Feel the water as it gently sprays over your body. Feel the water wash tension from your body. That's right . . . any tension in your body washes right off and goes down the drain. You feel relaxed as the warm water gently flows over your body.

Now, reach for the bar of soap. It has a lovely scent . . . not too much . . . just right. It smells very fresh. See yourself hold it under the spray of water and make some lather. Spread the lather over your head and neck. Feel how good the lather feels, washing away any stress . . . washing away any tension . . . making your head and neck completely relaxed. Now spread the lather over your shoulders and chest. Feel how good the lather feels, washing away any stress . . . washing away any tension . . . making your shoulders and chest feel completely relaxed. Now spread the lather over the top of your back. Feel how good the lather feels as it flows down your back, washing away any stress . . . washing away any tension . . . making your back feel completely relaxed.

Now spread the lather over your stomach and abdomen. Feel how good the lather feels, washing away any stress . . . washing away any tension . . . making your stomach and abdomen feel completely relaxed. Now as you spread the lather over your arm, hands, and fingers, you feel how good the lather feels, washing away any stress . . . washing away any tension . . . making your arms, hands, and fingers completely relaxed. Now take a deep satisfying breath, hold it for a moment, and gently exhale. You continue to feel the warm water flow over your body. It feels so wonderful.

Now continue to spread the lather over your hips and buttocks. Feel how good the lather feels, washing away any stress . . . washing away any tension . . . making your hips and buttocks feel completely relaxed.

Now feel yourself spread the lather over your thighs and legs. Feel how good the lather feels, washing away any stress . . . washing away any tension . . . making your thighs and legs feel completely relaxed.

Now feel as you spread the lather over your feet and toes. Feel how good the lather feels, washing away any stress . . . washing away any *tension . . . making your feet and toes feel completely relaxed. Stand under the water spray and allow yourself to rinse away any stress or tension that might have remained. That's right . . . any stress or tension simply washes off and floats down the drain. You are feeling clean, refreshed, relaxed, and wonderful.*

Now see yourself step out of the shower and pick up a thick towel. Feel how soft the towel is as you dry off every part of your body. The towel feels soft against your skin . . . it caresses you as you dry off. See yourself as you wrap yourself up in a warm, comfortable robe and leave the bathroom.

See yourself as you walk down the hall to a room. As you enter this room, you notice a warm, cheery fire burning in the fireplace. There is a comfortable chair pulled up right in front of the fire. Sit down in the chair and relax. Just curl up and be comfortable. The fire is warmly burning . . . making you feel toasty and comfortable . . . and so very relaxed.

As you sit before the fire, you notice that the walls of the room are covered with bookcases. There are books everywhere . . . books on every possible subject. All you have to do is pick a subject, pull out one of the books, and read it. Any time you are at a loss for an idea, simply visualize yourself in this special room. Picture yourself sitting down in the chair before the fire with a book on the subject you need ideas for. Simply open the book, and the ideas will flow just as though you were reading the pages of that book.

Creativity Conference

In ad agencies, ad developers often sit around a large table and have a brainstorming session. In that way, different ideas are generated.

This technique is very similar to the Conference Table technique in the chapter on habit control and smoking cessation. To use that technique for creativity, you will invite all the parts of you that are creative. They will identify themselves and tell you their names. For example, Mr. Color may explain how he likes to use colors and drawings. Ms. Storyteller may tell you a story. When all the parts are at the table, allow them to brainstorm for ideas. Each part may have a unique way of expressing its creativity.

Listen to all the ideas. They are really coming from you, this is just a way to allow them to come to the surface.

Chapter Sixteen

Goal Setting

We often *think* we know what we want, but the truth is we aren't always very clear about it.

Let's take the case of a man we'll call Gary. Gary wants a new job. He's in a dead-end job and is very dissatisfied with it. Up until now he hasn't done much about it; he's simply gone to work day in and day out. However, having recently read a book about meditation, he eagerly tries out a technique designed for successful goal achievement. He allows himself to reach a meditative state and then simply states that he wants a new job. He faithfully spends time each day working with meditation, each time stating that he wants a new job.

This helps motivate him to take action. He reads the employment ads in the newspapers. He updates his résumé and sends out quite a few. The interview requests pour in. However, as he goes on those interviews he finds that each job opportunity has a drawback. The hours are too long, the commute is too time-consuming, or the pay isn't very good.

Gary wonders what he's doing wrong. He's followed the advice in the book about visualizing reaching his goal—that of finding a new job. Why isn't he having any luck? He thinks, "I guess this meditation stuff doesn't really work."

The problem lies in the fact that Gary wasn't very specific. Setting a goal simply of finding a new job is too general. Yes, the example above is very hypothetical; most of us are smart enough to realize we have to take into account our education and job experience when we look for employment. Still, if one simply sets a goal of "I want a new job", we aren't being very clear to our subconscious.

Our subconscious mind is very literal. If we "tell" it that we simply want a new job, it doesn't know that there might be conditions attached. We need to take the time to define our goals. We need to let our subconscious mind know exactly what we want. By taking the time to do this, we make the process of reaching our goals a lot easier.

Meditation can be a wonderful and useful tool for goal setting and achievement. But consider the computer term, GIGO. That stands for Garbage in—garbage out. If you are serious about achieving your goals, take the time to figure out exactly what you want, as well as what you *don't* want.

Here are steps that will help you achieve that goal:

1. Identify your goals.
2. Why those goals?
3. Identify negative programming or thinking.
4. Set realistic goals.
5. Work toward those goals.

IDENTIFY YOUR GOALS

Write down your goal. What would it be like if you achieved your goal? Allow yourself to visualize what that would be like. We'll use Gary as an example. He wants a new job. What would it be like for him if he had a job? He pictures himself in a job where he feels appreciated. Great, he needs a job where his efforts will be noticed. That's a good first step!

He continues his visualization and notices that congenial people surround him and that they all work together and help one another. Here is another clue to what he wants. He wants to be in a workplace where there is a team effort.

Next, he notices in his visualization that he has time to spend with his friends, and that he is not too tired to do so. This helps him realize that he needs a job where he doesn't have to put in extremely long hours.

Finally, he pictures himself being able to pay his bills each month. Now, this might go without saying, but it is important. Gary realizes that he needs a job where the compensation is enough to support him.

WHY THOSE GOALS?

This step may not seem to be very important, but it is. In Gary's case, he has put down a new job as his goal. Why does he want a new one? In our scenario, we pointed out that he felt he was in a dead-end job. Is that really the case, or is that just his attitude toward it? It helps to know if the situation can be changed to a more positive one.

Maybe he feels that way because he hasn't made the effort to get his work noticed. Perhaps he has not shown his superiors that he would welcome the opportunity for greater challenge. Gary takes the time to think this over objectively and realizes that there is no room for advancement in his present job. He is bored by the job and the thought of staying does not appeal to him.

IDENTIFY NEGATIVE PROGRAMMING OR THINKING

Watch out for negative thinking: "I'll never get another job; I don't have enough experience." "I can't compete with the college graduates." "I'm too stupid, ugly, shy." You can give yourself a myriad of negative suggestions. Here it helps to write down the reasons why you think you might not be able to achieve your goal. Take them one by one and objectively decide whether there is any validity to them.

SET REALISTIC GOALS

In Gary's case, he may want to work at a job that requires a Master's degree, but he only has a Bachelor's degree. That is a valid reason why he may not be able to compete for some jobs. However, he has many years of experience working in his field, and for some jobs that may make a difference.

WORK TOWARD THOSE GOALS

Using meditative techniques is only part of it. You can meditate every day, but if you don't take positive steps toward reaching your goal, it isn't going to help. Meditation can motivate you and help you see yourself as a successful person, but you actually have to take the steps. It's like standing in front of a door. You know that if you only open the door, you'll get to where you want to go. You can meditate and visualize yourself opening the door, but this won't open it *for* you. Meditation can give you the courage and motivation to do so, but you still have to take action.

Now that Gary is armed with more specific goals, he can be clearer in his meditation, as well as in his actions.

MOTIVATION

What happens when you haven't any goal in life? Usually you don't go anywhere and you stagnate. You don't even try.

Using meditation, especially visualization techniques, can help overcome a lack of motivation. Picturing doing things, reaching your goals, and seeing the results is very powerful. When we are not motivated, we sit back and do nothing.

RELATIONSHIPS

You may wonder what a section on relationships is doing in a chapter on goal setting. It makes perfect sense, for most of us want a good love relationship. If we aren't in one, we probably want to be in one or have one someday. Even if we are already in a relationship, we generally hope for it to be better. In each case, those are realistic and normal goals to have.

However, much like Gary in our example of goal setting above, we often aren't very specific. We may think we know what we want in a partner, but very few of us realize what we *need*.

What we think we want is usually colored by previous relationships. We may think that we know what we want in a relationship, but usually it's not a very good yardstick. It's closer to the truth to say that what we end up with is a "hit list" of what we don't want. We aren't positive in establishing what we do want and need.

I remember, many years ago I dated a successful and intelligent man. He was a very nice man, and I think I'm a nice person. But we just weren't suited for each other. We had different views of what was important in life. I'm a jeans and sweatshirt type of girl. Take me out for a hot dog and a walk in the park and I'm happy. But he liked women who dressed to the nines and liked to go to elegant parties. Not a real good match here! But did we see that? No, we blamed each other when our needs were not met. I felt that he was critical of everything I said and did. He felt I was stubborn, aggravating, and unwilling to listen to what he had to say.

When that relationship failed, I decided to use meditation to find what I thought would be a better partner. Since I felt that the relationship had failed solely because he was too critical, I decided that I wanted was a man who worshiped me.

Well, needless to say, I got exactly what I thought I wanted. And, needless to say, it wasn't what I needed.

We should approach relationships in a thoughtful way. We have wants, but we also have needs. It's not wrong to admit those needs; they are vitally important. If people admitted that before going into a relationship, it would save a lot of heartache.

Wants and needs can easily be confused. Wants are what we desire or wish. Needs are what we require and have to have. Wants and needs do not always match; in fact, they can be diametrically opposed to each other. However, we think of our wants first and sometimes relegate our needs to a back seat. Sometiomes we want something but don't need it. When a want and a need do match, it's very powerful.

The first step toward a better relationship is establishing what both partners need and want.

Identify what you want.

Identify what you don't want.

Identify what you need

Identify why previous relationships failed.

Identify What You Want

How do we know what we want in a mate? What qualities are we looking for? A good way is to ask yourself what is important to *you*. What things matter most? What areas of your life are most important? Sit down and write out a list of those areas. Also put down qualities that matter to you. Don't try to write down what you *think* you should put, write down what you think you want. Make this list as complete and as honest as possible.

Here are some suggestions:

Hobbies and interests

Career

Religion and spirituality

Looks

Intelligence

Kindness

A sense of humor

Identify What You Don't Want

This might not seem all that important, but it is! We all have things that we would not like or accept in a partner. We probably already know the big issues. Yet, if we take the time to really think about it, we will probably discover that there are other things not so obvious. Be as complete and honest as possible when making this list. Here are some of them:

I don't want a partner who is racist.

I don't want a partner who is physically abusive.

I don't want a partner who does not listen to what I have to say.

I don't want a partner who dislikes cats.

I don't want a partner who is a sports enthusiast.

I don't want an overweight partner.

I don't want a partner who travels often.

Identify What You Need

This will take some thought. Put down only the things you *have to have* and the things you *require.* You will be listing areas of your life, as well as qualities. Identifying what you want and don't want first will give you real clues as to what you need. You may find that you have some of the same items on this list as you did on your list of wants.

Here are some needs that might be on the list:

Religion and a spiritual life

Family values

Similar ethical and moral standards

Financial security

Independence

A *sense of adventure*

Affection

Respect

Strong work ethic

Play time

Children

An *animal lover*

Identify Why Past Relationships Failed

This next step is critical. It is truly difficult to do because it requires honesty as well as objectivity. The purpose is not to place blame either on yourself or your former partner, but rather to find the real reasons why the relationship failed. This is a two-step process.

First, look at the question in relation to the lists you've compiled of your wants and needs. Perhaps some relationships didn't work because not enough of your needs and wants were fulfilled. Maybe others failed because truly important needs were unmet.

Second, look at your lists for specific reasons why past relationships have foundered. Perhaps you were trying to maintain a long-distance relationship and being separated didn't make either of you happy. Maybe you were not ready to make a commitment, but your partner was.

Some of those reasons may now seem to be silly. They may seem trivial, but on some level they mattered. A seemingly trivial reason is often linked with a more important want or need. For instance, you may not have liked your partner's table manners. How someone acts in public may be important to you because your job requires you to attend business functions. If career is one of the more important areas in your life, it is easy to see why what initially seemed silly is a valid consideration for you.

Some reasons no doubt struck at a real core issue: something that really matters, that you cannot work around.

A by-product of this process is that it helps to identify patterns. Have you continually engaged in relationships of a destructive or an abusive nature? Have you sought out domineering partners, or have you been domineering? Have you allowed yourself to put your needs ahead of others, or vice versa?

Putting It Together

Compare your lists of wants and needs. Now that you have clearly defined them, you will find that some items will be listed in both sections. This will help you set goals for achieving fulfilling relationships.

If negative patterns in your relationships have emerged while going through this process, you can work with meditation to prevent them from reoccurring.

But I'm IN *a Relationship*!

Even if you are in a relationship, the process outlined above is important and useful, especially when both of you take the time to work with it. Together, you can establish the problem areas that need to be opened up to healthy discussion. You will gain information that can help you be more understanding of each other's wants and needs.

It's often the little things that undermine a relationship. Failure to recognize the existence and importance of these things can destroy a relationship. When you have that knowledge, you might find that you are a bit more tolerant.

Now when you use a meditation technique to help achieve a good relationship, you will have clear ideas and information on which to base the suggestions and imagery you use.

MEDITATIONS FOR ACHIEVING YOUR GOALS

The following meditations will help you achieve a goal. Simply insert whatever goal you wish to achieve, such as finding a new job, or perhaps completing a project that is due.

The Flower Garden

Eye fixation can be a useful technique for starting a meditation, especially if your mind wanders as soon as you close your eyes. Simply find a spot on the wall in front of you and stare it at.

Find a comfortable place to sit or lie. Take a deep breath. Hold it for a moment, and then gently exhale. Find a spot to focus your eyes, perhaps a picture on the wall. Place all your attention on this spot. Continue breathing in and out naturally. As you breathe in and out, know that with each breath you take, with each breath you exhale, you are becoming more and more relaxed. As you breathe, it becomes easier and easier to place all your attention on the spot you have picked to focus on. Keep focusing on the spot. Think about that spot, directing all your thoughts on that spot.

Other thoughts may come into your mind. That's all right, just allow them to gently drift away as you return to focusing on that spot. Continue to breathe in and out. With each breath you take, you find yourself becoming more and more relaxed. With each breath you exhale, you are becoming more and more relaxed.

As you continue to focus on the spot you may find that your eyes are getting tired. You might feel like you need to blink or that your eyes are watering. That is all right. With each blink you take, you find yourself becoming more and more relaxed. With each blink of your eye, the more relaxed you become. Worries and cares simply fade away as you become totally relaxed physically and mentally.

Now, just close your eyes and take a deep breath. Hold it for a moment, and then gently exhale. That's right, you are feeling very, very relaxed and comfortable. It feels good to close your eyes. And as you close your eyes you enter a deeper relaxed place.

As you feel yourself being relaxed, you know that you are feeling good. Feeling good about you. You are feeling safe and secure. There is nowhere you have to be, and nothing you have to do right now except relax. It feels very good to be relaxed. You deserve to be relaxed. You deserve the good things in life. And as you become more and more relaxed, you realize just how wonderful it feels. You are a confident and happy person, the type of person who sets realistic goals and reaches those goals easily and effortlessly.

Imagine yourself in a field. It's a beautiful field with tall, flowing grasses gently blowing in the breeze. There are flowers of many varieties. The flowers are very colorful and smell so sweet. That's right, take a deep breath and enjoy the sweet and fresh fragrance of the flowers.

Allow yourself to walk closer to the flowers. There are many, many flowers, each more beautiful than the last. And as you walk closer to the flowers, you know that you are allowed to pick some of the flowers. You can make a bouquet of bright, beautiful flowers. Allow yourself to walk around and look at all the flowers you have to choose from. As you do so, you notice that one of the flowers has writing on it. As you bend down to read the writing, you notice that this flower has your goal written on its petals.

You smile and pick this flower. Notice how lovely it is, how beautiful it smells. It feels soft in your hand. Feel how soft it is. Allow yourself to lift the flower to your nose and inhale the beautiful scent of the flower. Imagine a special flower just for you.

As you look around the field, you notice another flower with your goal written on its petals. You walk over to it and smile. Imagine another special flower just for you. You smile and pick this flower too. Notice how lovely it is, how beautiful it smells. It feels soft in your hand. Feel how soft it is. Allow yourself to lift the flower to your nose and inhale the beautiful scent of the flower.

Now you have two lovely flowers. Allow yourself to continue walking in the field, enjoying all the flowers. As you walk around the field, you notice yet another flower with your goal written on its petals. You walk over to it and bend down to smell its sweet fragrance. How lovely, yet another special flower just for you. You smile and pick this flower too. Notice how lovely it is, how beautiful it smells. It feels soft in your hand. Feel how soft it is.

Allow yourself to continue walking in the field of flowers. You discover many, many flowers that are just for you. Each of these flowers has the goal you wish to achieve written on its petals. You are allowed to pick these flowers, and you do so, one by one. With each step you take, you can pick another flower. As you pick each flower, you realize you are getting closer and closer to having your goal right in your hands. With each flower you pick, you find your goal to be within your reach. Your goal is right within your hands.

Now you have walked through the entire field, and you have a lovely bouquet of flowers, each with your goal written on its petals. You hold your goal right within your hands. Allow yourself to look at the bouquet you have picked. See how it feels, vibrant and alive. The colors are bright and clear, just like your goal. Imagine a special bouquet just for you. As you look at the bouquet of beautiful fragrant flowers, take a moment to honor each individual flower. Each flower is like a step toward your goal, and you hold it within your hands.

Stairway to Success

Here is another meditation filled with metaphorical imagery and suggestions. With each step you take, you move closer to your goal. How many steps you climb is up to you, you can do from twenty-five to a hundred or more. It's particularly good, for the longer you do this meditation, the deeper the level you will reach. It is highly repetitive, which helps anchor the suggestion that you are taking decisive steps to reach your goal.

Find a comfortable place to sit. Take a deep breath. Hold it for a moment, and then gently exhale. Feel the chair you are sitting on, feel your arms relaxed in your lap. Feel your feet comfortably placed on the floor. Breathe in and out naturally and rhythmically. Take a deep breath, hold it for a count of three, and then exhale for a count of three. Take another breath, hold it for a count of three, and then exhale for a count of three. With each breath you take, you feel your body becoming relaxed. Take a deep breath, hold it for a count of three, and then exhale for a count of three. Take another breath, hold it for a count of three, and then exhale for a count of three. With each breath you take, you feel your mind becoming relaxed. Feel your arms becoming relaxed in the chair. Feel your feet becoming relaxed on the floor. Take a deep breath, hold it for a count of three, and then exhale for a count of three. Take another breath, hold it for a count of three, and then exhale for a count of three. With each breath you take, you feel your whole body and mind becoming even more relaxed. You feel very safe and secure and relaxed. You have plenty of time to allow yourself to sit here and relax. Continue to breathe in and out, knowing that with each breath you take, you become more relaxed. With each breath you take, you feel even more peaceful. That's right, just breath in and out, in and out.

Now imagine yourself in a very large airy room. The temperature is just right; it's a warm and inviting room. It's a very safe and peaceful place. It's the most beautiful room you have ever been in. It's so beautiful that you want to explore it. Allow yourself to walk into the room, feeling very safe and secure. In the middle of the room you notice a large, wide, beautifully carved staircase. It's of a beautiful sturdy wood in a soft pol-

ished color. It stretches up, up, upward to the ceiling, so far that you can't even see the top. As you look up at the staircase, you realize at the top of it is your goal. All you have to do to reach your goal is to walk up the steps.

Feel yourself placing a foot on the first step. Then feel yourself placing your other foot on the first step. You are one step closer to achieving your goal. Take a deep breath, exhale, and allow yourself to feel how wonderful that feels. You are one step closer to your goal. Feel yourself placing a foot on the second step. Then feel yourself placing your other foot on the second step. You are one step closer to achieving your goal. Take a deep breath, exhale, and allow yourself to feel how wonderful that feels. You are another step closer to your goal. Feel yourself placing a foot on the third step. Then feel yourself placing your other foot on the third step. You are one step closer to achieving your goal. Take a deep breath, exhale, and allow yourself to feel how wonderful that feels. You are another step closer to your goal. Feel yourself placing a foot on the fourth step. Then feel yourself placing your other foot on the fourth step. You are one step closer to achieving your goal. Take a deep breath, exhale, and allow yourself to feel how wonderful that feels. You are yet another step closer to your goal. With each step you take, you are getting closer and closer to reaching your goal. Now feel yourself placing a foot on the fifth step. Then feel yourself placing your other foot on the fifth step. You are one step closer to achieving your goal. Take a deep breath, exhale, and allow yourself to feel how wonderful that feels. You have taken another step closer to your goal. Feel yourself placing a foot on the sixth step. Then feel yourself placing your other foot on the sixth step. You are now one step closer to achieving your goal. Take a deep breath, exhale, and allow yourself to feel how wonderful that feels. You are getting closer and closer to your goal. With each step you take, you are getting closer and closer to reaching your goal. Feel yourself placing a foot on the seventh step. Then feel yourself placing your other foot on the seventh step. You are now one step closer to achieving your goal. Take a deep breath, exhale, and allow yourself to feel how wonderful that feels. You are getting closer and closer to achieving your goal. Feel yourself placing a foot on the eighth step. Then feel yourself placing your other foot on the eighth step. You are now one step closer to achieving your goal. Take a *deep breath, exhale, and allow yourself to feel how wonderful that feels. You are getting much closer to reaching your goal. Feel yourself placing a foot on the ninth step. Then feel yourself placing your other foot on the ninth step. You are now one step closer to achieving your goal. Take a deep breath, exhale, and allow yourself to feel how wonderful that feels. You are getting so very close to reaching your goal. Feel yourself placing a foot on the tenth step. Then feel yourself placing your other foot on the tenth step. You are now one step closer to achieving your goal. Take a deep breath, exhale, and allow yourself to feel how wonderful that feels. You are within sight of reaching your goal.*

Now you are at the top of the stairs. You have come a long way; you have gone a long way toward reaching and achieving your goal. You have come far; you have gone a long way to making your goal real. Now, stand at the top of the stairway and allow yourself to embrace your goal. It is here, right in front of you. Know that it is yours, you have worked for it, and you deserve it. Know it, feel it, sense it. You now know it's possible, simply by taking it a step at a time. You have done it; you have reached your goal. You have climbed the Stairway of Success.

Meditation for Relationship Success

This meditation is a nice one to record on a cassette tape. Talk slowly and clearly. If you wish, simply substitute the word *someone* with either *a man* or *a woman*. It also helps to leave some pauses on the tape during the scenes to give yourself plenty of time to visualize the scenes fully.

Find a comfortable place to sit or lie. Take a deep breath and close your eyes. In a moment, I am going to count from ten to one. With each decreasing number you will find yourself going deeper and becoming relaxed. Ten. Feel your head becoming relaxed. Feel your neck and shoulders relaxing. Nine. Feel your back becoming relaxed. Allow yourself to go deeper and deeper. Eight. Feel your arms, hands, and fingers becoming relaxed. Feel yourself going even deeper. Seven. Feel your chest and stomach becoming relaxed. Allow the feeling of relaxing to gently wash over your body. Six. Feel your hips and thighs becoming relaxed. Relaxing . . . relaxing . . . deeper and deeper. Five. Feel your legs becoming more and more relaxed. Go even deeper . . . and deeper. Four. Feel your feet becoming relaxed. Three. Feel your entire body becoming relaxed. Go down . . . down . . . deeper and deeper. Two. Feel your mind becoming quiet and relaxed. You feel so very relaxed. More relaxed than you have ever been before. One. You are now completely and totally relaxed.

Imagine yourself out with your friends. You are out at a gathering, a picnic. The day is warm and sunny, a perfect type of day. You feel very happy and relaxed. You are happy being with your friends for they like you, admire you, and respect you. Feel how good that makes you feel inside. Allow that good feeling to wash over your entire body. That's right, it feels wonderful. Feel the sensation of being cared about. Allow that feeling to wash over you from your head to your toes. Feel it fill your body with joy.

Now you notice one of your friends walking toward you. He is smiling and glad to see you. Your friend is very happy that you came to the picnic. You can hear him tell you how happy and glad he is to see you. You can see his face. It's lit up with joy at seeing you. Another friend joins you. She is smiling and happy to see you. She is very happy that you came to the picnic. You can hear her tell you that she is delighted to see you. You can see her face. It's beaming with happiness to see you. Allow yourself to take some time and talk with your friends. It's a wonderful day, it feels wonderful to be with them. Just allow yourself to take some time to listen to your friends. Hear them? They are telling you how wonderful it is that they can spend some time with you.

Your friends walk off, and you drift toward another group of friends. You can hear them. They are talking about you. They are saying what a lovely, warm, caring person you are. They are saying that you deserve someone very special because you are a special person. Notice and feel just how good that makes you feel inside, how special that makes you feel. Allow those feelings to wash over your entire body from your head to your toes.

After a while, you walk off. The air smells fresh and clean. You can hear the birds singing in the trees, even the birds sound happy to see you. You take off your shoes and walk in the soft green grass. Feel the grass between your toes. It's cool and refreshing. As you walk along, feeling the grass gently touch the bottom of your feet, you notice a cool, inviting pond. You sit down beside the pond and look into the surface. It's very calm and sparkles with the sunlight. See how it reflects the trees above. As you sit there, you stare into the pond's surface. It's very calming and relaxing. It feels very peaceful. You look into the surface of the water, and you can see the clouds reflected from above. You can see an occasional bird fly by reflected in the water. After a while, you notice a scene slowly start to form in the water. It's a picture of you and someone else. You can't quite see the face, but you see and know the person is happy to be with you. As the scene unfolds, you notice the things you and this person do together. They are the things you like to do. Scene after scene floats by in which you and this person are doing interesting, fun, and wonderful things together. You share each other's joy in doing these things. You share joy in doing them together. Take some time and allow yourself to see the pictures and scenes of the things you are doing together. They are all of your favorite things to do, your favorite places to go. Feel how wonderful it is to have someone to be with, someone who likes to do the same things you do. Allow those feelings to wash over your entire body from head to toe.

As you continue to look at the scenes unfolding on the surface of the water, you notice that in scene after scene you and this person are talking about interesting, fun, and wonderful things. You can hear yourself and this person talking together. You share each other's joy in the conversation. Take some time and allow yourself to hear the conversation you are having. It's a conversation about all of your favorite things. Important things. Trivial things. Feel how wonderful it is to have someone to be with who likes to discuss the same things you do. Feel how wonderful it is to have that person think you are smart, funny, and interesting. Allow those feelings to wash over your entire body from head to toe. As you continue to look at the scenes unfolding on the surface of the water, you notice that scene after scene floats by in which you and *this person meet your friends and family. Notice how happy your family and friends are that you have met someone special. Friends and family members come up to greet this person and tell him (her) how happy they are to meet him (her). Then they come up to you and tell you just how pleased they are for you. You are a warm and loving person, and you deserve someone as warm and loving as you are. And as you continue to look at the scenes unfolding on the surface of the water, you notice that scene after scene floats by of you and this person meeting his (her) friends and family. Notice how happy family and friends are that he (she) has met someone special like you. Allow the wonderful feelings to wash over your entire body from head to toe.*

Existing Relationships

Here is a similar meditation, but geared toward working with an existing relationship. If you wish, just replace the words *special person in your life* with *boyfriend, girlfriend, wife,* or *husband,* or with a name. Substitute *she* for *he* if appropriate. If you record it on audio tape, use pauses between each sentence. Use the deepening method you prefer. Use one from a meditation in this chapter or any other chapter.

Imagine yourself at a lakeside cabin. You are with the special person in your life. It feels wonderful to have some time alone together, to spend time just being together. It's just the two of you. There are no distractions. There is nowhere that you have to be . . . nothing that you have to do. You have plenty of time just to spend with each other.

Allow yourself to take some time and talk with that special person in your life. It's a wonderful day, it feels wonderful to be alone with him, just the two of you. Just allow yourself to take some time to listen to what that person has to say. He is telling you how wonderful it is to spend some time with you. How wonderful it is to be able to get to know each other again. Notice how he listens to everything you say. He is attentive and interested in what you have to talk about. Notice how he looks at you, how he leans toward you, interested in your every word. Hear the

*things that you say to each other, and the loving way in which you speak
and look at each other.*

Love Meditation

Use the deepening method you prefer with this script. You can use
one from a meditation above, or from another chapter.

> *Let all your doubts about being deserving of love, being lovable, wash
> away just like a gentle rain washing over your body, cleansing away
> any doubts. And as any remaining doubts are simply washed away, the
> sun comes shining through the clouds, bringing the light of love into
> your life. You are love and as the sun shines light upon you, you know
> that you, too, can share that love. And as you allow that light to flow
> over you, you become a full vessel, so full that you realize you have
> plenty of love to give. And as you give that love, you realize your capac-
> ity is endless. You realize the more love you give, the more you receive.
> And as that love flows, you realize that love is like a circle. When you
> send it out, it flows away from you and continues on its path. That path
> leads back to its beginning, and its beginning is you. Love flows and
> grows in your life.*

The Discovery Channel

Use the deepening you prefer with this script. You can use an example from one of the meditations above, or from another chapter.

> *Imagine yourself in a video store. It's a very large store and has
> many rooms totally devoted to different categories. As you walk around
> the store looking at the signs over the entrance to each room, you notice
> one that has your name on it. Imagine, a room devoted to you. As you
> walk around you notice that there are many sections. There is a section
> devoted to your childhood . . . there is a section devoted to your school
> days . . . there is a section devoted to the jobs you have held . . . there is
> a section devoted to your talents and abilities. What a large room, it is*

filled with many, many videos from the areas of your life. As you look at
the many sections, you notice that one has the word, **relationships**
printed above its shelves. You walk closer to this section, and as you do
so, you notice that your name is on each video and also the name of
another. There is one for every relationship you have ever had.

Each of these videos has been produced by a well-known director who
has taken all the events of those relationships and made a documentary
of them. All the important highlights have been included. You notice that
there is a comfortable chair in front of a television and VCR right next to
this shelf of relationship videos. Next to the chair is a box. See yourself
sitting down in this comfortable and very relaxing chair. That's right . . .
just allow yourself to get comfortable.

Now imagine yourself selecting a video from the shelf and inserting it
into the VCR. Push the Play button and sit back comfortably in the
chair. As the video starts to play, you see yourself in one of your first relationships. Allow yourself to view all the events of that relationship from
the beginning to the end. Notice the feelings and emotions that wash
over you. Simply gather those feelings and emotions and place them in
the box that is by the chair. Now place that box beside you on the floor
and continue watching the video. Now you can watch the movie on the
video without being distracted by feelings and emotions. If at any time a
feeling or an emotion arises, you can simply place it in the box and continue watching the movie. It's as though you are a movie critic reviewing
a movie.

As you watch the movie, you can easily pick out the good points in
the movie. As you watch the movie, you can also pick out any of the bad
points. Picture yourself writing a review of the movie, just like a movie
critic. What makes it work? What doesn't work well? Now take a deep
breath, and take that movie out of the VCR. Look over at the shelf and
look over the remaining videos. Pick one that you would like to view, perhaps one of a very important relationship in your life. Put that video in
the VCR, push the Play button, and sit back comfortably in the chair.
As the video starts to play, you see yourself in that very important relationship. Allow yourself to view all the events of that relationship from

the beginning to the end. Notice the feelings and emotions that wash over you. Simply gather those feelings and emotions and place them in the box that is by the chair. If at any time a feeling or an emotion arises, you can simply place it in the box and continue watching the movie. It's as though you are a movie critic reviewing a movie. As you watch the movie, you can easily pick out the good points in the movie. As you watch the movie, you can also pick out any of the bad points. Picture yourself writing a review of the movie, just like a movie critic. What makes it work? What doesn't work well?

And now when you are done watching your relationship videos, take a deep breath, and pick up the box where you have placed your feelings and emotions. Close up the box and tie a brightly colored ribbon around it. There are a lot of feelings and emotions in there, but it is a very light box and is easy for you to pick up. Imagine yourself carrying that box outside into the garden, which is right next to the video store. Within this garden there is a beautiful sunny spot with a small bench. See yourself walk over to it and place the box on it.

Notice how the sunlight shines softly on the box. How very beautiful it is! Now sit down quietly in front of the bench. Take a deep breath, exhale, and allow yourself to honor all the feelings and emotions that are placed within that box. They all have been important to you and have had their place in your life. Honor their existence and thank them for having been a part of your life.

Now undo the ribbon and open the box. All of the negative or unhappy feelings you have had simply rise to the top of the box and pour out into the sunshine. Watch as the sunlight transforms those feelings into bright, beautiful butterflies. You watch with wonder as they spread their wings and fly away. Now look into the box where all the good, happy, and positive feelings have remained. As you look inside the box, you notice that they've been transformed into sparkling warm water. Pick up the box and let the warm water flow over your body. Feel how good it is to pour the warm water over your body, filling you with happiness, security, and love.

Eliminating Negative Relationship Patterns

If you find that you keep having the same type of relationship over and over, this meditation can help you work toward not repeating that pattern. Use the deepening you prefer with this script. You can use an example from one of the meditations above, or from another chapter.

You are a deserving person, a person who deserves love in their life. You deserve to be treated well, as you treat people well. You deserve to be respected and cared about, and you attract those to you who will treat you with that respect and care. You are a powerful person and you feel safe and secure with the knowledge that you deserve to have those in your life who will honor that power and who will respect and care for you. Feel yourself drinking in the power that you have, like drinking the waters of a sacred fountain. Your body is sacred just like the fountain, and you deserve to have your body treated with respect, love, and care. Feel yourself standing in the light of the eternal sun. Feel the rays of the sun flow over you sharing its power, its energy and its radiant love. You are filled with that love and deserve to share that love with someone who will respect, love, and care for you. Know that from this day forward you attract to you those who will honor that power and love within you.

Affirmations

I set realistic goals and I am able to reach them.

Every day brings me closer and closer to my goals.

I strive to reach my goals, and my goals strive to reach me.

With each breath I take, my goals become clearer and clearer.

I am a warm and loving person.

I deserve to have love in my life.

Love flows and grows in my life.

I attract love into my life.

Chapter Seventeen

Pain Management

Pain can be good. I get reactions of surprise when I tell that to those who attend my workshops. Pain has a purpose, and an important one at that. It's an alarm system that tells us, "Something's wrong, something's wrong!" Without pain, we might not be aware of serious injuries. We could cut ourselves seriously and bleed to death if we were not aware of it. Pain gets our attention.

The sensation of pain is both a chemical and a physical reaction. When we are injured, a series of events take place in our brain and body. Nerve endings cover almost every inch of your body. If you accidentally hit your thumb with a hammer, the nerve endings on your thumb instantly send a message to your brain, directing it to take action: "Warning, injury has occurred." Your brain then sends back a message of pain in your thumb. You then notice that you have been injured and that you need to take action.

Meanwhile, your brain also sends a message to your body, telling it to produce various chemicals. These chemicals help cause swelling, which aids in the fight against infection. Your brain also produces additional chemicals that tone down the amount of pain.

To elaborate on this example, you have now been notified that your thumb has been injured. You take the appropriate action to ensure that the situation will not be ignored, thereby decreasing the chance for further injury. Pain has served its purpose. It has done its job and is no longer needed. Yet it's still there and you still feel it. Here is where meditation can help.

MEDITATION AND PAIN

It would be unethical to suggest that all pain can be eradicated simply by using meditation. Yet this is an area where meditation is an extremely powerful tool.

I became involved with using meditation techniques for pain management several years ago when my brother, Michael, broke his neck in a car accident. He was in constant and intense pain, and it bothered me to see him suffering. I wanted to be able to do something to help.

The doctors gave him pain pills, and those helped at first. However, he soon became dependent on them. The use of painkillers for long-term situations can cause a major new problem, that of drug addiction. There are countless stories of people who have drug addictions not to recreational drugs, but to prescription medications.

There is another problem with taking painkillers long-term: that of building up an immunity to them. As a person builds that immunity, he requires higher and higher doses in order to relieve pain.

When someone is in extreme pain, it can be difficult to divert their attention from their pain. Simple meditation may not work. But meditation can be used, especially if the person can learn to go into a deep meditative level. Layering is an effective way to achieve this.

Layering Technique

This technique requires two people. One person will facilitate the meditation. The effect of this guided meditation is to allow the subject to reach a deep meditative level in the theta brain wave. It is done by means of "layering." The subject is brought down to a meditative state, brought part way back to a higher level, and then immediately brought back down, back up again, and then back down. The effect is to help the subject attain the deepest meditative level without falling asleep. After this meditation is done once, the subject can then work on his own.

By working in this manner, the subject can get past the pain, and then learn to reach that same meditative level again quickly.

First have the person lie down. Although this exercise works best if the person lies down, it can be modified if necessary. The deepening method used is counting stairs, elevators, or steps. Start at ten and go down to one.

When the number one is reached, say, "Now I want you to open your eyes, but when I gently touch your shoulder, you will immediately close your eyes and allow yourself to enter a very deep relaxing place."

Then count down from ten to one, and repeat the process. This should be repeated for a total of three times.

After the third time, say "You are now at a deeper level of relaxation than you have ever been before. It will be easy for you to return to this level whenever you wish simply by counting from ten to one. From this time forward, whenever you need to go to as deep a level as you are now, you can do so quickly."

The person can then use any pain control technique he wishes.

Body Focus

This is a good meditation to practice *before* you feel pain. Then, when you do experience pain, you can use this technique to help alleviate it. You do not need to use a deepening technique, for the very nature of this meditation is focus, which will bring about a meditative state. Therefore, it's also a good exercise for improving your ability to focus.

Start this technique by thinking only of your hand. Think about your hand getting very, very cold. Keep focusing on feeling your hand getting cold. When your hand feels cold, focus on its becoming very, very warm. Do this until it feels warm to the touch.

Go through the same process with your other hand. Once you have mastered that, you can direct your attention to other parts of the body. Then, if you have an injury, you can simply focus on that area of the body.

Coldness will feel better for some injuries. Warmth may be more soothing for other injuries or pain. In this way, you can have use of both.

Peeling Away Pain

Imagine your pain to be like an onion. An onion has layers to it. You can peel away layer after layer. Now concentrate on your pain so that you can roll it into a little ball, just like an onion. Your pain is compressed into a small onion. And now that you have moved your pain to this round onion, you can peel your pain away. Just peel away each layer. With each layer you peel away, you feel less and less pain. You may peel away as many layers as you need. With each layer that you peel away, your discomfort becomes less and less. Just keep removing layers until you have no discomfort

THE MOTHER OF ALL MEDITATIONS

Before my son Scott was born, I'd listen to other women and their war stories. You know the ones: "I was in labor for two days and they could hear me screaming for miles away. It hurt so bad I thought I'd never go through this again." I knew I wanted a child, but that didn't sound like anything *I* wanted to go through. I was scared of having to endure such extreme pain. I wondered why we couldn't have children without pain.

My son is now twenty-three years old. At the time, there weren't any books that talked about meditation and childbirth. Natural childbirth had come into vogue, but most of what I'd heard seemed to suggest that the natural method found ways around the pain. It seemed to me that childbirth still would be painful.

I knew there had to be a better way. I didn't tell anyone, but I used meditation techniques to give myself suggestions that labor would be easy and natural. I didn't focus on the pain, but rather on how easy and effortless the experience would be. I didn't have a guide to go by; I simply made it up as I went along. I pictured myself going through delivery and focused on visualizations of a pain-free process. I also used affirmations, such as, "Labor is simply the birthing process, which is natural and easy," and "I will be comfortable and relaxed during the birth of my child."

When the big day arrived, it happened just that way: easy and effortless. My son helped matters by being impatient to see the world; my labor was very short. Actually, I didn't even realize I was in labor at first! I felt mild contractions, but they didn't hurt at all.

At the hospital, the delivery was just as easy and effortless. The doctor and the nurses and I told jokes during the whole procedure.

I felt no pain at all! I was very relaxed throughout the entire delivery. My doctor was amazed. I wasn't.

Childbirth is an individual matter. Just as varying methods of pain management work for different people, the same goes for childbirth. You can modify any of the pain management techniques in this chapter to suit your tastes and preferences. We all have different views, perceptions, beliefs, and expectations.

I didn't understand why there had to be pain in childbirth. I refused to believe that it was a necessary part of childbirth. Therefore, that conviction became part of my belief system. It shifted from just a hope or wish to what I truly believed and expected. Those beliefs, in turn, helped to suggest to my subconscious mind that I would not feel pain.

Marie ("Mickey") Mongan, a leading expert in the field of HypnoBirthing, said to me recently, "When a woman in labor brings herself into a profound relaxation and meditative state, all of the birthing muscles become relaxed, endorphins are released, and she is better able to call upon her natural birthing instincts. The result: a safer, easier, more comfortable birthing. All pregnant women should strive to learn this technique."

Childbirth Meditation

I see and feel myself having the first contraction! I know that contractions are my body's signal that my child is ready to be born. My body has done its job: making me aware of the fact that my child is ready to be born. Contractions are a signal; and I have heard that signal. This helps to relax me, for I know that the process of having my child has started. Each further contraction I have is simply my body's way to help my child be born. It's a natural and wonderful experience. With each contraction that I feel, I am able to relax even more, for I know that is helping my child to be born easily and effortlessly. With each contraction that I have, I simply take a gentle breath, hold it for a moment, and then gently exhale. It's a wonderful feeling, knowing that I soon will have a child to hold in my arms. A child to share the wonders and the joys of life with.

As I enter the delivery room, I am feeling completely relaxed. Should a feeling of discomfort come over my body, I will simply take a deep breath, and that discomfort will wash away like rain washes away leaves on the ground. With each contraction my body feels, I know I am one step closer to giving birth to my child. With each passing contraction, I am one step closer to seeing my child, and holding my child in my arms. With each contraction, I am feeling more comfortable and relaxed. I know that childbirth is a natural process, a process of bringing a new life into the world. I am able to find a comfortable position; I am relaxed and comfortable.

And as I relax, I know that I am helping my child to be born in a way that will make the child's experience a wonderful thing. By being relaxed, I am helping my child enter the world healthy and strong. I am helping my child come into the world in a peaceful manner. I feel joy for my child and myself. I feel confidence in my ability to bring my child effortlessly into the world.

I feel love in my heart for my child, and I allow that feeling of deep love to spread throughout my entire body. I feel it flow from the top of my head, down my neck and shoulders, down through my chest, over my back, down my stomach and abdomen, down my hips and thighs, down my legs, all the way down to my feet and toes. This feeling of love spreads through me just like a warm, gentle light. And as that light of love spreads throughout my body, I know I have plenty of love to share with my child. I am feeling confident, peaceful, and sure of my ability to share my feelings of love with my child.

I see myself smiling and those around me are smiling too. I see them offering words of encouragement. The doctors and nurses around me are offering encouragement. Everyone around me is pleased and happy to be part of the experience of bringing this child into the world. I can see their faces, how pleased they look. They are happy to see that it is such a natural and easy process. I can see and hear them as they tell me how happy they are that it is such an easy and natural process for me. Looking at their faces and hearing their words of encouragement allow me to become even more relaxed, even more confident.

I see myself in the birthing process . . . I look relaxed, strong, and joyful. I can see myself breathing perfectly . . . just the right number of breaths to feel comfortable. I can see myself looking calm and relaxed. I can see myself pushing exactly when I need to push. I can feel that I am able to brush away any feelings of discomfort should they arise. I can simply brush them away . . . and return to the feeling of being relaxed and calm. I know exactly what I need to do to help my child be born.

And now I can see my child being born. How relaxed and calm my child looks as he or she takes that first breath. How strong and healthy my child is! And now I see myself holding my child . . . How wondrous and joyful it feels. Feelings of love and joy wash over me as I hold my strong and healthy child.

Chapter Eighteen

Self-Esteem and Self-Confidence

Do you lack self-confidence or have low self-esteem? This is a more common problem than you might think. Almost everyone has at some point in their life suffered from a lack of confidence or from low self-esteem. It's compounded by the fact that we may be quite confident in some areas of our life, but not in others.

A COMMON PROBLEM: SELF-DOUBT

Think about it. You may be very comfortable when talking and doing things with your friends. However, when you are in a work situation, you suddenly feel inadequate. On the other hand, you may be outgoing with friends and family, but are tongue-tied and feel stupid when you meet a member of the opposite sex.

Low self-esteem and a lack of self-confidence go hand in hand. We build a low self-esteem through time and events, which result in our not being as confident as we could be.

Meditation can help in both cases. We can change the negative programming we have received from ourselves and from others and substitute positive programming instead. The mind is similar to a computer. It accumulates the information that has been given to us. Statements, whether negative or positive, which are stored in the subconscious, in effect, "program" how we think, act, and feel.

Low self-esteem is usually a long-term condition. It takes years to develop. Much of it is the result of childhood experiences. Did we receive positive reinforcement? Self-confidence, on the other hand, can be a momentary thing. Even a person with healthy self-esteem can momentarily lack confidence.

In their book *Self-Esteem,* Matthew McKay and Patrick Fanning have this to say: "One of the main factors differentiating humans from animals is the awareness of self; the ability to form an identity and then attach a value to it." We are aware of ourselves and instinctively compare ourselves with others. How do we measure up? Where do we rank in relation to others?

As children, we may have had a parent or role model who wittingly or unwittingly played a major role in our perceptions of how we measure up. In truth, we are usually our own harshest critic. We often set impossibly high standards for ourselves and then chastise ourselves if we do not meet them. We label ourselves stupid, bad, or ugly. We also make the assumption that everyone else must or should view us that way.

Take the case of a woman we'll call Sally. She was a beautiful and intelligent young woman. She had an older sister named Julie. Julie excelled at everything she set out to do. She received straight A's in her schoolwork. She was homecoming queen, and often won the leading role in plays. Of course, she sang well, danced well, and was proficient in several musical instruments.

Sally always felt that no matter what she did she was not as good as Julie. Although Sally did very well in whatever she set out to do, she did not feel that way. She measured her own self-worth by what Julie did and consequently had very low self-esteem.

New Hampshire school counselor Steve Scarfo recently said this to me: "When we are teenagers we are a bubbling mass of insecurity. If we could have ESP while in a room full of teenagers, we'd hear thoughts such as 'I wonder what they think of me?' Even the ones who look confident are likely thinking, 'I wonder what they are thinking about me?' They all feel that way even if they don't show it."

We take feelings like these into our adult life. We may not be quite so focused on ourselves, but many of our thoughts still concern how people react to us. If we feel we are being well received, it boosts our confidence. If we don't feel we are well regarded, our confidence level drops dramatically.

It's like acting. If we act confident, that is the way we will be perceived. How many times have you heard someone give a speech? The speaker stands up straight and tall, speaks eloquently, and makes direct eye contact. She oozes self-confidence. Yet, if you spoke with her afterward, you might find that she felt scared. Nevertheless, she projected self-confidence. That is what people perceived, therefore, it was assumed the speaker felt confident in what she was doing. You are, in effect, what you project.

How we *perceive* things colors how we feel about them. Do you remember the game you played as a child where one person would whisper a statement to another and that person would whisper the statement to someone else? The game would go on and on until the last person would say the statement out loud. Usually that statement was very different from the original!

Similarly, the attitude with which we approach things affects how we perform. If we start out thinking we won't do well, chances are we won't. If we start out thinking we can, we have a good chance of doing well.

Let's take the two following scenarios:

Scenario One

You have been picked to speak to a group of your colleagues. You are apprehensive because you don't like public speaking. What if you appear not to know what you are talking about? What if you stutter? Everyone will laugh at you and talk behind your back.

You start to prepare your speech. As you write, all you can think about is how people will view you. Why did you have to be picked? You try to work on your speech, but ideas just will not come to you.

The day of the speech dawns, and you wake up with a queasy stomach. You race through breakfast while still working on your speech. You are sure it's not a good one.

The moment of truth arrives. You are standing in a room where everyone is looking expectantly at you. If only the podium would just cover all of you—then no one could see you. You look out at the sea of faces and start to talk. The microphone makes feedback noises. Darn!

As you start talking you look at everyone. Suddenly, every thought you had just flies out of your head.

Scenario Two

You have been selected to speak to a group of your colleagues. The speech is about a topic you know well, so you feel quite confident and comfortable. As you prepare your speech, you envision that you will deliver it confidently and that people will enjoy your talk. You look forward to it, for you know you have much to say.

The day of the speech dawns, and you are confident and excited. Your speech is all written, and you know the material. In fact, you know your speech so well, you could give your talk without notes.

The moment of truth arrives. You are standing in a room where everyone is looking expectantly at you. You look out at the sea of faces and start to talk. You see everyone smiling at you, for your speech is very interesting. What a wonderful day!

USING REAL LIFE AS AN ANCHOR

With meditation, we can use real life events to help eliminate negative programming. Using real life experiences in our meditations can be powerful because they have the ring of truth. The meditation is familiar because it is based on something that has happened. It also anchors in the effect we want to have. Because it is something our mind can relate to, it is reinforced much more strongly.

Toward the end of writing this book, I went to a conference I go to every year held by the National Guild of Hypnotists. This year was a wonderful experience; everyone I met and talked to was nice to me. I didn't have one negative experience during the entire four days. It's not that people were less pleasant in other years. Not at all! It was because this year people seemed to be even friendlier.

Perhaps it was because things flowed smoothly and there were very few glitches. People were just in a good mood. The mood was contagious, and it was a very positive experience for me.

I came home feeling very self-confident. I had four days of reinforcement of positive feedback. I came home from that conference feeling very happy and self-confident. Since I am always working to find new ways to incorporate positive statements into meditations, it occurred to me that here was a perfect example. I could use this real life example in my meditations.

Positive reinforcement can go a long way toward our building confidence. Conversely, a negative experience can dramatically shatter it. Have you ever been in a situation where something you have done was rejected? You probably didn't feel very confident about yourself, and it may well have affected other areas of your life.

Many meditations utilize imagery. It can be very effective to imagine and visualize scenarios in which you receive positive reinforcement, but just imagine the benefit when you are able to use a real experience. You can remember the feelings and bring them into your meditation.

Remember that self-esteem and self-confidence go hand in hand. If you are confident, you will have good feelings about your ability to succeed and you will be motivated to continue your efforts.

But what happens when you are not confident? It can be a vicious circle, for you can find reasons why things are not going well, which just reinforces your behavior. You stop trying.

Self-image—how we feel about our appearance—can have a tremendous impact on your self-confidence. If you do not feel attractive—let's say you are a few pounds overweight—you often judge yourself by that criterion. True, you may be overweight, but that has nothing to do with your intelligence, your talents, or your abilities.

Therefore, you need to pull out what you do well and concentrate on those feelings. By being positive, you can stop dwelling on the things you don't do well. And when you do not dwell on them, you can *do* something about them. Getting stuck on negative feelings will get you nowhere. Being confident can help you get past the stumbling blocks you face.

THE GAME OF LIFE

Make a list of your good points and abilities. Focus on what you do well. Most of us have *something* that we do well. Make a game plan.

Again, don't dwell on what you don't or cannot do well. If it's possible to improve it, then work to do so. If you can't, work to have a sense of humor about it. Humor goes a long way toward diffusing negative feelings about something that you cannot change. In *Battlefield of the Mind*, Joyce Meyer has this to say: "Even a person who is really positive won't have everything work out the way he would like all the time. But the positive person can go ahead and decide to enjoy himself no matter what happens. The negative person never enjoys anything."

For instance, I have always wished that I could sing well. The truth is I sing very badly. I have learned to find humor in it. I'll joke that my cat used to put his paws over his ears when I sang in the shower. I have even found a way to use my lack of ability to my advantage. Once I was cast in a play where my character had to sing rather badly. That was easy for me to do—I didn't have to act at all!

If necessary, spend time each day looking at the list of things you do well. Be your own cheerleader. Then find ways to use those good points.

THE PARENT TRAP

A lack of self-esteem may well have deep roots in childhood. However, don't fall into the blame game trap. Yes, some parents don't encourage their children or favor one child over another. It is wise to remember, though, that children don't come with instruction manuals. Parents make mistakes, often unwittingly. And it is also wise to remember that many of our experiences are colored by our perception.

Even if we have had negative programming in our early years, we can choose not to let it affect us now. We can work to overcome this.

SUCCESS

When we lack confidence and have low self-esteem, we can sabotage our attempts at success. This can influence every area of our lives. It can affect our relationships, our business and career, as well as our health. It can sap our motivation. We don't always see this; we may blame setbacks on luck, on others, or some other excuse.

How many times have you refused to try to do something because you automatically decided you would fail? Let's take for example a man named Bill. Bill is intelligent, talented, and well thought of at the company where he works. Yet Bill doesn't have a lot of self-confidence. Every time someone gives him a compliment, he brushes it off.

There is an opening for a supervisory position, one that would mean a substantial raise in pay. But Bill feels that it would be a waste of time to even try for it. He feels that "there are others who are better than I am; if I put in for the job and don't get it, it'll look bad." So, he never even apoplies.

Bill never gave himself a chance to succeed. He may have been perfect for the opening. He did fail, but not because he didn't have what it took to get the job. He failed because he didn't have what it took to even try. He sabotaged himself.

Self-Esteem Meditation

(You may substitute another method for deepening, such as one from another meditation in this book).

> *Find a comfortable place. Sit or lie down, whichever is more comfortable for you. Close your eyes. Take a deep breath, hold it for a moment, and then exhale. Imagine yourself at the top of a stairway. There are ten steps, and each step will help you go into a deeper level of meditation. Step onto the first step and allow yourself to become more relaxed.*

> *One. Feel your body become relaxed. As you step down the second step, your body becomes even more relaxed.*

Two. Your mind is becoming relaxed. Now you step onto the third step, going even deeper into a relaxed state of mind.

Three. Take a deep breath, and hold it for a moment. Now gently exhale. Allow yourself to move down to the fourth step, and as you do so, you notice that your body feels very relaxed.

Four. You step down onto the fifth step. As you do so, you notice that your mind is even more relaxed. It feels very good.

Five. Now step down onto the sixth step, and as you do so, you are entering an even deeper state of relaxation.

Six. Take a deep breath, and hold it for a moment. Now gently exhale. Feeling very relaxed, you step down onto the seventh step. With each step your body and mind become more and more relaxed.

Seven. Now step down onto the eighth step, and as you do so, you notice that you are more relaxed than you have ever been before. It feels so very good.

Eight. And as you notice how relaxed you feel, you step down to the ninth step. Take a deep breath and hold it for a moment. Now allow yourself to gently exhale.

Nine. Now step down to the tenth step. You are feeling totally relaxed, mentally and physically. Ten.

See yourself at the bottom of the stairs. As you do so, you notice that you are in a room. You are feeling relaxed and comfortable. There is nothing you have to do, nowhere you have to be. You have plenty of time to enjoy this feeling of peace and relaxation. You are safe and secure in this room. As you look around the room, you notice that there are photographs on the wall. You walk closer to examine them. They are photographs of you. There are many, many photographs.

You move to look at the first photograph. You notice that it is one of you as a very young child. You are smiling. There are people in the photograph and they are smiling as well. It is easy to see the photograph was taken during a celebration. Everyone is happy. You are happy and feeling good. Listen. You can hear the people in the photograph saying, "What a wonderful child." "What a nice smile." Take a deep breath and allow yourself to feel those wonderful feelings flow with your breath, right into your body. That's right, feel them in your entire body. It feels so very good.

Now you walk over to the next photograph. It's a photograph of you when you were just a bit older. You are smiling in this photograph too. It's a photograph of you when you were in school. It is a special day. There are people in the photograph and they are smiling and look proud of you. Listen. You can hear them saying, "I am proud of you." "You did so well." "I know you worked hard." It feels so very good. Take a deep breath and allow yourself to feel those wonderful feelings flow with your breath, right into your body. That's right, feel them in your entire body. It feels so very good.

Now, feeling very happy, you walk over to another photograph. Yes! You are smiling in this photograph as well. It's another special day. There are people in the photograph and they are smiling and looking very happy and pleased with you. Listen. You can hear them saying, "I knew you could do it." "What an accomplishment!" It feels so very good. Take a deep breath and allow yourself to feel those wonderful feelings flow with your breath, right into your body. That's right, feel them in your entire body. It feels so very good.

Allow yourself to go from photograph to photograph. You are smiling in each one of them. Each one represents a special day, a special time or event. There are many, many photographs. Look at all the happiness you have created on the walls. There are many more photographs than you can count.

As you move around the room, looking at the photographs, feeling happy and good, you notice that there is one wall with no photographs. It is painted with bright rainbow colors. It is ready and waiting for more photographs. Look at all the space you have to place more photographs. You are a confident, happy, and positive person. You will have many, many more photographs to place on the wall.

Each day is a special day. You can fill your wall with more photographs of the wonderful things you can do that show the wonderful, confident person you are.

Self-Confidence Meditation

Meditations do not have to be set meditative scripts or affirmations. Storytelling can be a very effective technique. I like to write my own stories and record them on tape. It works very well if you include a deepening exercise at the beginning. Here is a story that I use often:

Find a comfortable place. Sit or lie down, whichever is more comfortable for you. Close your eyes. Take a deep breath, hold it for a moment, and then exhale. Imagine yourself standing near a boat. The boat is floating next to a dock on a calm, peaceful lake. You can hear the water softly lapping up against the shore. The water in the lake is a beautiful deep-blue color. The trees surrounding it are leafy and green. You can hear the sound the leaves make in the breeze. You can hear the birds singing in the trees. As you look up into the sky, there are puffy white clouds slowly drifting by. The sun is shining warmly down upon your face. You can feel the gentle breeze on your skin. You can smell the flowers in the meadow behind you.

You step inside the boat. It has a very comfortable seat to sit on, and you feel very safe and secure. You untie the boat from the dock and allow the gentle current to move the boat.

As the boat moves slowly and gently across the lake, you notice that off in the distance is an island. It is very beautiful, with tall trees swaying in the breeze. The sandy shore is golden and inviting. As you float nearer the shore, you notice that there are people standing there waving at you. They are smiling and are very happy to see you.

The boat gently drifts onto the shoreline. One of the people who was waving at you steps up and helps you out of the boat. Everyone there takes the time to take your hand, greet you, and tell you how happy and honored they are that you have come to visit their island.

They invite you to share their dinner with them around a campfire. During the meal they tell stories of the things they have done, what they have accomplished. As they tell their stories, you notice that no matter what each person has to say, everyone else listens intently. Every achievement, no matter how big or how trivial it might be, is met with encouragement. Every person is important.

When it comes time for you to tell a story, you hesitate. You say, "But I have no achievements to speak of. What have I done in my life? I have no story to tell."

An old man who has been sitting there listening to the stories looks at you and says, "You are you! What greater accomplishment can there be but to be yourself, with all of the things that make you special?"

You reply, "But I am not special. I know people who are, but I certainly am not. I don't seem to do things right the way others do."

The man replies, "In our land everyone is special. They may have their own ways of doing things, but each one is right for them. We honor that uniqueness, for that is what makes each of us special. And since everyone has their own way, their way is the right way."

It is now time for you to return to the boat. As you sit back in the boat, each person gives you a gift. When you return home, you open up

*each of the boxes that the people on the island gave you. As you open the
first box, you notice a colorful folded piece of paper. You unfold the piece
of paper and read the words written on it. It says, "I give to you the gift
of your story. You only have to look inside yourself to find it." You smile
and remember the person who gave it to you. You then open the next
box, and in it also is a colorful folded piece of paper. You unfold the piece
of paper and read the words written on it. It says, "I give to you the gift
of your story. You only have to look inside yourself to find it." You then
pick up and open the next box, and in it is a colorful folded piece of
paper. You unfold the piece of paper and read the words written on it.
It says, "I give to you the gift of your story. You only have to look inside
yourself to find it."*

*Each box has the same words written on a piece of paper, except for
the last box, which the old man gave you. Instead, on the colorful folded
piece of paper are the words, "You now know you have a story. Now give
the gift of telling it."*

Success Meditation

Many good meditation scripts are like highly metaphorical riddles.
Lying within the script itself are phrases that are themselves positive hypnotic suggestions.

*Find a comfortable place to sit in or to lie down, whichever makes you
feel more comfortable. Close your eyes. Take a deep breath, hold it for a
moment, and then gently exhale. I am going to count from ten to one;
with each number you will feel yourself going deeper and becoming more
and more relaxed.*

*Ten. As I say the number ten, you feel yourself going deeper. That's
right, you are feeling more relaxed mentally and physically.*

*Nine. As you hear the number nine, you feel yourself relaxing even
more, allowing your body and mind to relax.*

Eight. As you hear the number eight, you feel your body releasing any tension. Your body becomes relaxed. Loose and relaxed.

Seven. As you hear the number seven, your mind becomes as relaxed as a feather floating in the breeze.

Six. As you hear the number six, you are becoming even more relaxed.

Five. As you hear the number five, you continue to go deeper and deeper.

Four. As you hear the number four, your body and mind become yet more relaxed.

Three. As you hear the number three, you go deeper, and deeper, and deeper.

Two. As you hear the number two, your mind is relaxed completely.

One. As you hear the number one, your body is completely relaxed. Now you are completely and totally relaxed.

Imagine yourself in a place where there is a large, stone wall in front of you. Imagine yourself walking down the length of the wall. As you walk, you notice that there is a gate. On the gate are the words, "Open this gate for success." You notice that the gate is locked and there is a keyhole, but there is no key in sight.

You wonder how you will open the gate if there is no key. You look around for something you can use to open the gate. You lift a rock and notice that on its underside there is an inscription that reads, "The Key to Success Lies in Your Mind."

Puzzled, you think, "How can the key to success lie in my mind? There is a keyhole, there must be a key somewhere!" You look around and do not find a key anywhere. You continue walking down the wall until you nearly trip over a big rock. On the rock you notice these words painted in big letters: "Go back! You were standing right in front of success." You are even more confused, for you didn't see a key. How will you get into the gate? How could a key be in your mind?

You walk back to the gate and sit down in front of it, scratching your head. You know you want success, but how will you open the gate? You sit for a long time still wondering how you can get into the gate. After a while you grow sleepy and fall asleep.

In your dream a wise man comes to you and asks why you have not opened the gate to success when you are sitting right in front of it. "Don't you want to be successful?" he asks. You tell him, "Yes, I do, but I don't know how to open the gate; I don't have a key."

The wise man replies, "Of course you have a key, it's right in your mind." In your dream, you ask the wise man, "How can it be in my mind?" The wise man replies, "If you think you don't have the key, then, of course, you don't. But what do you think would happen if you did?" And with that the wise man disappears.

Now you wake up from your dream, still a little puzzled. But you decide to give it a try. You stand up in front of the gate and say, "I have the key, I want success." And to your surprise, the gate opens wide! The key was not a physical key . . . but lay in your thinking. The key to opening the gate was believing that you could.

Chapter Nineteen

Weight Loss

There are some words in our language that have really negative connotations. *Diet* is a case in point. What a nasty word! Diet means restriction, that we can't have something. The more we think about what we can't have, the more focused we become on it. It is far healthier to think of a diet as incorporating healthier eating habits into our lives, rather than thinking that we can't have chocolate, or ice cream, or french fries.

We can be obsessed with our weight. We are surrounded by ads for diet companies, diet drinks, diet food, and the latest diet books. Watch television, especially during the day, and you will be bombarded by diet ads. Have you ever noticed that they are usually right before or after junk food commercials?

The media have much to do with our perception of what is an acceptable weight. One only has to look at supermodels or actresses to see this. We are made to feel that we aren't attractive unless we are fashionably thin. Many psychologists feel that the rise in cases of bulimia and anorexia have much to do with this mind-set. Oddly enough, years ago it was considered attractive to be a bit heavier. Look at paintings from the Renaissance, and you will see that most of the people are much heavier than what is considered attractive today.

Weight is not a gender-specific issue either. Obviously, since I am female, I relate to weight as a woman. Women often feel that a man who is overweight is judged far less harshly than an overweight woman. A woman who is ten or twenty pounds overweight may feel ostracized, whereas a man who is just as much overweight can "get away with it." Yet, men are also concerned with their appearance. I am sure that many males reading this will say, "Of course we think about our weight and worry about not being attractive!" It may not appear to women to be the case because a man's worth as a human being isn't so tied up with their weight.

I am reminded of a skit I saw recently on television. A group of men were getting ready to go out. One man, standing in front of a mirror, said to his friend, "Do these jeans make my butt look fat?" Everyone in the room with me laughed hilariously, for let's face it, that type of behavior is associated with a woman.

To my way of thinking, here is a disadvantage that women do not face. A man's desire to lose weight is not taken as seriously as a woman's unless he is obese. A woman's self-image is often directly related to her weight, and she understands another woman's plight. But are we as compassionate toward a man? Think about it. Women do not feel the same way toward a man who wants to lose weight as they do toward a woman.

WHY DO WE GAIN WEIGHT?

Weight issues tend to be complicated. It would be easy to assume that being overweight is simply a matter of overeating. How many times have you seen a seriously overweight person and thought, "If he just ate less, he'd lose weight"? It is interesting to note that a large percentage of people who are overweight eat much less than those at optimum weight. With weight issues, there are often other factors at work, including metabolism, heredity, and psychology.

I am not a psychologist, nor is this a book on psychology. However, in many cases the amount of food consumed is not the cause of a weight problem. In those cases, meditations to limit food consumption will simply not work. For instance, some people hold weight as a means of protection. In some cases of sexual abuse, some women and men will subconsciously allow themselves to gain weight. In this way, they feel they will not be attractive and can "protect" themselves from a sexual relationship.

Some people have low self-esteem; they feel small and insubstantial. Having weight subconsciously gives them a feeling of substance. Subconsciously, they feel that being overweight is the only way to be noticed.

The people around you can have a strong impact on your weight. A spouse may encourage you to have dessert even though he knows you want to lose weight. He may fear losing you if you were too attractive. You have someone sabotaging you. You may not realize it, nor may he.

Some people do eat too much, especially certain types of food. They may have a weakness for sweets, pasta, or junk food. We often make fun of our weaknesses. I'm sure you've heard the expression, "I'm a chocoholic." Meditation can be very successful with this, for it can help decrease the desire for food or a type of food.

We may eat at times that are not healthy for us. Raiding the refrigerator in the middle of the night, or eating late night snacks in front of the television can add unwanted pounds very quickly. Sampling while cooking can add calories without our realizing it.

It is very helpful to have some idea why you are overweight. This will help you find the type of meditative technique that will be most successful.

For those whose weakness is a specific food, meditation can lessen the desire for that food. Some people eat when they are stressed. Stress reduction techniques can be effective in those situations. Others use food for comfort. Techniques to improve self-esteem may help these people. At times, simply using a "feel good" meditation can work. Meditating has fewer calories than chocolate chip cookies!

Metabolism can be a factor in weight issues. Metabolism changes as we grow older. We have to be realistic and realize that this happens. We may not be able to eat as much as we did when we were teenagers. Exercising can help boost our metabolism and burn extra calories. Meditation can help with the motivation to exercise.

As you can see, it helps to know why you are overweight so that you know what techniques will work best for you. There is no one diet, no one technique that will work for everyone.

Taking the time to do this can save time trying the wrong diet or the wrong approach. You need to find out the causes. By keeping a daily eating journal for a week, you can go a long way toward discovering why you are overweight.

JOURNAL OF EATING

Use a notebook. Each time you eat, whether it is a meal or a snack, write down the following:

Name of the food(s)

Is it a regular meal or a snack?

Reason for eating: Are you hungry? Is it a meal? Is it a snack? Did someone offer you a snack and you just took it without thinking? No reason at all?

What activity were you doing: Watching TV? Cooking?

Where were you: Dinner table? Your desk at work?

Your mood: How are you feeling? Happy? Depressed? Anxious? Fearful?

Time of day

Keeping a journal will help you pinpoint when, where, what, and why you are eating. To be the most effective, you need to write down every morsel you eat, even if it's one M&M while walking past a coworker's desk.

The first step is to find out if you can rule out overeating as the *sole* cause. The cause may well be a psychological factor *plus* overeating. This is not said to discourage you, but rather to help you be successful. If you use a technique that is geared solely toward limiting food intake when other factors are involved, you are likely to fail. I want you to be successful. Keeping the journal will help pinpoint if overeating is the cause.

If overeating is the main factor, willpower alone is often not enough. It's easy to say "I'll just eat less," but following through is not. We all start with good intentions. How many times have you said in the morning, "I'll be good today, I'll eat only low calorie, healthy foods," only to binge later in the day? Meditation can keep you motivated and help you prevent that.

WEIGHT-LOSS TECHNIQUES

I'm including a wide variety of weight loss techniques. Feel free to modify any of these, or mix and match them.

The No-No Table

For those who have problems with specific foods or specific types of foods, such as fried foods, sweets, or junk food, this technique can be effective. Use the deepening technique of your choice, or use this technique at the end of another meditation of any kind.

Imagine and see yourself in a large room. In the room are two tables. One table has a great big sign with a red X over it (you can substitute the universal sign of a circle with a line running through it). This table is over in the corner, where it is very dark. It has a dark brown tablecloth made out of very coarse material.

The other table is in the other corner where it is brightly lit. There is a large sign hanging over it with a great big smiley face. The tablecloth is a stunningly clean white tablecloth. The table even seems to have a glow about it.

Visualize yourself placing on the dark table all the foods you know you should not eat. Each time you place a food on the table, mark a great big red X over that food. Keep placing foods on the table until you have placed all your problem foods on it. All those foods have gigantic red X's over them. Notice how dark and dingy the table is. Even the foods placed on the table looks unappetizing . . . they are all dark and heavy-looking.

On the other table, the bright and glowing table, place all the foods that you know are good for you . . . that will help you maintain your desired weight. See how wonderful they look. As you place each and every item of food on the table, it's as though they are lit up from above . . . as though they each were wearing a halo. Notice how bright this table looks! The food on this table looks tasty and fulfilling.

See yourself eating foods from the light table. Whenever you want to eat a food from the dark table, just visualize it with a big red X over it. It's dark and unappetizing. You would much rather select foods from the tasty table . . . the table of light. See yourself eating only the light, tasty food. See and feel yourself feeling satisfied and happy.

Rooms of Change

One of the things we do to ourselves is set unrealistic goals, ones that seem too ambitious to reach. Even if we do need to lose large amounts of weight, trying to scale that mountain all at one time may be too difficult. It is better to set a goal of losing ten pounds. Even if you do need to lose twenty-five, fifty, or even one hundred pounds, taking a step at a time makes it seem like a goal that can be reached. I've started this exercise with the number five, but you can start with ten if you'd prefer. The number of rooms you go through in this meditation should be close to the number of pounds to be lost to reach your desired weight. Each room equals five pounds. If you want to lose ten pounds, you need to go through two rooms. Twenty pounds would be four rooms.

Find a comfortable spot and sit or lie down. Take a deep satisfying breath, hold it for a moment, and then gently exhale. Close your eyes and picture a very large fat red number five. See how big it is! As you see the number five, watch as it shrinks. See it getting smaller and smaller and smaller until you can no longer see it. It has now disappeared completely. Now, picture a very large fat red number four. See how big it is! As you see the number four, watch as it shrinks. See it getting smaller and smaller and smaller until you can no longer see it. It has now disappeared completely. Now, picture a very large fat red number three. See how big it is! As you see the number three, watch as it shrinks. See it getting smaller and smaller and smaller until you can no longer see it. It has now disappeared completely. Now, picture a very large fat red number two. See how big it is! As you see the number two, watch as it shrinks. See it getting smaller and smaller and smaller until you can no longer see it. It has now disappeared completely. Now, picture a very large fat red number one. See how big it is! As you see the number one, watch as it shrinks. See it getting smaller and smaller and smaller until you can no longer see it. It has now disappeared completely

Now imagine walking into a large building. As you walk in you can see that it is a large room with a doorway at the far end. The walls in the room are covered with mirrors. As you walk in, you can see yourself. Perhaps you aren't all that happy with your reflection, for you would like to lose weight. But, this is a magic house . . . each room is special. The further you walk into the house, the more rooms you will be able to enter. Each and every time you enter a new room, you will be five pounds lighter.

See yourself taking the walk to the far end of the room. Feel yourself putting one foot in front of the other . . . taking one step at a time. It seems like a long walk to reach the far end . . . but you know you can do it . . . it's right within sight. Keep placing one foot in front of the other. Finally, you have reached the door. Open the door and walk into the next room. This room too has mirrors . . . but look, you are five pounds lighter! Turn around and admire yourself. See how great you look and feel. Wow! Five pounds really does make a difference! But perhaps you need to lose a bit more weight. You can do it, you can see the door at the far end of this room. See yourself taking the walk to the far end of the room. Feel yourself putting one foot in front of the other . . . taking one step at a time. It seems like a long walk to reach the far end . . . but you know you can do it . . . it's right within sight. Keep placing one foot in front of the other. Finally, you have reached the door. Open the door and walk into the next room. This room too has mirrors . . . but look, you are another five pounds lighter! Turn around and admire yourself. See how great you look and feel. Wow! Another five pounds really does make a difference!

Now imagine and see yourself going out of the house into the outside world. Notice how everyone is smiling at you. They all think you look attractive. Feel how good this makes you feel, how proud! Stop and talk to anyone you'd like . . . you will hear them tell you how good you look, how proud they are that you reached your goal. You feel and look terrific!

OTHER TECHNIQUES

Adapting the Conference Table technique from the chapter on habit control and smoking cessation to a weight-related technique would work well. Simply change any dialogue to sentences that relate to weight.

Affirmations

Every day I am one step closer to my goal . . . to my final goal of weighing _____ pounds.

I eat healthy and I feel healthy.

I am slim and thin.

Chapter Twenty

Sports and Performance

Athletic superiority takes practice as well as talent. Superstars in any sport spend hours on the courts and playing fields. Simply imagining and visualizing winning the Olympics certainly won't ensure a gold medal. But many of those same athletes practice mentally when they aren't actually playing their sport. They give it their all, physically and mentally.

Larry Bird, former Boston Celtics star and now a coach for the Indiana Pacers, once said that he used to practice shooting baskets over and over in his mind, as well as practicing on the court. There is no doubt that he has talent and practiced on a real court for endless hours. But he also had the drive to rehearse mentally as well. Most exceptional performers of any kind excel because of that total devotion. They work at their sport both physically and mentally.

BUT WHAT IF YOU'RE A KLUTZ?

Most sports require concentration as well as physical ability. Tennis and golf are such sports. While meditation can't guarantee that you'll become as good as an Andre Agassi or a Tiger Woods, it can help you to improve your game.

Years ago I studied karate. I wasn't too bad at it, except when it came to the forms. They consist of a series of steps and moves much like a choreographed dance. I was horrible at them! For some reason, I had great difficulty turning the correct way. Of course I constantly practiced the forms physically. But I kept turning the wrong way, going left when I should have been going right. My instructor was polite, although at times I could see him struggle to keep a straight face. I'm sure he wondered how anyone could be such a total klutz.

My instructor suggested that I practice my forms mentally. I was quite surprised, for I wasn't a klutz in my visualizations. I could envision myself doing the moves in the correct directions. I kept mentally rehearsing the forms over and over. Soon I found that my actual moves improved dramatically. It was as if my body "remembered" the moves I had done in my mind.

Scientists have studied this phenomenon and have concluded that we do indeed have muscle memory. It's like riding a bicycle. Once we know how to do it, the body remembers what muscles need to move. We perform these activities without conscious thought. Practicing physically builds muscle memory. Remember that we have talked previously in this book about the mind not knowing the difference between reality and fantasy. Practicing mentally while using meditation will be as real to the mind as doing the activity. Of course, we have the benefit of being able to do it correctly in our mind! We can be perfect.

Tennis Meditation

Imagine dressing for a tennis match. As you put on your outfit, you realize that helps you prepare for the game. Putting on your tennis outfit serves to mentally ready you for the upcoming match. See yourself lacing up your tennis shoes. With each shoe that you tie, your mind becomes more focused. You are preparing yourself physically and mentally for your game.

Now, see yourself stride out onto the tennis court. See yourself as you confidently pick up your racket. Feel the racket in your hands, and feel how that racket serves to make you feel even more confident. Holding your tennis racket is a signal to you that you are focused and ready to concentrate on the game. With each breath you take, you will be able to focus and concentrate better. You are able to concentrate on the moves you need to make. You are able to concentrate on the movement of the ball as it comes to you . . . and goes away from you. You will be able to keep your focus completely on the ball.

Now see yourself as you start the tennis game! . . . see yourself as you make the serve. See and feel as you hold your arms up high . . . the racket and ball in the perfect position. See as you throw the ball up into the air, see as you move the racket to strike the ball. You can see, feel, and hear as the ball makes contact with your racket. And as you strike the ball with your racket, see the ball as it flies over the net. As it flies over the net, you can see it approaching your opponent. See and hear as the ball makes contact with your opponent's racket and it returns over the net toward you. See and feel as you move into the perfect position to return that volley. See as you move to the spot on the court you need to be to meet the ball. See as you find the ball and are in the perfect position to return the volley. Notice how agile and in control you feel. See, hear, and feel as your racket strikes the ball and sends it flying once again over the net. Notice how good it makes you feel to have hit the ball so perfectly. See the joy on your face as you realize that you are playing very well. See the excitement on your opponent's face, for he enjoys playing with you . . . he enjoys playing with a good opponent. And you are good.

See as the ball is repeatedly returned to you . . . and see yourself repeatedly returning the volley to your opponent. With each volley of the ball, you are able to move to the spot on the court where you need to be. Each time you hit the ball with just the right amount of speed and strength. It feels so wonderful to be this agile . . . this strong . . . this focused on your game. You are able to maintain that concentration throughout the entire game. With each stroke of your racket, you are better able to concentrate . . . to focus.

And you know that each time you play tennis, you will become better and better at it. With each game your stroke will improve . . . your ability to return the ball at just the right speed and velocity will improve . . . and your agility to run wherever you need to be on the court will improve.

Tennis Volleys

A large part of tennis is hitting the ball, or volleying. Mental rehearsal works well for this activity. Simply imagine hitting a ball over and over. Visualizing that you are standing in front of a ball-throwing machine is excellent. See the ball coming toward you and see yourself making the shot every time. Work not only to see yourself making the shot, but to make the visualization real by getting involved with all your senses. See and feel yourself making the shots. As you concentrate on an exercise such as this one, you will go from seeing yourself hitting the shots to imagining that you are *doing* it.

Perfect Golf Swing

I am told that one of the more important things in golf is to master a proper swing. It doesn't just involve the arms; it's a total body activity. Meditation can help you perfect your golf swing. If you need to know the exact moves to be made, you may want to purchase a golf video that shows someone demonstrating good form. Look at it in slow motion several times until you know the exact sequence of moves and the proper body positions. Then imagine *yourself* in that video. See yourself executing a perfect golf swing. If necessary, slow down the action to make sure you are doing it perfectly. When you are, keep running that mental image over and over. It's like actual practice; the more you work at it, the better you will be. The good thing with mental practice is that you don't need to get out your clubs. You can fit in a few minutes of practice during a break at work or while sitting on the subway or riding in a car.

Putting

Putting in golf takes a great deal of concentration as well as physical dexterity. This meditation works both with concentration and mental rehearsal of making the putt.

Concentrating on the Putt

See yourself standing on the green. Each and every time you hold a golf club, you are able to concentrate and focus. See yourself as you have a shot lined up. You can see the hole and the ball in front of you. See yourself position your body perfectly. Feel yourself position your body perfectly. Take a deep breath, hold it for a moment, then gently exhale. Each time you take a breath, it will help you keep your focus . . . your concentration. You are able to easily focus on the ball . . . on the hole. You can shut out any distractions. Noise does not bother you; in fact noise helps you to concentrate. Noise, such as the conversation of another golfer or the sound of a golf cart in the distance, merely helps you retain your focus. You can concentrate on the ball and the hole in which the ball is going to go. See yourself standing in front of the ball with your club lined up for the perfect shot. See and feel yourself mentally finding the correct path for the ball to take to go into the hole. Feel your body instinctively move into the proper position to make that shot. Every breath you take helps you to retain your concentration. Each and every time that you hold a golf club, you are able to concentrate and focus. See yourself line the shot up perfectly. Feel yourself move your body into the perfect position. You are able to concentrate fully and totally on the task at hand . . . the task of putting the ball . . . the task of hitting the shot perfectly . . . the task of making the shot . . . the task of seeing the ball fall perfectly into the hole. Each and every time you hold a golf club, you are able to concentrate and focus. Now see yourself putting . . . hitting the ball with the right amount of speed and pressure. See the ball rolling toward the hole . . . and now see the ball dropping into the hole.

Batting Practice

Imagine standing at the plate . . . see yourself standing with bat in hand. Feel as you move your body into the correct position. Feel and see yourself as you hold the bat in the position that is best for you to make a perfect swing. See yourself holding the bat at just the right angle . . . with just the right grip. See as the pitcher throws the ball. See and feel as you instinctively know when to swing . . . or not to swing. You are able to focus on the ball coming toward you. You can easily shut out any distractions so you can focus totally on the ball. You will instinctively know and be able to see if this is a ball you should swing at. And when you see a pitch you should take a swing at, see yourself move into exactly the right position . . . holding the bat with exactly the right grip. See the ball coming closer. See and feel yourself as you swing at just the perfect time. See and hear as the ball makes contact with the bat. And see as the ball flies out straight and strong.

Bowling

See yourself as you pick up the bowling ball. See and feel yourself holding the ball in the correct manner and grip for you. Feel yourself lift the ball and hold it in the position that is best for you. You are able to concentrate on the pins at the end of the alley. Noises will not distract you; in fact, noises will only serve to help you concentrate. You are able to focus completely on the ball you are holding, the lane, and the pins at the end of the lane. Feel and see yourself standing at just the right spot for you to make a strike. See and feel yourself going through the exact sequence of moves necessary to place the ball onto the lane at just the right spot. See as you place the bowling ball exactly on the right spot . . . see the ball roll down the lane . . . and hit the pins in just the right spot for a strike. See the pins fall down . . . all ten of them. See as you have made a strike.

MEDITATION AND OTHER SPORTS

Most sports can be mentally rehearsed. The ones above are just a few examples. To use meditation, see and feel yourself going through all the necessary moves to accomplish your goal. Perhaps it's surfing. Run a mental picture of yourself knowing the correct wave to pick, and then picture youself standing in the correct position to ride the wave to the shore. It could be rollerblading, parachuting, or skiing. Just about any sport can be mentally rehearsed.

MENTALLY REHEARSING OTHER ACTIVITIES

Mentally rehearsing can work for other activities as well. Want to learn how to do the electric slide? Mentally practice the steps, and you'll find that you are able to do them on the dance floor more easily. Basically, any activity that requires physical movement can be rehearsed and often improved.

Chapter Twenty-One

Habit Control and Smoking Cessation

A habit is something we do repeatedly, usually without conscious thought. We just do it. We can be, as the saying goes, creatures of habit. We get up the same time each day. We drive to work taking the same route each time. Even our morning routine is likely to be the same day in and day out. Think about it for a moment. I bet many of you do the same things each morning when you get up. Do you get out of bed, go grab a cup of coffee, and turn on the television for the news? You probably don't even think about it; you just automatically go about these activities.

Not all habits are negative. For instance, we might have a habit of smiling at people when we meet them or we might make our beds as soon as we get up in the morning. Some habits are neither negative nor positive. For instance, maybe you have a habit of eating your food in a certain way, such as eating one food at a time. Someone else might do it differently, eating a bite of each food in turn.

However, there are many other habits that are bothersome and interfere with people's lives. Habits can become compulsive/obsessive disorders. Some people repeatedly wash and scrub their hands until they are raw. There are others who must do things in a certain order. In the recent Academy-award-winning movie *As Good As It Gets*, Jack Nicholson's character had such a disorder. He had set ways of doing everything. He had to lock the door in a certain way. He walked in a certain way, and, of course, avoided cracks in the sidewalk. Every day he ate the same foods at the same restaurant. In the movie this was funny, but in real life such behavior can be troublesome.

When we think of negative habits, smoking usually comes to mind. The last part of this chapter is devoted to smoking cessation. Other habits, however, are no less burdensome. Nail biting, hair pulling, teeth grinding, bed wetting, head banging, and procrastination are just a few. Some cause great embarrassment, guilt, or shame.

Nail biting is one of the more common habits. When I was younger, some of my classmates bit their nails. I remember several of them putting bad-tasting liquids on their nails. I'd watch them make horrible faces, but they'd still bite their nails. The late Princess Diana reportedly bit her nails. Early photographs show her holding her hands so the nails didn't show. It must have caused her embarrassment, for everything about her was exposed to public view. Apparently, she conquered the habit. Later photographs show her with her hands exposed and her nails nicely manicured.

With any habit, it helps to understand why and when we do it. Do we do it at times of stress? Has the habit become so ingrained that one does it many times a day, regardless of mood? The next step is to become aware of when it happens. Since many habits are done without conscious thought, it can take some real work to become aware of when you actually do it. Keeping a diary or a journal is a great help. It can show you when you do a habit and allow you to note down your emotions and feelings. Are you stressed? Nervous?

It is true that many habits have a psychological cause and can be difficult to break. Many habits are formed at a time of stress or trauma and are deeply ingrained. We reinforce those habits by doing them over and over again, yet that does not make them impossible to break.

Meditation can help control or alleviate bad habits. There are two things to consider when utilizing meditation to control habits: First, many habits are caused by stress. By using meditation to relieve stress, we can work to eliminate the habit. Second, with meditation we can work on framing a more positive behavior for ourselves. We can replace the old behavior with a new one.

SMOKING

If I asked you to guess the habit people would most like to break, and you answered smoking, you would be correct. I do not need to list the reasons why smoking is unhealthy. You only need to read the newspapers or watch television to understand the impact that cigarette smoking can have on health. Even if we do not smoke, we can be affected by second-hand smoke.

Therefore, a large part of this chapter will be devoted to smoking. Many of the techniques can be adapted for other habits, so even if you are a nonsmoker, you may find the information useful.

I consider smoking to be very close to drug addiction. Scientifically, it does not fit the criteria for a true drug addiction. A person with a true drug addiction *must* have that drug. The need is both psychological and physiological. While we may need to have a cigarette, we can go without one. A drug addict, on the other hand, may not be able to sleep through the night without the drug. It is not just a psychological craving.

Most of us who smoke are able to sleep and not wake up craving a cigarette. Oh, we may wake up and want a cigarette, but very few of us wake up *just* to have a cigarette. We don't wake up shaking with withdrawal symptoms.

Smoking is, in large part, a psychological addiction, but there *are* physical factors as well. A drug addict's whole focus is on obtaining and using a drug. Smokers may focus a large part of their lives on smoking, but it is not their only focus. The life of a drug addict revolves around their next fix. However, smoking comes close to a drug addiction.

With smoking, there is also reinforcement. While we smoke, we are often in a meditative state. Think about it. When we smoke, we often are thinking about something else. We may be daydreaming. We are more suggestible in that brain wave pattern. Each cigarette and each puff we take reinforces the habit. We are giving ourselves a strong hypnotic suggestion to continue smoking.

I will give a large variety of techniques for smoking cessation.

Some of them will be nonmeditative. Smoking is a big problem, and it should be attacked from every angle. Now, I have known people who have quit smoking easily. One day they smoke, and the next day they don't. Some use a meditation technique or go to see a hypnotist, and suddenly they are a nonsmoker. Others quit smoking simply by sheer willpower.

Many smokers have tried a variety of techniques. It's a highly individual problem. My advice is to read the techniques I have included here and combine those you feel will work for you. Start small and then add from there.

The first step is to figure out why you persist in the habit. Why did you start smoking? What would it take for you to stop? What would you miss about smoking? At what times do you smoke? What situations make you want to have a cigarette?

Sound like a lot of work? Consider that you have put a lot of work into smoking! Even if you have only smoked for a short time, you still have put considerable effort into smoking. Lets use an example of a smoker who smokes one pack a day and has been smoking for a year.

That's twenty cigarettes a day for 365 days. That works out to 7,300 times you have had a cigarette. That is a *lot* of effort.

These are some habits we don't want to change even if we say we do. Smoking is a good case in point. As a hypnotherapist, I have many clients who contact me for smoking cessation. Their desire to quit is not always as strong as they think. A statement like "My wife wants me to quit, she's tired of the house smelling" usually indicates that the person is not doing it for himself. A person like that can see a hypnotherapist, and then blame hypnosis when he fails to quit: "I tried, but it didn't work for me."

I am going to make a revelation. I feel your pain. Yes, I know you've heard that before. Truly, I do, no matter how you might feel about that *other* person. Why? Until very recently I was a smoker. I was going to tell you that I planned to quit by the time this book was published. As it turned out, I quit before finishing the first draft. It is not easy, I know. I've been there.

I knew all the reasons for quitting. My mother had part of a lung removed due to lung cancer. I was scared by all I read and heard. Yet I continued to smoke. Trust me, I used every excuse there is: "I smoke when I am stressed," "It calms me," "It helps me think," "I'll quit later." Of course, I *know* better. After all, I am a hypnotherapist and here I was writing a book on meditation. It was beginning to sound a lot like "Do as I say, not as I do."

For those of you who perform well when motivated by pressure, here is a wonderful technique. Tell people who matter to you that you've set a date by which you intend to stop smoking. I told a few people that I was going to declare in this book that I would quit before it was published. I usually do well under pressure. For me, it was a matter of pride as well. If that kind of reasoning works for you, use it. I'm all for using what works. Each person is different, though, which is why no one smoking cessation plan will ever work.

If you do not do well under pressure, keep your goal to yourself. Just quietly go about your business. Then when you have succeeded, you can tell people what you have done. In that way, you won't have to deal with people who give you that look if you do happen to smoke a cigarette.

It can be quite important to allow room for failure, especially psychologically. In that way, it can be viewed as a small setback rather than a total meltdown. I do not mean that you should set yourself up *to* fail, but rather leave room for that possibility. Allow for failure, and you can dismiss it as just a small incident. However, if you set impossible goals and fail, you'll view them as insurmountable.

Smoking can be tricky when it comes to stress. We smoke more when we are stressed. We think it calms us. What it actually does is increase blood pressure and reduce the flow of oxygen to the brain. That is hardly relaxing or calming.

Smoking is a complicated habit. There are many reasons why people start and many other reasons why they continue. Some habits have what is known as secondary gain—there is something gained by the habit. The reasoning behind the gain may not seem logical to the conscious mind, but it does to the subconscious. For instance, many young people start smoking because of peer pressure. A teenager may start because he wants to be "cool." Many years later that reason may seem silly.

The subconscious mind can be very childlike. The person who starts smoking as a teenager to gain social acceptance still wants to fit in as an adult. That has not changed, even though he has matured. We need to shift the secondary gain to a healthier one and still fulfill its desires and needs. Using a visualization where people come and give their approval can be very powerful. Right now it's politically correct to be a nonsmoker. This can be a strong incentive to give to the subconscious mind. It still wants to be "cool," and now it can be by changing the habit.

Smoking Meditation

Find a comfortable spot and close your eyes. Picture yourself walking down a path. The air is fresh and clean. Allow yourself to take a deep breath, hold it for a moment, and then slowly exhale. Feel how wonderful and crisp the air is. It smells clean and fresh. Continue walking down the path. Notice the flowers, the trees, and the birds singing. The sun is shining; there are puffy white clouds in the blue sky. The temperature is pleasant. As you continue walking, you notice that a little further down the path is a gathering place. There are people there. As you get closer, you recognize many of them. They are smiling at you and beckoning you to come closer. When you are close enough to see and hear, one of them calls you by name, shakes your hand, and tells you how pleased he is that you are now a nonsmoker. You walk over to the next person and she gives you a big hug. She tells you that she is very happy to hug you now that you no longer smell like cigarettes. Feel how proud you feel. You are a successful person, and here is one more success you have to your credit. You are a nonsmoker. Notice how wonderful you feel, how strong, how vitalized. You know you will continue to be successful. Each breath you take reminds you that you are successful. Each breath you take, reminds you that you are now a nonsmoker. You feel special because you are special. You have successfully done something that was difficult . . . but you did it . . . and you did it well. You are successful . . . you are a nonsmoker.

See as you go to your home and stand in front of your closet. Lift out an article of clothing . . . one of your favorite outfits. Notice how fresh and clean it smells. Now that you are now a nonsmoker all your clothes will smell fresh and clean. See how wonderful your clothes look . . . they even seem brighter. Go ahead and try on several of the outfits in your closet. See how wonderful you look in them. You know that it is just an old wives' tale that people always gain weight when they quit smoking. You know that isn't true, and you can see that it isn't simply by trying on the outfits in your closet. See how great they fit . . . notice how fresh and clean they smell. You are happy, for you know you look great . . . and you smell better. You no longer smell like cigarette smoke. You have reached your goal, and you have done it well.

Think of how wonderful it is to face each day as a nonsmoker. You can appreciate the crisp scent of the air. Your house smells fresh and clean now that you are a nonsmoker. The windows are even cleaner, and you can appreciate the sun shining in the windows. See how clean they are! Your car is fresh and clean. You breathe easier in so many ways now. You have quit smoking, and have done it for all the right reasons. Therefore, you now will be a nonsmoker for the rest of your life. And you will be able to enjoy that life fully. You can breathe deeply. You know you will have more energy. That's right, say to yourself, "I have more energy; I am a nonsmoker; I am successful."

See yourself facing every kind of situation without needing a cigarette. You can do anything without needing a cigarette. If you ever feel the desire to have a cigarette, all you have to do is take a deep breath, hold it for a moment, and then gently exhale. When you do that, you can breathe easier knowing that you are a nonsmoker and it will be easy for you to stay a nonsmoker. You feel wonderful, proud, and successful.

See all your friends and family coming up to you and hugging you. See how proud they are of you. You deserve it!

Thirty-Day Technique

Some people need to ease into quitting. That is fine; each person is different. With this technique, pick a date that you will quit smoking. You can use thirty days, or sixty days if you'd prefer. Picture a calendar in your head with that date. See yourself standing next to the calendar pointing to that date. Hear yourself say, "On (fill in the date) I will be a successful nonsmoker." Each night before you go to sleep, visualize that scene again. You are standing next to a calendar marked with the date you picked to quit smoking. Hear yourself say, "By this date I will be a nonsmoker." Whenever you have a moment or two during the day, you can also quickly visualize this same scene. Know that you *will* quit smoking by that date.

Conference Table

There are many reasons why we smoke, and many parts of us that still might have the desire to smoke. This technique allows all those parts (subconscious reasons) of you to have their say. For a deepening method, I would suggest a very long body relax with a mental vacation relax added. This is done as a free-form meditation. Below are some of the particulars that should be included:

> *Imagine that you are entering a large conference room. When you come into the room, you notice that there is a large round conference table . . . just like King Arthur's Round Table. Sit down in one of the chairs at the table. You've previously invited to this conference all the parts of you that want to continue smoking, and all the parts that want you to quit. Each part will have its say. As each part walks into the room and sits down, it will identify itself. For instance, there may be a part that will call itself "Mr. Cool." Mr. Cool is the part of you that wants to fit in with the crowd. Another part called "Ms. Thinker" might want you to continue smoking because it "helps" you think. Don't force this part of the meditation or try to second-guess; allow the parts to reveal themselves naturally. During the meditation, another part or two may come in later on. Allow this to happen.*

When all the parts (that come in at this time) have indicated their name, give each one a chance to speak. Let each part say why you should quit, or why you should not. The parts can converse and reason with each other. You may invite "The Referee" if you think the parts need to be controlled so they don't talk out of turn. No part can attack another part in this conference.

You may also find people in your life who want to come into the conference room, for instance your mother or spouse.

The purpose of this exercise is to help you discover hidden reasons why you continue to smoke. You may uncover things you were not aware of, things that will help you decide which techniques will work best for you.

Affirmations

I am a nonsmoker.

With every breath I take, I am closer to being a nonsmoker.

With every breath I take, the less I desire a cigarette.

I am successful in everything I do, and I am a successful nonsmoker.

Chapter Twenty-Two

Fears and Phobias

Fear is a necessary emotion. It can protect us from harm. If we hear a strange noise in the middle of the night, fear can make us cautious. However, fear can limit our lives if we let it take over when it's not necessary. Many of our fears don't signal present danger.

A large number of our fears are rooted in past events. These events may be traumatic, or they may just have made a strong impression on us at the time. When I was a young child, a bee stung me. It hurt, and I remember not feeling very well afterward. It wasn't a traumatic event, but I developed a fear of bees. I became fearful of hornets and wasps as well. Whenever a bee came near me, I'd freeze and stand still, afraid to move. It must have looked pretty comical to those around me. I thought that if the bee couldn't see me, it wouldn't sting me. I'd break out into a cold sweat, my heart would pound furiously, and I could barely breathe. All intelligent and logical thinking and action just went right out the window.

I would never have thought I had a phobia. I just knew I was afraid of bees. However, I went out of my way to avoid them. I made sure to keep my distance from flowers. If I went running or walking through a field, it was always with this thought in the back of my mind: "Be careful, there could be bees."

My phobia wasn't pronounced enough to limit my life. I still don't like bees very much, even though I know they are a necessary part of our ecological system. But I am no longer afraid of them. I worked with meditation techniques to decrease the effect that the mere sight of a bee had upon me.

My mother has always been afraid of birds. When she was a young child, she witnessed her brother being mauled by a rooster. Since that time she has been terribly afraid even to be in the same room as a bird. Even if it was only a parakeet in a cage, she would still tremble with fear. Clearly, this is a case of a traumatic event producing a fearful reaction, even when there is no danger. My mother logically doesn't think of parakeets as dangerous, but her body and mind still react as though there is danger. Her subconscious is remembering the mauling incident she witnessed as a child.

What is the difference between fears and phobias? In the book *Self-Hypnosis, The Complete Manual for Health and Self-Change*, authors Alman and Lambrou have this to say: "The difference between a fear and a phobia is mostly one of degree. A phobia is something that causes you to change your way of living to avoid the object or situation. A fear can be something only mildly interfering; it does not control your life."

Some of us aren't aware that a fear has become a phobia. We just don't allow ourselves to be in situations where we would be faced with it. People have fears that they don't consider problems, such as fear of mice, spiders, or snakes. For instance, a person who is afraid of the dark will just use a night-light and forget about it. It doesn't interfere with their lives.

Yet some fears *do* interfere with a person's life. Take agoraphobia, which is often described as an abnormal fear of being in open places. Actually, agoraphobia is more realistically a fear of fear. People who have agoraphobia often stay at home. They may experience extreme symptoms if they leave the house, such as fainting spells, nausea, or blurred vision—or what is known as a panic attack. Therefore, they are afraid of having those attacks.

In effect, these people become prisoners in their own home. Spouses, children, or relatives end up doing all their errands for them; they cannot do them for themselves. There are many stories of those who have lost jobs because they couldn't face going out into the world. Clearly, people such as these need professional help. Health care professionals may well use meditation techniques to help these people regain control over their lives.

Fears can interfere seriously with people's lives without their realizing it. They simply take extreme measures to avoid those situations. For example, those who are afraid of bridges will sometimes drive long distances to avoid going over one. If asked why they took that particular route, they often give a reason that has nothing to do with the bridge: "There's always so much traffic that way, I prefer this way."

FEAR OF FLYING

It has been said that what people really fear is not flying so much as *not flying*. Funny as that may be, it really is true. People who are afraid of flying fear that the plane will crash. Flying still evokes great fear in many people, and it is one of the major fears people will admit to.

I've sat on planes next to people who are afraid to fly. It's easy to see the fear on their face. They usually are perspiring heavily and have that panicked look in their eyes. Most try to hide the fact that they are fearful. If we could see what they were visualizing, it would probably be the plane torn and twisted on the ground. You can tell such a person that statistics show flying to be much safer than driving, yet that doesn't help.

Meditation techniques can help. Mental rehearsal techniques, such as the ones used in the chapter on sports performance, can be effective. Visualizing the entire trip from start to finish as safe and uneventful can decrease anxiety. Generally, it is best to start several weeks or even a month or two before a trip.

When I work with clients with a fear of flying, I have them start from the very beginning of the trip. I don't have them start at the airport. I have them visualize themselves purchasing the tickets, packing their clothes, and driving to the airport. I also don't have them stop with just getting off the plane. I have them visualize the purpose of the trip. If they are going to see their grandchildren, I have them visualize hugging them. The point is to not make the airplane flight the whole focus. People usually fly somewhere because they want to do something or be with someone. The plane ride is just a small part. It's simply a way to get there. I want them to focus a large part of their attention on that part of the trip. This also helps to reduce the magnitude of the fear.

FEAR OF PUBLIC SPEAKING

I do quite a bit of public speaking and even travel to do lectures and workshops. I also teach at conferences, sometimes very large ones. However, if you had told me many years ago that I would do this for a living, I would have said you were crazy!

I delayed taking a public speaking course in college for as long as I could. Whenever I had to stand and speak in front of a group, my stomach would get queasy, my voice would quiver. Worse still, my face would turn beet red. I looked like I was blushing furiously, and of course everyone noticed. I used to dread speaking in front of a group. It wasn't just a matter of being nervous right before a speech; I would think about it constantly for several weeks in advance.

I used a combination of techniques to reduce my fear. I used affirmations such as these: "I enjoy speaking and people enjoy listening to me," and "I speak clearly and effectively."

I also used mental rehearsal techniques, envisioning myself actually giving the speech. As it turned out, there were several additional benefits to using that technique. I was able to memorize the material because I started practicing several weeks before giving the speech. My creative abilities were sharpened because I envisioned an audience that participated. I even found instances where the audience's reaction indicated that certain areas could be written or presented better.

MONSTER-SIZE FEARS

Some fears loom larger than life . . . literally. For instance, a few years ago, if you had asked me to imagine a bee, I'd have visualized a bee of epic proportions. Godzilla would have had nothing on that bee! Interestingly, in talking with people who have fears of objects, I have found that they often have dreams about them. And in those dreams—in a large number of cases—the thing they fear is visualized as much larger than normal.

A woman I know started having nightmares about gigantic ants. She understood exactly where the dreams were coming from. A short time before, she'd moved into a newly constructed house. She had hired someone to install a dryer vent in the basement. The person had to pull back a bit of insulation in order to drill a hole, and when he did, thousands of ants were covering the surface underneath. As she watched, the ants fell all over the carpenter, covering him. Now, that didn't thrill *him* by any means, but she found it made her squeamish. She started having dreams about ants that were ten feet tall. Her subconscious mind magnified them out of all proportion.

Even though she understood why she was having the dreams, she still had them every night. She also was beginning to be afraid of going down into the basement, fearing that she might see an ant. She used the following meditation.

The Amazing Shrinking Fear

In this meditation, simply substitute the example given with the object of your fear.

Find a comfortable place to sit or lie down and close your eyes. Take a deep breath, hold it for a moment, and then exhale. Imagine yourself in an elevator on the tenth floor. As you push the down button, with each descending floor you will go deeper into a deeper level of meditation.

Ten. Feel your body become relaxed. As you step down the second step, your body becomes even more relaxed.

Two. Your mind is becoming relaxed. Now you step onto the third step, going even deeper into a relaxed state of mind.

Three. Take a deep breath, and hold it for a moment. Now gently exhale. Allow yourself to move down to the fourth step, and as you do so, you notice that your body feels very relaxed.

Four. You step down onto the fifth step. As you do so, you notice that your mind is even more relaxed. It feels very good.

Five. Now step down onto the sixth step, and as you do so, you are entering an even deeper state of relaxation.

Six. Take a deep breath and hold it for a moment. Now gently exhale. Feeling very relaxed, you step down onto the seventh step. With each step your body and mind become more and more relaxed.

Seven. Now step down onto the eighth step, and as you do so, you notice that you are more relaxed than you have ever been before. It feels so very good.

Eight. And as you notice how relaxed you feel, you step down to the ninth step. Take a deep breath and hold it for a moment. Now, allow yourself to gently exhale.

Nine. Now step down to the tenth step. You are feeling totally relaxed, mentally and physically.

Ten. See yourself at the bottom of the stairs. As you do so, you notice that you are in a room. You are feeling relaxed and comfortable. There is nothing you have to do, nowhere you have to be. You have plenty of time to enjoy this feeling of peace and relaxation.

As you step into this room, you know that it is a very safe room. Nothing can harm you or hurt you in this place. This room has every-thing you need to be safe and secure from anything and everything. It's a very powerful magic room, and you are always in control when you are in this room. You control everything that happens to you. Nothing can happen that you don't wish to happen. You are completely safe and secure. As you look around this room, you notice that it is comfortably furnished just the way you would like. Maybe you would like a fireplace over in the corner . . . why yes . . . there is one! And look, there is an oversized stuffed chair . . . just the type that you can curl up in and be comfortable. Everything in the room is designed just the way you want. Allow yourself plenty of time to look around. If there is something that is not in the room that you would like . . . you have the power to change it . . . and just simply place it in the room. It's your room and you can furnish it any way you please.

Over on one wall, you notice that there is a large movie screen. You sit and settle down on the comfortable chair and proceed to watch the screen. Next to the chair is a remote control. It has many clearly labeled buttons on it. It has fast forward . . . rewind . . . volume control . . . a button to change the channels—all the usual features. But there is an additional button on the remote control. This button says "shrink." You hit the play button, sit back and watch the movie. As the scene comes up, you notice it's a (fill in the object you fear). You are just a bit uncomfortable until you remember that you are in a special room. You control everything that happens. Nothing can harm you or hurt you in this room. You are always in control. So, as you watch the screen, you know you have nothing to be afraid of. Watch as the (fill in) appears on the screen. See it as it moves around. You can sit back and watch it, knowing that it cannot leave the screen. You are safe in the chair . . . safe in the room.

As you watch the (fill in), you realize that it has no power to hurt you. You do not have to be afraid of it. You also remember the special button on the remote control. Out of curiosity, you want to see what that button does. You pick up the remote and aim it at the screen. See yourself push the button marked "shrink." As you do so, the (fill in) on the screen gets smaller. That makes you laugh! See the (fill in) get smaller. Go ahead, push the button again. Watch as the (fill in) becomes even smaller. That is even funnier, for it is getting quite small now. See as the (fill in) wanders around on the screen. As it does so, you notice that it doesn't make you feel afraid at all. It actually looks rather comical as it trys to walk all over the much bigger screen. It's getting very, very, very tiny. Go ahead, push the button again. Now the (fill in) is so tiny that you can hardly see it! Why, you'd probably need a magnifying glass to do so. If you wish, you can go ahead and push the shrink button one last time. And now the (fill in) disappears completely!

Anytime you see a (fill in), all you have to do is mentally pick up the remote control and push the shrink button. You can shrink your fear . . . you have complete and total control from this time forward.

Now count from one to five. At each number you will feel more and more in control. One . . . coming out. Two . . . more and more awake. Three . . . you are even more aware and feeling in control. Four . . . wide awake. Five . . . totally aware and in control.

Unwrapping Fear

Whenever you are feeling fearful, simply imagine that fear has different layers, just like the skin of an onion. Imagine that you can peel away each layer one at a time. With each layer you peel away, you feel more confident and less fearful. Take time as you remove each layer to notice how you feel. Let your confidence and fearlessness build with each layer you remove.

Some fears will have many layers, others will have only a few. As you work with this technique, a fear that once had many layers will most likely produce far fewer layers.

Affirmations

I am feeling strong and confident.

I can face my fears.

I am in control of all areas of my life.

I am a warm, loving person who is comfortable around people.

Whenever I feel fearful, all I have to do is take a deep breath, and that fear is not so big.

Part Four

And Beyond . . .

Chapter Twenty-Three

The Spiritual Realm

Since the dawn of civilization, humankind has believed in the existence of spirit guides. I feel that we all have spirit guides. How many do we have? It depends, but we usually have quite a few. Some guides are with us from birth, and others come and go at various times in our lives. They are with us whether or not we are aware of them, and even if we do not believe in them.

They come in various forms. There are human, animal, and nonhuman guides. What are nonhuman guides? Angels are one example. Although we tend to personify them, that is, to give them human form and identity, angels are considered nonhuman. Animal totems are another example. It is important to remember that *human* does not imply any kind of superiority. To say a guide isn't human certainly is not an insult or a slight.

Can guides be dangerous? It's important to remember that wisdom isn't automatically conferred upon a guide. As with people, some guides are wise and some are not. There are many philosophies with respect to spirit guides. Some people feel that no evil or harm can ever come through a guide. Others believe that is true only of *genuine* guides, and that lower entities can and do pass themselves off as spirit guides.

Most philosophies, however, agree that there are different *levels* of guides. Some guides have recently passed on to the spirit level, dead relatives for example. There are also master teachers, who were special during their lifetime—people like Martin Luther King and John the Baptist. I feel that someone of the caliber of Mother Teresa will certainly become a guide.

There are ascendant masters, gatekeepers, and more. Then there are the guides who are closest to the highest spiritual realms. The closer the guide is to the higher source (God, the universe), the less chance there is that ego, judgment, and human personality traits will be involved. However, the more humanlike guides have personalities just as we do. Like us, they are not perfect or infallible.

I feel that no guide is dangerous *if* approached with common sense and discretion. No matter where a guide comes from, do not blindly accept any statement. Ask questions such as these: "Are you a true guide? Do you come from the light and the truth?" A true guide will never shun outright questions, nor will they hesitate to answer them plainly.

You may ask your guide for a name. Here is another area where there are incredibly conflicting opinions. A guide may give you a name you feel comfortable with, one that will be easy for you to remember. That may or may not be the guide's real name. Perhaps you will be given the name of someone famous, however, that does not mean the guide *is* or was that person. Certain philosophies believe that is possible, while others feel it could only be an *aspect* of that person.

People can get quite egotistical about the names and identities of their guides. Believe me, name-dropping is not unheard of in spiritual circles. The belief that one's own guide is better, more powerful, higher, more famous, or more spiritual than other people's guides is all too prevalent.

Guides will not make direct contact with us without our permission. They may subtly give us direction, such as influencing our dreams. They will not directly participate, nor will they interfere in our lives. Once they do have permission to make contact, they make their presence known in a variety of ways.

Spirit Guides are just that . . . guides. They are not there to tell us what to do or determine every step we take. We retain the ability to act and, more importantly, the responsibility for our own actions. I have heard people who start just about every sentence with "My guide said." It reminds me of those who constantly pepper their sentences with "My therapist said I should." Guides and therapists aren't there to run our lives. Their purpose is to help *us* benefit from our own experiences. They are not supposed to be crutches.

It is true that I am opinionated about this. I could be wrong, I suppose. But guide or no guide, *we* each live our own life. Living as though we dare not take a step without consulting our guide isn't realistic or healthy. This is real life, and we have to deal with that. A guide's purpose is not to give us an excuse for not doing something.

If you do run into a guide who tries to make decisions for you or tell you what to do, it's probably not a true guide. It could be a lower entity or just a bit of fantasy or wishful thinking on your part. Guide-work needs to be done with common sense, as well as an open and questioning mind. We have the right to dismiss guides. If you have attracted a guide or an entity you feel uncomfortable with, you should firmly tell him to leave.

You will hear the terms grounding, centering, and protection in regard to spirit guides, psychic abilities, channeling, astral projection, and myriad other New Age topics. As with any field, there is jargon that isn't always clear. It seems that everyone expects you to know instinctively what those terms mean. Do we need to ground ourselves? And what is it? What is centering? Why would we need protection?

GROUNDING

Think of grounding as a fairly literal term. You need to keep yourself "on the ground," and able to deal with things realistically. Being grounded keeps you from flying off in a million directions. Grounding also connects you with planet Earth.

Grounding Meditation

For this exercise you should sit in a chair. The chair should have good back support so you can keep your spine fairly straight. You should also be able to place your feet firmly on the ground. If you cannot do so, use telephone books or a box to rest your feet on. It is important that your feet are not dangling in the air.

Sit in the chair with your feet on the ground or the floor. Take a deep satisfying breath and close your eyes. Place all your awareness on your body. Feel your back against the back of the chair. Feel your buttocks on the seat of the chair, and feel your feet on the floor. Notice how your body feels against the chair. Feel every part of your body. Feel your head . . . feel your neck . . . feel your shoulders . . . feel your chest . . . feel your stomach and abdomen. Feel your arms . . . all the way down to your fingers. Go ahead and wiggle your fingers if you would like. Now notice and feel your back . . . the top of your back . . . down along your spinal column . . . all the way down to the small of your back. Notice how it feels to be sitting on the chair. Feel the backs of your legs against the chair. Feel your legs . . . feel your ankles and the tops of your feet. Notice your toes . . . go ahead and wiggle your toes if you wish. Feel your feet firmly on the floor. Feel how they feel touching the floor. And as you are aware of your entire body . . . sit up straight and feel a warm white light from above you enter into the top of your head. Feel it flow throughout your body . . . down the trunk of your body . . . down your legs and down through your feet. Feel this white light go out of the soles of your feet all the way down into the earth. It is as though you can see and feel this light connecting all the way down into the center of the earth. Know that you are a part of this light and energy and that you are connected and grounded to the earth's energy. You and the earth are together. Feel its pulse . . . feel how alive the earth is. You are part of this energy and are tapped into its center. You are one with this planet and its sacred energy.

CENTERING

Being centered while meditating simply means being aware of your inner world calmly and objectively. To be objective, you focus on the inner world without being judgmental or egotistical. Centering is difficult to explain without resorting to a somewhat vague description. I like to think of it as finding a quiet place within and then focusing on that "spot." *Spot* does not mean an actual physical location, but more of an inner spot. By focusing on that spot within you, you are able to balance your energy and become "centered."

Centering Meditation

I like to use the heart chakra in centering meditations, for the heart chakra is near the center of the body. It also relates to feeling, emotion, and love, and therefore is the center of our core being. I often use both a centering and a grounding meditation at the beginning of other meditations.

> Sit or lie comfortably. Take a deep, cleansing and satisfying breath. Hold it for a moment and then gently exhale. Throughout this meditation, continue to breathe in and out gently and naturally. Place your attention . . . your awareness . . . your focus on the area of your heart chakra. You may even feel it as it gently spins. Feel the place of your heart chakra, and place all your attention and awareness on this spot. Imagine or visualize some loving pink light flowing through your heart chakra. Feel this energy flowing . . . gently . . . right in the center of your being. Concentrate your awareness and your attention on this spot, and allow yourself to become calm and relaxed. Continue to breathe in and out very gently . . . as you become aware of this spot . . . and only this spot. Take a few minutes and place all your awareness on this spot. Should other thoughts or other areas come to mind, simply brush them away for now. For right now, all your awareness is on the area of your heart chakra. The energy in this area is smoothly and gently flowing within you. Know that this brings you to a balanced and centered place.

PROTECTION

Not all agree that we need protection when working with spirit guides—or any psychic work for that matter. Like many things, there are a wide range of opinions as to the necessity for protection. Personally, I prefer to place a "white light shield" around myself. This can be done at the beginning of any meditation, and can be done throughout the day if you wish.

Protection Meditation

Visualize or imagine a force field of light surrounding your entire
body . . . the field of light is a brilliant white glowing light, and that light
surrounds you completely . . . This field of white light prevents any neg-
ative energy or entity from harming you. Simply visualize this light sur-
rounding you.

MEETING YOUR GUIDES

If you are serious about meeting and working with your guides, meditation is one of the best ways to begin making contact. I highly recommend keeping a journal of your impressions and, in time, the
information you are given. In the beginning you probably will get impressions rather than feeling you have made direct contact. As you
work with meditation exercises, you will be able to recognize and communicate with your guides.

Imagine yourself standing at the top of stone stairs. They go down
and curve around, and you can tell they wind down and around . . .
farther than the eye can see. This stairway of stone leads to another time
and place. A place you have been before; perhaps you've seen it in your
dreams. Perhaps you can remember it from far distant memories that
vaguely whisper and flow through your mind. It's as if you can hear
those memories like a song . . . soft and lilting on the wind and breeze.

You take the first step on the stairway of stone and start down on
your journey. Feel your feet step upon the first step. You place your
hands upon the railing and it feels cool and smooth upon your hands.
You breathe in the air that has an unknown . . . but familiar sweet
scent. Place your foot upon the next step, and allow yourself to descend
the stairs of stone . . . these stairs that lead to the place where you will
meet your guide. And as you walk down these stairs you feel safe and
secure . . . relaxed and at peace. You wish to meet your guide. You know
your guide has been there for a long time . . . silently helping you each

day. Place your foot upon the next step and allow yourself to go further down the stairs of stone . . . downward on this journey. Feel how safe and serene you are . . . and continue down the stairs and onto the next step . . . and the next step . . . down, down, down, you continue down the stairway of stone. You continue on your journey . . . down the stairs . . . down and around as the stairway winds its way deeper and deeper and closer and closer to the place you have been before.

And as you get to the bottom of the stone stairway, you see that there is a path. This path goes far off into the distance, curving around farther than the eye can see. You feel safe and secure and want to walk along this path . . . and as you do so you hear the birds singing . . . and you notice the smell of flowers upon the light gentle breeze. You walk along the path noticing all the scenery . . . a field of flowers, a fence way off in the distance . . . sheep grazing past the fence . . . trees in full leafy bloom. It's a peaceful day . . . the sun is warm and inviting. You continue to follow the path until you come to a clearing. It seems so familiar . . . this place to which you have come. You are drawn to this place and know you have been here before at some other time. You instinctively know that this place is safe, secure, and yes . . . it feels very sacred. It feels like a sacred place and you feel honored that you have been allowed to come to this place.

As you walk around this serene and sacred place, you notice that there is a seat made from vines and branches and other materials that you have no name for. This seat is covered with flowers and greenery. The flowers are blue and white lotus flowers . . . they have such a heavenly scent. And now you know you are in a very special place . . . a spiritual sanctuary . . . the place of all knowing and all being. A place where time has no meaning. All that has been, all that will be, and all that is . . . are right here in this place. You sit down on the seat and just allow yourself to be in this place . . . there's nothing to do . . . nothing to be . . . you just are. Everything you are is perfect for this place and time, and all that is in this place in time is perfect.

And as you sit on the seat, you start to notice that what you thought was silence is really a kind of music . . . so very soft like a whisper. It

sounds like angels singing . . . it's so very beautiful and unusual . . .
unlike anything you have heard before. It's so very, very soft, yet so
comforting, peaceful . . . and somehow . . . familiar. It soothes you . . .
right to the deepest part of you. Allow yourself to sit and listen for a
while, drinking in the serenity. And as you listen to this music, you look
around and notice things . . . notice how soft the colors are . . . the grass
. . . the flowers . . . even the light is somehow very soft.

And as you continue to look around at your surroundings you notice
that there is a path that leads to the spot where you are sitting. You gaze
down the path and it stretches as far as the eye can see. It is winding
and flows off into the distance like a ribbon. It seems to flow right off into
the heavens beyond. And as you sit there gazing down the path, listening to the music, and feeling very safe, serene, and comfortable, you notice a glow way down the path. As you gaze at this glow, you notice that
it is slowly making its way toward you. It's a warm, golden glow . . .
soft and beautiful. This glow seems to float right toward you . . . slowly
and gently. Soon, it is fairly near . . . just outside of the clearing. It
stops for a moment and then you can see a form. You can clearly see
this form within the gentle golden glow.

As you gaze upon the form, you realize that this is your spirit guide.
Your spirit guide has come to you. As your guide stands just outside the
circle of this sacred place, you realize that you must give permission for
your guide to enter . . . for no one can enter this sacred place without
your permission. You grant permission by saying, "Guide of mine, if
you come from the light and are from truth, you may enter this sacred
place." You feel comfortable knowing that only a guide who is truthful, a
true guide and one from the light of goodness will be able to enter this
sacred place.

And when you know that this is a true guide, your guide enters this
sacred place and sits beside you on the seat. Your guide is silent, allowing you as much time as you would like to gaze upon his face. Notice
how having your guide sitting next to you makes you feel. Take all the
time you need to look, sense, and feel your guide. And if you would like,

you may now speak with him. It is permissible for you to ask your guide his name. Ask, "Guide, what is your name, how may I call you?" Allow yourself to listen to the answer you receive. Whatever answer comes into your mind is the correct one. Just listen quietly and allow your guide to tell you his name.

Now that you know your guide's name, you may ask other questions. Take time to ask questions of your guide. [pause] When you have asked the questions you wish, speak with your guide about how you would like him to contact you again. [pause] Your guide will tell you how he will contact you, and you will be able to recognize when he does. Gaze once again upon the face of your guide. Before your guide leaves for now, he has a gift for you. Allow yourself to receive this gift. It may be a symbol or a visual picture of something. It will be something that you will find within the physical world within the next few days. It could be anything from a flower you have never seen before . . . a feather . . . or a pretty stone . . . You will know what it is when you see it. You will know that it is a gift from your guide.

And now, before you say good-bye, allow yourself to feel the love that your guide has for you flow over you like sunshine. Thank your guide for being in your life. Know that your guide will be with you always . . . And from this day forward, you will be able to call upon your guide, this true guide who has revealed his presence to you today.

HUGGING YOUR INNER CHILD

There is a childlike part of us that remains even when we have grown into adults. It's the child we once were . . . our "inner child." It is an archetype, which means it is a representation of a part of you. I have found that most of us still feel like "a little kid" no matter how old we are. Emotionally, that young insecure child is still with us.

A meditation that can be emotionally comforting is to hug our inner child. That part of us can be almost inaccessible, and it can be emotionally uplifting to be able to hug that part of ourselves. I've used a female child, but you can change that if you are male. Use the deepening method you prefer.

Imagine yourself walking down a long hall with several doors. The doors have small nameplates on them. Walk down the hall until you find the door with the nameplate that reads CHILDHOOD. *Open the door and walk inside. As you do, you notice you are in a playground. There are lots and lots of children smiling and laughing and playing. You can see can that some children are playing on the swings. Watch as they swing back and forth, and notice how happy they look . . . swinging back and forth, feeling free and light as air. You look to your left and you see children sliding down a slide. You smile, for you remember doing that as a young child. Allow yourself to walk all around the playground and notice all the children and the things they are doing . . . the fun they are having.*

As you walk around the playground, you notice a young child off in a corner. This child is sitting by herself on a rock. She is swinging her feet back and forth, looking a bit forlorn. All the other children are playing, yet she is not. She is sitting by herself with no one to play with. You walk closer to this child, and you notice that she looks a lot like you did as a child. Allow yourself to walk even closer . . . now you notice . . . this child is you. You are looking at yourself as a young child.

You go and sit next to the little girl . . . and as you do so . . . you smile at her. She doesn't recognize you, but she instinctively knows you somehow . . . she knows that it is safe to be sitting with you. See yourself smile at this little girl. Know that this little girl is you . . . your inner child . . . and you have been blessed to be able to spend time with her. She looked so lonely before you came to sit with her . . . and now she looks happier. Someone has come over and is paying attention to her. Talk to her and show that you very much like to listen to what she has to say. She tells you the things she has done today. You tell her stories of many things . . . fairies and dragons and magical places. See yourself spending time with this little girl and the two of you talking.

And as you talk with this little girl you see her face light up, for she is now feeling special. Someone is taking the time to listen to her, to talk to her, to care about her. She had felt that no one cared and was feeling very sad until you came along. As you look into her eyes you know she isn't feeling sad any longer. She feels happy and cared about . . . and special. Now allow yourself to hug this little girl. Feel how wonderful that feels! See how happy this little girl feels to have someone hug her. Immerse yourself in this wonderful, fulfilling feeling of hugging this little girl . . . this little girl who is you . . . your inner child.

MEETING YOUR ANGELS

Angels have always been viewed as special beings. In paintings they are usually depicted as glowing and smiling. There is something magical about an angel. Many religions and philosophies believe in angels and in guardian angels that watch over us. Working with angels can be joyful and exhilarating . . . and yet also peaceful and comforting.

Stories abound about angelic interventions at times of crisis. "An angel must have been watching over you" is an expression we often hear. We also read and hear stories about mothers being alerted to danger to a child.

I believe angels are around us all the time, not just in times of danger. We can contact our angels just as we can our guides. Angels and spirit guides are not very different from one another. Angels are guides that are closest to the highest spiritual plane.

Angel Meditation

Take a deep satisfying breath, hold it for a moment, and then gently exhale. Close your eyes and take another deep satisfying breath, hold it for a moment, and then gently exhale. We are about to go upon a journey, a journey in which you will meet your guardian angel. Your angel has been beside you since the day you were born. There may have been times when you knew of your angel's presence. Today, here and now, you are going to meet your angel. Now take another deep satisfying breath, hold it for a moment, and then gently exhale. Imagine yourself standing on the shore of a sparkling lake. See how the sunshine dapples the surface of the clear blue lake. Hear birds sing, hear leaves rustle in the gentle breeze, hear insects buzzing in the distance . . . hear the sound of water lapping against the shore. Yes, this is a restful, serene, and magical lake, unlike any lake you have ever seen. Now allow yourself to look around and see the scenery . . . the beautiful colors of the flowers, the clear blue color of the water, the blue of the sky, the white of the clouds that are scattered here and there in the warm, sunny sky . . . see how the water sparkles. Yes, this is a restful, serene, and magical lake, unlike any lake you have ever seen. Take a deep satisfying breath, hold it for a moment, and then gently exhale. Feel how wonderful it is to be in this place . . . at this magical lake. Allow time for these feelings to soak in, to know how peaceful, safe and secure you feel. [pause]

As you stand at the shore, you notice a dock. Tied to the dock is a small boat, just the right size for you to sit in. See yourself walk down the dock and get into the boat. You feel very comfortable getting into the boat and you sit down in the middle. As you do so, the breeze gently floats you away from the dock. The boat is gently floating . . . pushed along by the breeze. Slowly, gently . . . and as the boat floats along you sit back and allow yourself to relax. You have plenty of time to enjoy this ride . . . there is nowhere you have to be . . . nothing you have to do . . . all you have to do is sit back in this magical boat and enjoy the ride. You are happy because you know this boat will take you to the place where you will meet your guardian angel.

You allow yourself to drift awhile in this boat, pushed along by the breeze. You aren't quite sure if it has been a few minutes . . . or forever . . . or if it's only a dream . . . but the boat has come a long way from the shore. As you look to see where you are, you notice an island ahead of you rising out of the mist. The most beautiful mist you have ever seen surrounds the island. The mist is blue . . . it is white . . . you can't quite tell. You just know the mist feels so peaceful and looks so hauntingly beautiful. As you draw nearer you hear music . . . light . . . soft . . . sort of unearthly and heavenly.

The boat reaches the shore of the island, and you notice that the sand is an unusual shade of gold . . . softly glowing in the sunshine that filters through the mist. There are flowers unlike any you have ever seen before. Everything looks different . . . but somehow familiar. As you get out of the boat to stand on the shore, you notice a light moving toward you. As the light draws closer, you see that it is a form. And as this form draws even nearer, you can see that the form is a person . . . no . . . it's an angel! No person could look so glorious . . . so heavenly . . . so peaceful . . . so angelic. You know immediately that this is your guardian angel, the angel who has been with you since the day you were born . . . your true angel from the light.

Your angel takes your hand, and the two of you walk toward a garden on the island. As you walk, you notice that this garden, too, is magical. There are plants, flowers, vegetables, and fruit trees that you have never seen before. There is a glow about everything on this island. As you walk hand in hand with your angel, you come to a small clearing with a bench next to a fountain. You and your angel sit down on the bench. For a few moments neither one of you speaks . . . you just take in the magic of your surroundings . . . the peaceful feelings . . . You listen to the sound of the fountain, the songs of the birds . . . the breezes rustling the leaves of the trees. At last you turn to your angel and you are able to speak to this wondrous angel. See and hear yourself thanking your angel for having been with you each and every day. Take all the time you need to talk to your angel. [pause] Your angel has something to say to you . . . that's right . . . just allow yourself to listen to what your angel has to tell you . . . [pause]. See and hear yourself and your angel talking together. You have plenty to say to each other. So much to talk about . . . but you have plenty of time in which to do this. Just allow yourself to talk to your angel as long as you need and want to do so.

And now take a deep satisfying breath, hold it for a moment, and then gently exhale. Look upon your guardian angel and tell him anything you need to before you go back. [pause] See your angel smile down at you. You know that your angel is with you at all times. You may talk to your angel anytime you wish . . . in your prayers . . . your dreams . . . your meditations.

And now walk back to the boat and get inside. As you do so, you see
your angel smiling at you. You feel special . . . you know you have had
a special experience. Feel how this makes you feel. Drink in all the feelings from this experience of meeting your angel. Yes, that's right . . . it
feels unlike any experience you have ever had before. Now . . . just sit
back in the boat as it moves away from the shore. The boat will float you
back to the other shore . . . the shore you started from. The breeze will
gently float the boat back to the shore where you began. Feel as you
gently drift over the sparkling water. Now you are there . . . and when
you step onto the shore you know you have indeed taken one of the
most magical journeys of your life. You have met your guardian angel.
Know that your angel walks with you always.

Chapter Twenty-Four

Spirituality and Health

In this chapter I address the issue of creating our own reality. Most illnesses are thought to have origins that are largely psychosomatic. However, I have found in much New Age thinking a tendency to blame everything that happens to us on our ability to "create our own reality."

Yes, I truly believe that meditation and positive thinking *can* do much to improve health. I have witnessed many instances where ill health has been dramatically turned around. Yet I feel it is careless and can be downright hurtful to suggest that those who are ill have *purposely* "done it to themselves."

It is often suggested that we choose a particular illness or handicap in life. On a deep level that might or might not be true, I have no proof either way. If we do choose our challenges for each lifetime, I do not believe it to be a question of reward and punishment. I have heard many people say that their life-threatening illness was ordained by karma. They are then told that if they dealt with those karmic issues, they would no longer "need" the illness and could cure themselves.

That *may* be true on a deep level. Our soul may embrace certain challenges. But that is our soul, and not the conscious self. How do we know what the soul has chosen for that challenge? Perhaps it was not the challenge of an illness but something else. Either way, I don't believe one's karma is cut in stone. We make our own decisions and take our own actions. I don't believe we are fated by karma to illness or good health. Karma is not a reward or a punishment for deeds done in a previous life.

My feeling is that karma means that the soul goes through various incarnations, choosing to experience life in different ways. Perhaps in one lifetime we were not very nice. Maybe we were downright evil. I don't believe, though, that we are punished for that. It isn't correct to say that "things never go right for me because in a previous life

I was mean." We do not get to evade responsibility for our actions in this lifetime.

Some people believe they are ill in this life because they did something horrible in another lifetime, but this just doesn't ring true. To tell someone that simply knowing and accepting their karma will free them from illness is unfair and cruel. This implies that if someone fails to beat an illness, they have done something wrong karmically.

I also find it distasteful when someone blames a person for making illness a "reality." They imply that the person could simply *choose* not to be ill, think differently, and suddenly be cured. That means the person fails to heal himself because he is thinking incorrectly and therefore wishes to be ill.

I do not criticize the belief that it may well be possible to create a healthy life for ourselves. I believe we can mentally work towards good health—even from a place of ill health. What I do object to is the belief that the person who is ill has willed or chosen to be so.

We do create much of our own reality by our actions. If we take an action *a* and an action *b*, we usually get result *c*. If bad things happen to us, it's often the result of something we have done, and it's the same with good things that happen. However, this is not *always* the case, for we must take other people and their actions into account.

Some New Age thought suggests that every single thing that happens to us is our own doing. But that theory falls apart because other people are out there doing their thing just as we are doing ours. And their actions inevitably have an impact on us. Therefore, it is impossible for us to create our own reality. We can influence it, but we cannot create it. By the same token, we cannot undo everything that happens to us.

There is medical proof that stress and lifestyle can cause illness. However, I do not believe that psychosomatic illnesses are that simple. Nor do I believe that one chooses to have a specific illness, and can make it go away by admitting that they created it. Psychosomatic illnesses are very real. While interesting research is being done using meditation and hypnosis to help achieve remissions and cures, I believe that making patients feel they are to blame for their illness is not at all spiritual or positive. Helping someone to use positive thinking techniques is more compassionate.

Recently I overheard two practitioners talking about clients with muscular dystrophy. One said that one of her clients refused to "accept the fact that she had the disease and that it was of her own creation." The practitioner felt that once this woman accepted her condition and admitted that she had created it, she'd be on her way to recovery. What bothered me most was the practitioner's tone of voice—it was critical rather than supportive of her client's mental process. The implication was that the client's biggest problem lay in her refusal to admit creating the illness.

The practitioner went on and on, saying that once this woman admitted that she had created the illness, she'd be able to cure herself. This mind-set bothers me because it implies that when someone fails to recover or go into remission, it's because they have not "thought correctly." That's a lot of needless guilt to place on anyone!

Chapter Twenty-Five

Aromatherapy and Meditation

The practice of aromatherapy has increased in popularity within the last few years. Aromatherapy and the use of essential oils have been around for centuries. In *Aromatherapy: The Essential Beginning,* D. Gary Young says this: "According to the translation of Egyptian hieroglyphics and Chinese manuscripts, priests and physicians were using oils thousands of years before the time of Christ."

What are essential oils? They are liquids taken from various parts of plants, trees, and bushes. The oils are taken from the roots, stems, bark, flower, leaves, or fruit.

During meditation the sense of smell can be very powerful. Certain smells are relaxing or soothing, while others are vitalizing. The sense of smell can create a mood and spark a memory. Think about how certain smells evoke memories of other times and places. The use of essential oils to trigger a deep meditative state works well for those who do not like smoky incense.

I introduce essential oils into the air with a diffuser. A diffuser is a unit with wells into which the essential oil is poured. A glass tube called a nebulizer, which is shaped much like a Christmas icicle light, fits into the unit. The essential oil is poured into the well and then is forced by air from an air pump into the glass tube. It is then diffused into the air.

Aromatherapists believe that essential oils have numerous health benefits, emotionally and physically. I find certain scents to be very relaxing. Others make me feel calm and peaceful. Oils can be used one at a time or blended together. The brand I use blends oils with such names as Peace and Calming, Joy, Hope, and Harmony.

OILS AND THEIR PROPERTIES

ANGELICA
Calming; helps one let go of anger

BASIL
Helps one maintain an open mind

BERGAMOT
Releases anxiety, tension, and stress

CEDARWOOD
Spiritual communication and protection

CHAMOMILE
Calming; reduces stress

CLARY SAGE
Calming and clarity

CLOVE
Promotes a feeling of protection

CYPRESS
Relaxing

FIR
Grounding and security

FRANKINCENSE
Soothes nervousness; improves and elevates mood

GERANIUM
Soothes nervousness; relaxing; releases negative emotions

GRAPEFRUIT
Uplifting and refreshing

HELICHRYSUM
Soothes anger; uplifting to the spirit

HYSSOP
Releases nervous tension

JASMINE
Emotionally uplifting; reduces anxiety

JUNIPER
Promotes feelings of peace

LAVENDER
Reduces stress and tension; promotes feeling of peace

LEMON
Promotes feelings of well-being; releases nervousness

LEMONGRASS
Calming; increases intuition

MANDARIN
Peaceful, especially for someone who is tired due to lack of sleep

MARJORAM
Fosters peaceful feelings

MELALEUCA: (Tea Tree Oil)
Spirituality and purification

MELISSA
Calming; soothes nervousness

MYRRH
Spiritually uplifting

MYRTLE
Calms anger; soothes

NEROLI
Focus for the mind, body, and spirit

ORANGE
Fosters peaceful feelings

OREGANO
Promotes feelings of security

PATCHOULI
Promotes energy and feelings of prosperity

PEPPERMINT
Stimulates the conscious mind

ROSE
Fosters feelings of peace and harmony

ROSEMARY
Promotes an open mind

ROSEWOOD
Soothes; promotes feelings of peace and gentleness

SAGE
Lifts the spirits; reduces mental fatigue or lethargy

SANDALWOOD
Soothes nervous tension

SPRUCE
Releases emotional blocks; brings about balance

TANGERINE
Soothing and calming

THYME
Uplifting especially when one is physically and mentally tired

WHITE LOTUS
Highly spiritual oil; sacredness; calms emotions

WILD TANSY
*Uplifting; fosters feelings of well-being and
a positive attitude*

YLANG YLANG:
Relaxing and calming; releases anxiety

Chapter Twenty-Six

Chakras, Auras, and Meditation

There are points on the body that are considered powerful energy centers. These centers are called chakras. There are seven main chakras although there are up to twenty additional centers. These chakras run in a vertical line from the top of the head down along the center of the body. Although diagrams usually show the chakras on the front of the body, they are actually funnel-shaped in nature.

Chakra is the Sanskrit word for "wheel." The chakras spin clockwise through the body. When chakras become clogged or stuck, they result in disharmony or imbalance in the body. This imbalance can cause disease or illness. A chakra meditation can help restore the balance by unclogging and cleansing the chakras. It is not necessary to know much about chakras or even to believe in them to receive the benefits of a chakra meditation.

The chakras are numbered starting from the bottom and working upward. Each chakra corresponds to a color and governs parts of the body.

THE CHAKRAS

Root *The first chakra is located at the base of the spine and in the genital area. The color associated with it is red. The root or base chakra governs the adrenal glands, kidneys, spinal column, colon, legs, and bones. Balancing this chakra gives us roots. Vitality for the physical body.*

Sacral *The second chakra is located in the abdomen, below the navel. The color associated with it is orange. The sacral plexus or navel chakra governs the ovaries, testicles, prostate gland, genitals, spleen, womb, and bladder. Balancing this chakra helps us deal with issues that require change. Sexual vitality.*

Solar Plexus *The third chakra is located below the chest area and above the navel. The color associated with it is yellow. The solar plexus chakra governs the pancreas, stomach, liver, gallbladder, nervous system, and muscles of the body. Balancing this chakra helps us deal with emotional extremes. Emotional vitality.*

Heart *The fourth chakra is located in the center of the upper chest. Two colors are associated with the heart chakra: green is the major color, and rose/pink the secondary color. The heart chakra governs the heart, the thymus gland, the circulatory system, the lungs, and the arms and hands. Balancing this chakra helps us work with spirit and mind. The vital life force.*

Throat *The fifth chakra is located in the center of the throat. The color associated with it is blue. The throat chakra governs the thyroid, the parathyroids, and the hypothalamus, as well as the throat and mouth. Balancing this chakra helps us to speak what we may have held back or within. Vitalizes communication.*

Third Eye *The sixth chakra is located in the center of the forehead between the eyebrows. The color associated with it is dark blue, or indigo. The third eye or brow chakra governs the pineal and pituitary glands, the left eye, the nose, and the ears. Balancing this chakra helps us "see" what we may not have been able to see. Vitalizes the cerebellum and the central nervous system.*

Crown *The seventh chakra is located at the top of the head. The color associated with it is violet. The crown chakra governs the pineal gland, the cerebral cortex, the central nervous system, and the right eye. Balancing this chakra helps us strengthen our connection with the spiritual. Vitalizes the cerebrum (brain).*

Chakra Meditations

Most advise starting from the first chakra and working your way up, which, in effect, is from the ground up. Personally, I do it either way, depending on my mood.

During this exercise breathe in and out naturally and gently. Close your eyes.

Imagine that you can see and feel your root chakra. See it spinning clockwise. Imagine yourself drawing beautiful, glorious red energy into the root chakra as it spins. See this energy as though it were coming up from the earth, rising up and flowing into your root chakra. Imagine the root chakra opening wider and clearer and spinning smoothly. See it spinning very, very smoothly. If you find that there is any difficulty in allowing this chakra to spin smoothly, just examine any thoughts or feelings that come up. Let the emotional hold of these experiences pass away. Forgive yourself for anything you feel or think you did wrong, and let it pass away. Continue to allow this chakra to spin gently. Feel the warm red energy flow into the root chakra. Allow yourself to continue with the root chakra until you feel this chakra open and clear comfortably.

Next, imagine that you can see and feel your sacral chakra. See it spinning clockwise. Imagine yourself drawing beautiful orange energy up through and from the root chakra right into the sacral chakra. The energy swirls and spins, and as it does so, the sacral chakra opens and spins even more smoothly.

See it spinning very, very smoothly. If you find that there is any difficulty in allowing this chakra to spin smoothly, just examine any thoughts or feelings that come up. Let the emotional hold of any of these experiences pass away. Forgive yourself for anything you feel or think you did wrong, and let it pass away. Continue to allow this chakra to spin gently. Feel the warm orange energy flow into the sacral chakra. Allow yourself to continue with the sacral chakra until you feel this chakra open and clear comfortably.

Imagine that you can see and feel your solar plexus chakra. See it spinning clockwise. Imagine yourself drawing beautiful yellow energy up through and from the sacral chakra right into the solar plexus chakra. The energy swirls and spins, and as it does so, the solar plexus chakra opens and spins even more smoothly. See it spinning very, very smoothly. If you find that there is any difficulty in allowing this chakra to spin smoothly, just examine any thoughts or feelings that come up. Let the emotional hold of these experiences pass away. Forgive yourself for anything you feel or think you did wrong, and let it pass away. Continue to allow this chakra to spin gently. Feel the warm yellow energy flow into the solar plexus chakra. Allow yourself to continue with the solar plexus chakra until you feel this chakra open and clear comfortably.

Imagine that you can see and feel your heart chakra. See it spinning clockwise. Imagine yourself drawing beautiful green loving energy up through and from the solar plexus chakra right into the heart chakra. The energy swirls and spins, and as it does so, the heart chakra opens and spins even more smoothly. See it spinning very, very smoothly. If you find that there is any difficulty in allowing this chakra to spin smoothly, just examine any thoughts or feelings that come up. Let the emotional hold of these experiences pass away. Forgive yourself for anything you feel or think you did wrong, and let it pass away. Continue to allow this chakra to spin gently. Feel the loving green energy flow into the heart chakra. Allow yourself to continue with the heart chakra until you feel this chakra open and clear comfortably.

Imagine that you can see and feel your throat chakra. See it spinning clockwise. Imagine yourself drawing beautiful blue energy up through and from the heart chakra right into the throat chakra. The energy swirls and spins, and as it does so, the throat chakra opens and spins even more smoothly. See it spinning very, very smoothly. If you find that there is any difficulty in allowing this chakra to spin smoothly, just examine any thoughts or feelings that come up. Let the emotional hold of these experiences pass away. Forgive yourself for anything you *feel or think you did wrong, and let it pass away. Continue to allow this chakra to spin gently. Feel the warm blue energy flow into the throat chakra. Allow yourself to continue with the throat chakra until you feel this chakra open and clear comfortably.*

Imagine that you can see and feel your third eye chakra. See it spinning clockwise. Imagine yourself drawing beautiful purple and indigo energy up through and from the throat chakra right into the third eye. The energy swirls and spins, and as it does so, the third eye chakra opens and spins even more smoothly. See it spinning very, very smoothly. If you find that there is any difficulty in allowing this chakra to spin smoothly, just examine any thoughts or feelings that come up. Let the emotional hold of these experiences pass away. Forgive yourself for anything you feel or think you did wrong, and let it pass away. Continue to allow this chakra to spin gently. Feel the warm purple and indigo energy flow into the third eye chakra. Allow yourself to continue with the third eye chakra until you feel this chakra open and clear comfortably.

Imagine that you can see and feel your crown chakra. See it spinning clockwise. Imagine yourself drawing beautiful white light energy up through and from the third eye chakra right into the crown chakra. The energy swirls and spins, and as it does so, the crown chakra opens and spins even more smoothly. See it spinning very, very smoothly. If you find that there is any difficulty in allowing this chakra to spin smoothly, just examine any thoughts or feelings that come up. Let the emotional hold of these experiences pass away. Forgive yourself for anything you feel or think you did wrong, and let it pass away. Continue to allow this chakra to spin gently. Feel the white light energy flow into the crown chakra. Allow yourself to continue with the solar crown chakra until you feel this chakra open and clear comfortably.

When you finish with the chakras, feel the current of energy moving through your entire body.

THE AURA

All living things have an aura. The dictionary defines *aura* as "a distinctive quality that seems to surround a person or thing." The aura is thought to be an energy field arising from the chakras in the body. Recently, a great interest has arisen in Kirlian photography, developed in Russia by Semyon Kirlian in 1939. A Kirlian camera was developed in the 1980s. It photographs colored light around a body, which is believed to be a person's aura.

Different colors are thought to mean various things, although there is some disagreement as to what each color means.

Red *Vitality and energy*

Yellow *Intellect and the mind; represents openness*

Purple *Spiritual, visionary, and the higher realms*

Blue *Tranquility, peace, and balance*

Green *Healing energy and growth*

Pink *Love, sensitivity, and gentleness*

White *The highest source; universal power and love*

Gold *Higher source; universal power*

Aura Strengthening Meditation

Use the deepening method you prefer, although a breathing meditation is especially good with this exercise. I've used the healing color green as an example. You can go through each color one by one, or you can use just one or two colors. Use your intuition and feelings to guide you.

Sit down on a mat or on the floor. Take a few moments to concentrate on your breathing. Now visualize, sense, and feel the color green totally surround your entire body. Breathe in the color green, feel it absorb into your skin. Know it, feel it, sense it. Feel the green light within your body

*right down to the cell level. As you feel the green energy surround you,
it's as though you are green, you have become that green light.
Everything that this light is . . . you are. Feel the light enter you and
swirl all around you, giving you its power and energy. It strengthens
you, vitalizes you, becomes one with you. You are green . . . you are
strong. Feel how the light glows and radiates from you. For a moment,
it will be as though you can look at yourself. See how the green light
surrounds you, envelops you, giving you its energy and strength.
Now take a moment to pull in that energy, feel it become part of you.
Take a deep breath, and exhale slowly.*

In Conclusion

This book has touched upon several ways and areas in which you can meditate, but alas it has been just a featherlike touch. The uses of meditation could fill volumes. Why? Because the things we can do with meditation are only limited by our imagination! How far can you stretch your imagination? If you don't set limits, perhaps it could stretch forever.

It is said that we use less than 10 percent of our brainpower. What would it be like if we gained the use of just 1 percent more, or learned to use that 10 percent more fully? I think it would be an incredible world, one I'd very much like to see. I believe meditation can help us achieve this kind of life for ourselves.

Not only is there a whole world "out there," there is a whole world "in there." Imagine a world in which there are no limits to what we can do. Well, we already are living in such a world. We just need to realize it—and once realized—we are on our way to living our lives being the best we can be. We can make the most of our talents and abilities.

I would enjoy hearing about how meditation has worked in your life or interesting ways you have found to use it.

Feel free to contact me:

Holly C. Sumner, Ph.D.
P.O. Box 309
Cape Neddick, ME 03902
holly@hollys.com
http://www.hollys.com

Part Five

Resources

This part of *The Meditation Sourcebook* is divided into two sections. The first is Online Resources. Online resources can be found on the internet and include Web sites, discussion groups, chat rooms, and E-Zines.

The second section is Offline Resources, which can be found outside cyberspace and include your local bookstore, community groups, and educational institutions. Magazines and meditation associations will be listed.

Online Resources

There is a world of meditation resources on the Internet, including Web sites, discussion groups, newsgroups, and chat rooms. This section will list many of them. The main purpose is to bring you resources that are informational and useful. I'll add a few others that are interesting for other reasonsand a few are just plain fun.

No one list can ever be comprehensive. Especially in the online world, resources come and go. Between the time of writing this section and its publication, hundreds of new Web sites, discussion groups, and other resources will be born. Others will vanish into the night without a trace. However, I've tried to list the best of the best, as well as ways to help you find up-to-date sources.

The listings will follow the chapters wherever relevant. Not all chapters, however, will have resources listed.

WEB PAGES

Listed below are Web pages and their addresses. Please be aware that Web sites come and go. For that reason, I've listed sites that have been around for a while. There are a few other gems that I sincerely hope are still online when you read this!

Basic Meditation

Of course, your first stop should be my Web page on meditation. The URL is http://www.hollys.com/meditation. There will be information about the e-mail discussion group called Magic of Meditation, affectionately shortened to MOM. There also is a meditation chat room and much more!

Other URL's *to* Visit:

Monday Mom's Mandala Page:
http://ourworld.compuserve.com/homepages/CatAnna/mandala.htm

Meditation Learning Center:
http://www.learningmeditation.com/relax.htm

The World Wide Online Meditation Center:
http://meditationcenter.com/

The Meditation Lounge:
http://pages.infinit.net/tsungen/home.htm

Meditation Relaxation Exercise:
http://healing.tqn.com/library/weekly/aa082297.htm

Earth Healing Meditation:
http://www.newage.com.au/library/meditat2.html

Practicing the Presence:
http://www.netnow.micron.net/%7Emeditate/intro.html

Mountain Wind:
http://www.breath.org/

Meditation FAQ:
http://www.cis.ohiostate.edu/...usenet/meditation/faq/faq.html

Third Circle Website:
http://www.geocities.com/Athens/Acropolis/5715/

Daily Affirmations

Father Leo has a wonderfully inspiring site at:

http://www.fatherleo.com

Each day he brings a new affirmation and a short essay on the affirmation. This is a very uplifting site.

Motivating Moments:
http://www.motivateus.com/

AstroMind:
http://www.astromind.com/

The Human Brain

This site is geared toward children, but is quite good for people of all ages!

The Brain Is Boss:
http://www.kidshealth.org/kid/normal/brain.html

A Brief Intro to Light & Sound:
http://www.ecst.csuchico.edu/~andrewc/brf_intro_2ls.html

The Brain:
http://www.sciam.com/askexpert/medicine/medicine31/
medicine31.html

And for those who enjoy personality tests, here are sites that have lists of them, from the serious ones to silly ones:

Personality Tests on the Web:
http://www.2h.com/Tests/personality.phtml

Queendom of Tests:
http://www.queendome.com/test_frm.html

Positive Thinking

Success Dynamics:
http://www.hollys.com/success-dynamics

The Rainbow Garden:
http://www.io.com/~rga/rainbow.html

Positive Places:
http://www.realvoices.com/positive/posplace.htm

The Positive Place:
http://members.aol.com/bcruikindy/index.html

Stress Management and Relaxation

Relaxation Exercise:
http://healing.tqn.com/library/weekly/aa082297.htm

Breath & The Body:
http://www.transformbreathing.com/body/breath.html

Relaxation Techniques:
http://www.healthy.net/library/books/lark/relax6.htm

Health and Well-Being

HealthWorld Online:
http://www.healthy.net

Health WWWeb:
http://www.healthwwweb.com

Healthy Ideas:
http://www.prevention.com

Homeopathy Home Page:
http://www.cambr.force9.co.uk

Mayo Health Oasis:
http://www.mayohealth.org

Wellness Web:
http://www.wellweb.com

Alternative Medicine Digest:
http://www.alternativemedicine.com

OTHER MODALITIES

Reiki

The Center for Reiki:
http://www.reiki.org

Reiki Information Center:
http://www.tamoore.com/reiki

The Reiki Page:
http://www.crl.com/~davidh/reiki

Reiki:
http://www.spiralvisions.com/liz/reiki.htm

Yoga

American Institute for Yoga Science:
http://www.americanmeditation.org

YogaNet:
http://www.yogajournal.com

All About Yoga:
http://www.thriveonline.com/shape/yoga.index.html

Yoga Central:
http://www.yogaclass.com/central.html

Hypnosis

The National Guild of Hypnotists:
http://www.ngh.net

HypnoBirthing:
http://www.hypnobirthing.com

Aromatherapy

Essential Oils:
http://www.hollys.com/essential

AromaWeb:
http://geocities.com/~aromaweb/index.html

The Spiritual Realm

Spiral Visions:
http://www.spiralvisions.com

Centering and Grounding:
http://www.robinwood.com/GroundCenter.html

InnerSpace:
http://www.twelvestring.com/innerspace/

SpiritWeb:
http://www.spiritweb.org

Michael's Page:
http://www.hollys.com/michael

Golden Angel:
http://www.fantasyrealm.com/goldenangel.html

Hearts Afire:
http://www.dzn.com/~lhindi/Angels-Hearts-Afire.html

Angel Haven:
http://www.angelhaven.com

Angels on the Net:
http://www.netangel.com

Evolution:
http://www.netkonect.co.uk/evolution/

DynoWomyn:
http://www.angelfire.com/biz/DynoWomyn/

Alice in Wonderland:
http://www.fidnet.com/~whalenar/page4.html

Christian, Buddhist, Zen, and Hindu Meditation

The Association of Christian Meditators:
http://ourworld.compuserve.com/homepages/prothro/

Guide to Meditation:
http://www.nashville.net/%7Ekaldari/meditate.html

Zen Beginning Meditation:
http://www.mkzc.org/beginzen.htm

Dhyana Meditation:
http://www.sivananda.org/meditati.htm

Shambhala Meditation:
http://www.shambhala.org

Osho Meditation:
http://www.osho.org

Vispassana Meditation:
http://www.dharma.org

Dark Zen:
http://www.darkzen.com/zennist.html

Gangaji:
http://www.gangaji.org

Krishnamurti Foundation:
http://www.kfa.org

Ramana Maharshi:
http://www.satramana.org

NEWSGROUPS

alt.meditation
alt.meditation.moderated
alt.meditation.orsho
alt.meditation.shabda
alt.meditation.transcendental

MAILING LISTS

The Magic of Meditation (MOM)
To join send an e-mail to:
majordomo@hollys.com

Put in the body of the e-mail:
    subscribe meditation [put your e-mail address here]

    The Magic of Meditation is an open, friendly discussion group about basic meditation. It does allow off-topic conversation. No flaming is allowed. Slightly moderated.

The Psychic Discussion Group
To join send an e-mail to:
majordomo@happy-karma.com

Put in the body of the e-mail:
    subscribe psychic [put your e-mail address here]

    The Psychic Discussion group is an open, friendly discussion group about metaphysical and New Age topics.
    It does allow off-topic conversation. No flaming is allowed. Slightly moderated.

Vipassana
To join send an e-mail to:
listserv@maelstrom.stjohns.edu

Put in the body of the e-mail:
    subscribe vipassana [put your e-mail address here]
    Discussion group about Buddhist Insight meditation.
    Practical discussion rather than philosophical.

Insight
To join send an e-mail to:
majordomo@world.std.com

Put in the body of the e-mail:
  subscribe insight [your e-mail address here]
  This is a forum for discussion of Buddhist meditation
  practice, primarily from the Theravada perspective.

ONLINE MAGAZINES AND E-ZINES

WholeStar Journal:
http://www.inner-resources.com/success

Insight Magazine Online:
http://www.dharma.org/insight.htm

Healing Art Magazine:
http://www.healing-arts.com

Positive Health Magazine:
http://positivehealth.com

SpiritTalk Magazine:
http://www.spirittalk.com/

TranceNet Journal:
http://www.trancenet.org

RESOURCES FOR SOFTWARE

There are many sites that have shareware available:

Stroud's Consummate Winsock Apps:
http://cws.internet.com

C/Net Shareware:
http://www.shareware.com

Jumbo Shareware:
http://www.jumbo.com

APPLICATIONS SOFTWARE

E-Mail Programs

Pegasus E-mail:
http://www.pegasus.usa.com/

Eudora:
http://www.eudora.com

Browsers

Netscape:
http://www.netscape.com

Microsoft Explorer:
http://www.microsoft.com/ie/

IRC *Software*

MIRC:
http://www.geocities.com/SiliconValley/park/6000/index.htm

PIRCH:
http://www.bcpl.lib.md/us/~frappa/pirch.html

Newsreaders

Free Agent:
http://www.forteinc.com

My Deja News:
http://www.dejanews.com

Offline Resources

ORGANIZATIONS

Meditation

The American Meditation Institute
P. O. Box 430
Averill Park, NY 12018
(518) 674-8714
http://www.americanmeditation.org

The Inner/Outer Partnership
P. O. Box 1293
Pacific Palisades, CA 90272-1293
(212) 787-1281
http://www.innerouterpartner.org

Yoga

Ananda Yoga
The Expanding Light
14618 Tyler Foote Road
Nevada City, CA 95959
1-800-346-5350

Reiki

The Center for Reiki Training
29209 Northwestern Highway, #592
Southfield, MI 48034-9841
1-800-332-8112

MAGAZINES AND PUBLICATIONS

Explore Magazine
P. O. Box 1508
Mt. Vernon, WA 98273
(360) 424-6025

Yoga International
RR 1, Box 407
Honesdale, PA 18431-9960

Natural Way
P. O. Box 52170
Boulder, CO 80323-2170

Alternative Medicine
P. O. Box 10205
Riverton, NJ 08076-8205

Healthy Living (by *Country Living*)
P. O. Box 7467
Red Oak, IA 51591-2467

Healthy & Natural
100 Wallace Avenue, Suite 100
Sarasota, FL 34237-9977

Bibliography

Alman, Brian M. and Lambrou, Peter T. *"What Will Self-Hypnosis Do for You?"* New York: Brunner/Mazel, 1992.

The American Medical Association Family Medical Guide, 3d ed., New York: Random House, 1994.

Bloomfield, Harold H., and Kory, Robert B. *"Happiness. The TM Program."* New York: Dawn Press/Simon and Schuster, 1976.

Carrico, Mary. *"Yoga Basics, the Essential Guide to Yoga for a Lifetime of Health and Fitness."* New York: Henry Holt and Company, Inc., 1997.

Hadley, Josie, and Staudacher, Carol. *"Hypnosis for Change."* Oakland, Calif.: New Harbinger Publications, 1985.

Hogan, Kevin L. *"The Psychology of Persuasion."* Gretna, La.: Pelican Publishing Company, 1996.

———. *"The Miracles of Hypnosis."* Audio tape series. Eagan, Minn.: Network 3000, 1997.

Krasner, A. M. *"The Wizard Within."* Santa Ana, Calif.: American Board of Hypnotherapy Press, 1990.

McKay, Matthew, and Fanning, Patrick. *"Self-Esteem."* Oakland, Calif.: New Harbinger Publications, 1992.

Microsoft Encarta 97 Encyclopedia, Microsoft Corporation.

Myer, Joyce, *"Battlefield of the Mind."* Oklahoma: Harrison House.

Young, Gary D. *"Aromatherapy, The Essential Beginning."* Salt Lake City, Utah: Essential Press Publishing, 1996.

Index

Brain, 3–4
  right/left brain dominance,
    determining, 4
  Web sites, 277
Brain wave patterns, 5–8
  alpha state, 5–6, 29, 59
  beta state, 5
  delta state, 7
  theta state, 6–7
Breathing meditation, 39
Breathing, proper way to, 37–39
  exercise to promote, 39, 40
Bulimia, 205

Caffeine, impact on meditation, 51
Cancer, 138
Candle-flame exercise, to help with
  focus, 41–42
Candles, as a useful meditation
  aid, 62
Cassettes. *See* Audio tapes
Cats, meditation and, 52
Center for Reiki Training, 287
Centering, using meditation for,
  244–245
Chakras, meditation and, 245,
  265–267
  crown, 264
  heart, 264
  root, 263
  sacral, 264
  solar plexus, 264
  third eye, 264
  throat, 264
Chi (flow of energy), 68
Childbirth
  meditation for, 187–189
  pain management for, 186–187

Colors, using in meditation, 121–122
  auras, 268–269
Communication. *See also* Language
  different forms of, 13–16
  exercises to help stimulate, 14,
    15–16
  impact of unspoken, 13–14
Confidence. *See* Self-confidence
Contemplative meditation
  as a form of passive meditation, 25
Counting
  achieving meditative state by,
    29–30, 33
  using to help with insomnia, 124
Creativity, 155–158
  concentration and, 156
  developing, 155
  emotions and, 156
  habit control and, 158
  meditation for, 156–157
  running and, 156
  space for, 156–157
Criticism. *See* Self-criticism
Cults
  dangers of, 79–80
  meditation, use of, 64–66

Daily affirmations. *See* Affirmations
Daily meditations, using affirma-
  tions, 109–111
Dancing, 219
Daydreaming
  exercises to start, 28
  similarities to meditation, 25,
    27–29
Death, 145–146
Deepening method, 123–124
Delta state, 7